SUGAR-PLUMS AND SHERBET

I.T.
in memory

SUGAR-PLUMS
and
SHERBET

The Prehistory of Sweets

Laura Mason

PROSPECT BOOKS
2004

First published in paperback in 2004 by Prospect Books, Allaleigh House, Blackawton, Totnes, Devon TQ9 7DL.

BRITISH LIBRARY CATALOGUING IN PUBLICATION DATA:
A catalogue entry of this book is available from the British Library.

Typeset and designed by Tom Jaine.

ISBN 1903018285

Printed at the Cromwell Press, Trowbridge, Wiltshire.

Contents

Acknowledgements

MANY individuals have helped shape this book by discussing ideas and sources, providing encouragement and sharing their sweeties, especially Jane Baker; Peter Brown; Caroline Davidson; Doreen Fernandez; Mehdi Hojat; Richard Hosking; Philip and Mary Hyman; Charlotte Knox; Rachel Laudan; Caroline Lord; John and Kate Marsden; Kate Mason; Nuray Osalan; Ugo Palma; Graham Parker; Glynna Prentice; Joe and Emma Roberts; Ann Rycraft; Helen Saberi; the late Roy Shipperbottom; Jennifer Stead; and Joop Witteveen.

Elisabeth Orsini helped with translations from French; Ruth Grant and Agnes Winter read the manuscript and Peter Brears and Ivan Day generously shared their specialist knowledge. Other specialist help came from Graham Jones at the British Sugar Technical Centre in Norwich; the Coronation Rock Company, Blackpool; Richard van Riel, Pontefract Museum; the staff of John Rylands Library in Manchester; the John Johnson Collection at the Bodleian Library in Oxford; Special Collections at the Brotherton Library of Leeds University; the Borthwick Institute and the Castle Museum, both in York.

Andrew Millward lent me William Finemore's confectionery notebook and has allowed me to quote liberally from it. Permission to quote the verse from John Betjeman's poem 'The Liquorice Fields at Pontefract' came from John Murray (Publishers) Ltd; and material from MSS XVI.O.10 and Hailstone QQ5 is reproduced by permission of the Dean and Chapter of York. I am grateful to Nevin Halici, who allowed me to use her sherbet recipe, and to the Oxford University Press for permission to quote from John Ayto's *Diner's Dictionary*. The illustrations on pages 190 and 216 are reproduced by kind permission of Nestlé SA, and the cartoon on page 210 by courtesy of the Print Collection at the Lewis Walpole Library, Yale University.

Finally, but not least, thanks to Paul Sutherland, for his patience, and Alan Davidson, who started it all.

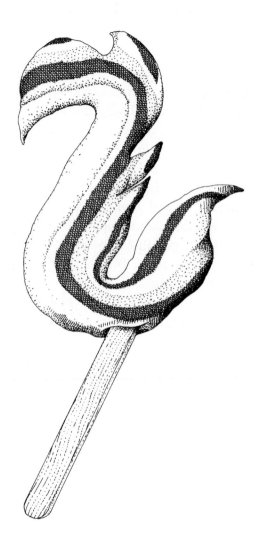

Figure 1. A Nottingham Goose Fair cock-on-a-stick, made of red and yellow pulled sugar. A fairing, no longer made.

Introduction

THE ORIGINAL intention of this book was a short investigation into some bizarre British sweets such as sherbet, liquorice, humbugs and gobstoppers. Soon I was trying to understand the history of sugar-boiling, from the first written recipes in English of the sixteenth century to the industrialization of manufacture a hundred years ago. How did Britain, a country which could not grow sugar-cane, chocolate or spices, come to be one of the most important global producers and consumers of sweets? The obvious answer is trade and empire. These were vital to the expansion of the industry but there were other more obscure but equally powerful factors at work from earliest times. To use the language of the market analyst, our medieval ancestors saw confectionery as a high-status, luxury consumer product, with the added advantage of a healthy image. These ideas derived from the first perceptions of sugar when it arrived in Europe.

For the twentieth-century observer, a curious point about early confectionery recipes is a general absence of chocolate. Originating in central America, this was first brought to Europe by the Spanish, but only developed into an important sweetmeat and competitor for sugar confectionery after about 1850. Chocolate has its own distinct history and skills which have been comprehensively explored by others; a good introduction is *The True History of Chocolate* by Sophie and Michael Coe (1996). It should be remembered, however, that many 'chocolates' and chocolate bars are based on traditional sugar confections coated in chocolate.

Another question which nagged me was why are so many sweets eaten in Britain? The question has preoccupied health professionals for years. Sugar is not essential for survival; dentists and nutritionists regard it as a dietary villain. We don't need the calories which sweets deliver so effectively in compact, concentrated form. The lure of the sweet shop and a notion that sweet equals good are usually considered enough justification for enjoying confectionery. Other, apparently sound reasons have been advanced—that humans have an inborn taste for sweetness, that sugar gives energy, sweetness is comforting, and that food manufacturers promote all things sugary. Good theories in their way but they are rationalizations from one side or the other.

Little about confectionery can be taken for granted. Older, odder reasons for the attractions of sweets emerged as I began to unravel their history. Embedded in our ideas of their value are notions of the expense and importance of sugar in the past, respect for the skills needed to work with it, and for the strange alchemy of the substance itself. Sugar is now very cheap and the skills of the magician have been appropriated by food technologists. Formerly elegant novelties, sweets have descended to trivia. Like nursery rhymes, they were once full of significance for adults but are now bits of nonsense for children.

The recipes

The main purpose of this book is to examine the hold which sugar, in the form of sweets, has on our subconscious. It is not intended as a craftsman's primer but a selection of tested recipes is included. In the text itself, I have quoted verbatim recipes from early manuals. At the end of each chapter, I have given modernized versions of these recipes that may be undertaken by readers in their own kitchens. They show the antecedents of such British favourites as fudge, seaside rock, barley sugar, acid drops, sherbet, liquorice and toffee. The distribution of recipes and emphasis on certain types of confection may seem erratic. Intrinsic interest was the first reason for inclusion; secondarily, the excellence of the results.

Relative ease of making (especially for those with little previous knowledge of sugar-boiling) was also borne in mind, but the whole point of confectionery is that it is a special skill. I have attempted to explain the processes as clearly as possible. To compose some recipes, a certain amount of guesswork was needed, as full instructions were rarely given in the originals. Practice is needed for the best results. Certain groups of sweetmeats, such as preserved fruit, are essentially based on the one formula, and I have only quoted a couple of examples, because more would have made tedious, repetitive reading. Other sweets are difficult and unrewarding to make at home, so recipes which need special skills and equipment, such as those for pouring comfits, are not given here.

Bibliographical note

Many confectioners recorded recipes and observations on their trade. These provide the basis for this book. Given the time-lag involved between developing skills, writing them down, and publishing the details, it is probable that many techniques and confections given here are of earlier origin than the dates of publications suggest. How much earlier is a matter on which I have not speculated at every turn.

The earliest recipes for sugar-working in English come from manuscripts, not printed books. One of them is in the Minster Archives at York. It is known officially as York Minster Library manuscript XVI.O.10, dated (by the handwriting) to *c.* 1500, and is thought to have been written by a northerner. I have referred to it in my text as 'the York manuscript'. The sweet recipes are bound into a collection of medicinal formulae, confectionery then being the province of apothecaries. A published transcription of this manuscript is in Elizabeth Brunskill, 'A Medieval Book of Herbs and Medicine, Part II' in *The North-Western Naturalist* (see the bibliography, below). Slightly later, the translation of work by Girolamo Ruscelli, an Italian alchemist and apothecary, became available in English as *The Secretes of the Reverende Maister Alexis of Piedmont* (1562). His book and those of his contemporaries show associations of confectionery with luxury and medicine (including a role as aphrodisiacs) tinged with quasi-magical skill.

Luxury and status were most important. By the start of the seventeenth century, confectionery became a smart accomplishment for ladies; printers fed a growing demand for books on the subject. Two publications set the tone: *A Closet For Ladies and Gentlewomen* (published anonymously in 1602) and *Delightes for Ladies* by Sir Hugh Plat (first published about 1605). Plat was a good example of a Renaissance man: cultured, learned, interested in art and science and enough of a polymath to be intrigued by the intricacies of confectionery and cosmetics.

Many of the English nobility retreated to the Continent after the Civil War. Here, some must have become aware of the increasing refinement of confectionery techniques. In publishing, this is reflected in *A Perfect School for Instructions for Officers of the Mouth* (1682), a translation by Giles Rose from French texts of 20 years earlier. French influence was to have a lasting effect through the next two centuries, from *The Court and Country Cook* by Massialot (1702) to *The Royal Parisian Pastrycook* by Carême (1834). Several British-born confectioners also published during the eighteenth century. Perhaps the best example is *The Experienced English Housekeeper* (1769) by Elizabeth Raffald, a lady of formidable energy, who established her own business in Manchester.

An important publication in the early nineteenth century was *The Italian Confectioner* by Guglielmo Jarrin (1820). Jarrin gave clear and detailed instructions, and revised his book several times. It represented the finest in high-quality craft confectionery, and remained a standard work for 30 years, but tells nothing of what journeymen were making for poorer people. By this time, a few small books appeared for those working in the provinces, such as S. W. Stavely's *Whole New Art of Confectionary* (published in Nottingham), showing that cheaper products had become established. I was also lucky to be given access to a manuscript notebook kept by William Finemore, who began as a confectioner in Devonport in the 1820s, but by 1840 had moved to London to be employed as a journeyman.[1] Supporting information came from *London Labour and the London Poor* by Henry Mayhew, a fascinating collection of reportage on the lives of ordinary people in the city, first published in 1851.

By the end of Victoria's reign, there were manuals to suit producers working on all scales. Of these, *The Confectioners Handbook* by E. Skuse (another work which went into many revised editions) shows confectionery as it went from a craft to an industry. Skuse obviously had much practical experience: he offered a postal service for materials, and appears to have acted as a consultant. At the other extreme was May Whyte, whose *High Class Sweetmaking* (c. 1910) was for the benefit of the young ladies who learned the skill of sweet-making from her, so that they, in turn, could earn a little money.

The books reflect different motivations, from apothecaries required to make aphrodisiac confections to ladies for whom fruit preserving was good domestic economy. They also show diffusion and rediffusion as fashions came and went, themes were forgotten, rediscovered and refined. Recipes were often plagiarized until vital details had been distorted or left out. The novice craftsman probably found them frustrating and unsuccessful, and the modern reader has to bear in mind that many reflect outdated practice and that instructions may be incomplete.

Other evidence about sweets and the status of confectionery comes from a multitude of sources. I have only outlined the books I found most useful; many others were consulted for details. References can be found in herbals, diaries, novels, and in books on shopkeeping. Information from other countries (especially France) is often illuminating. Artefacts such as moulds survive from the seventeenth century onwards, but as these could be used with several recipes, their messages about sweets are enigmatic. Still-life paintings, especially from Holland and Spain, show confectionery such as biscuits, comfits and candied fruit, but they too are silent about techniques.

Finally, confections can tell their own history. Names of some sweets can be traced through several languages and many centuries.

The products of past confectioners do not survive, but sweets are constantly being recreated. Ancient techniques, limited by the constraints of sugar chemistry, are glossed with novelty for new consumers. Confectionery preserves a remembrance of things past. Strange shapes and flavours, bright patterns and lurid colours are all remnants of former grandeur. The magic they once exerted over our ancestors finds echoes in unlikely places—on the sea-front, in souvenir shops and in children's Christmas stockings. But the best place to begin looking is the sweet shop.

CHAPTER I

In the sweet shop

THE CONTENTS of a sweet shop are an edible archive of social custom and technical expertise recorded in sugar. Aniseed balls were once valued as *digestifs*. Humbugs developed from medieval cold cures and liquorice strings were originally stored for coughs. Novelty chocolate figures are the descendants of marzipan or cast-sugar ornaments which provided diversion at medieval feasts. The predecessors of little floral cachous were used by court ladies as breath fresheners. Fruit-based sweets became popular through the keep-up-with-the-Jones's aspirations of Stuart housewives, and sherbet is an echo of a drink once considered as exotic as any cocktail. Our present view of bars of chocolate rarely plumbs these deep waters of the past.

In common with most British children, I began my sweet-buying career in a C.T.N. These initials stand for Confectioner-Tobacconist-Newsagent, a category of business recognized by experts in marketing. Every high street and suburb has at least one. A feature of the British life for much of this century, their history is obscure. Just after the Second World War, the firm of Cadbury Brothers wrote, 'It has always been something of a tradition that "SWEETS AND TOBACCO" shops and small "GENERAL STORES" are gold mines. The tradition has survived wars and slumps and considerable evidence to the contrary.'[1] That use of the word 'always' implied the retailing of sweets had remained unchanged for centuries. Yet tobacconists cannot have been common until people had the disposable income to smoke habitually; news-agents cannot have been a familiar sight until papers were cheap and the population literate.[2] The concept of the C.T.N. reflects, perhaps, the development of leisure pursuits in late Victorian and early twentieth-century Britain.

In my childhood memories of a mill village in Yorkshire in the 1960s, the best shop was the newsagent's. Small children ascending three steps from the street door saw first the sherbet flying-saucers and lucky-bags behind the counter of glass. They raised their eyes past massed ranks of chocolate bars to a vibrant backdrop of boiled sweets: sparkling towers of sugar. But there was competition for our custom. In the large general grocer's, a double row of tall glass jars filled with Rainbow Crystals, American Cream Soda, multi-coloured lollipops, toffees, and striped boiled sweets stood opposite the packets of tea and flour. A few doors away, the corner shop and off-licence offered four-for-a-penny chews, little bars of chocolate in purple foil, aniseed balls and gobstoppers. Even the greengrocer had a 'tray', a miscellany of cheap sweets in a wire basket, over which we could deliberate on the merits of 'spanish' (liquorice) and bubble gum, banana toffee and candy shrimps. Within 50 yards, there were four shops selling sweets, and another three scattered further down the main street. Even the chemist sold sticks of barley sugar. This was in a place with a population of about 2,000. Its collective sweet tooth was phenomenal.

The combination of sweets with some other retail activity has been a fact of modern life as garages, supermarkets and other unlikely outlets decide that confectionery is a profitable line. It is symbol of the erosion of confectionery's special place in our view of luxury.

Sweet shops once existed as separate entities. The 'sweetie wives' of Scottish towns early in this century were brilliantly evoked by F. Marian McNeill:

> There was always a sweetie-shop, to whose counter the bairns were lured by the delectable odour of boiling toffee that emanated from the kitchen behind. The sweetie-wives were usually known by some nickname as Candy Kate, Sweetie Annie, or Taffie (Toffee) Knott. Besides such homely sweets as gundy, glessie, cheugh jeans and black man, there were bottles of 'boilings' (Scotch Mixtures) that glittered like rubies, emeralds, topazes and all the jewels of the Orient, and tasted of all the fruits of the orchards and spices of the Indies. Striped rock in variegated colours and yellow spiral sticks of barley sugar were always prime favourites, and so was 'taiblet' of various flavours.[3]

One step down from the shop was the stall, the huckster's barrow, a survivor from a time before village stores provided constant supply, when seasonal treats were sold at great annual fairs through the land. Ginger-bread and comfits were fairings to take home to sweethearts or children. Or perhaps a 'cock on a stick', the boiled-sugar cockerels sold until recently at Nottingham Goose Fair, combining innocent reference to the purpose of the fair with characteristic innuendo. Thus shopping-mall administrators try to touch folk memory by installing the odd toffee-vendor.

A sweet stall once provided income for many journeymen sugar-boilers. Henry Mayhew, in his wonderful survey of Victorian street-life, estimated there were over 200 of these working in London. He noted, 'I never heard them called confectioners.'[4] Brought up to the trade, these people were 'sweet-stuff makers', and lived in some of the poorest areas of town, where Dickens described the crowding together of numerous trades: '"sweetstuff" manufacturers in the cellars, barbers and red herring vendors in the front parlours, cobblers in the back.'[5] The trade was open to the poor because small quantities of materials could be worked up for a quick turnover; and by this time sugar was cheap.

The aristocrat of the trade, however, was the confectioner. Not for him a shop that just sells sweets, nor was he a man who could merely do a little sugar boiling. The boundary may never be precise, but a confectioner and his shop imply skill, elegance and high prices. These shops are rarer than the C.T.N. and are found where people have money to spend, are in a mood to celebrate.

Few now exist in Britain, and many that remain concentrate on chocolate. The village of my childhood certainly never supported a confectioner, but the wealthy market town a few miles away did. This elegant shop followed the present trend and made chocolate a speciality; their thin chocolate wafers with chips of mint sugar, orange peel, or candied ginger were locally famous. They also sold breads and fancy cakes, something I never quite managed to reconcile with the concept of a chocolate shop (but would not have seemed strange to French children, accustomed to the *pâtisserie-confiserie*).

Another place I saw confectioner's shops—and where they still flourish—was by the sea. These had a brash and exuberant image. Trips to Blackpool or Bridlington yielded rock with letters running through it, and giant multicoloured lollipops. Oral or visual puns abounded: bacon and eggs or fish and chips and peas, the symbols of the seaside cafe, were wrought from sugar, as were baskets of gaudy yellow bananas and lacquered red apples. Sugar false teeth grinned beside huge babies' dummies and 'rock bottoms' made of hard sugar candy. Scallop shells held handfuls of pebbles which turned out to be sweets. Stacked high in surreal profusion, the contents of sea-front shops appeared little more than several hundredweight of sugar, combined with dye and flavouring, wrapped in wisps of Cellophane.

To get a flavour of an old-fashioned craft confectioner's in Britain, one has today to visit a museum. The few fittings that are preserved, such as those that used to belong to Terry's of York,[6] inspire questions. Why can we no longer buy the flavours of drops—damson, greengage, tangerine—displayed in shapely glass containers? Who provided the market for Superior Acid Drops, Linseed Lozenges, and White Acid Squares?[7] How many colds were soothed by Wintergreen Squares? (Terry's began as apothecaries.) Did Silver Cachous have their moment of glory on top of birthday cakes, as they had done at the parties of my childhood? What were Lemon Pennets? Gorgeous lace-lined boxes for fondants must have been treasured long after the contents were eaten. Perhaps the girls courted with these ordered their wedding cakes from this shop as well—for Terry's were patissiers too.

One can get an impression of what a working confectioner's shop might have been like before industrialization by looking beyond Britain's shores. In southern Europe such places have preserved their elegance and have more emphasis on fine hand-made sweets. Even quite humble French *confiseries* stock a rare choice of nougat, candied fruit, sugared almonds, fruit pastes and dragées alongside local specialities. Across the marble counters of Spanish *confiterias*, all gilt mirrors and glass shelves, one can take *turron*, candied fruit, *piñones* (sugared pine nuts) and cream cakes. Some concentrate on a single line; in Madrid, a tiny purple, white and silver bandbox mines the sweet possibilities of violets. A visit is an occasion, unlike the quick dash into a British C.T.N. to grab a bar of chocolate.[8]

One thing doesn't alter: indecision faced with apparently infinite choice. Dithering in a pastry shop in a small Sicilian town, I was pre-empted by a family who poured through the door and requisitioned the large almond-paste lamb I had been about to purchase. Then the children turned their attention to the astonishingly realistic display of almond-paste fruit and vegetables and after chattering debate each grasped a marzipan fig or head of garlic, like British children musing over the relative virtues of Mars bars and Kit-Kats. It did not matter to them that each shape was made from the same basic mixture: form was more important than content. Sugar is fantasy land.

In travels abroad, I discovered in Istanbul that there are 20 variations on *rahat lokoum* and in Amman the best coffee-house sold fantastic sugared pistachios. Crisp nougat full of almonds could be bought near the tomb of Moulay Idriss in Fès. In Manila, jars of syruped limes or citrons were on sale, with patterns incised in the peel, like the carved fruit I'd seen described in seventeenth-century cookery texts. Friends brought moulded gingerbreads from eastern Europe, exquisite fragile sugar flowers from Japan, and eggy confections from Portugal. Triangular brown paper bags full of strange salty liquorice lozenges and turquoise, pill-like mints turned up from Holland. Rumour reached me from Mexico of cast-sugar skulls, and funerals modelled in chocolate; and from India of sweets based on reduced milk or pulse flour, sold in temple courtyards.

The sweet shops of the world were obviously stuffed with curious confections, some of which were recognizably descended from the same tradition as British favourites. But they didn't have sherbet, or shiny black spanish, or toffee. It was time to read the contents of the sugar archives.

Figure 2. A setting for dessert, from François Massialot, *New Instructions for Confectioners*, an English translation published with his *Court and Country Cook* in 1702. The French original was first published in 1692.

CHAPTER II

Why sweets are not puddings: some definitions

WHAT IS a sweet? A curious, infuriating point is a lack of definition. The closer one looks, the more elusive the meaning. The British tend to think of sweets in the plural, and then resort to lists (humbugs, sherbet, liquorice, toffee...). Children standing in the sweet shop are sure of what is meant by sweets and know to distinguish them from puddings served at meal times. But is chocolate a sweet? Yes and no—we talk about 'sweets and chocolates'. Are biscuits sweets? Maybe not. What about marzipan? Perhaps, but why put it all over Christmas cake? Boundaries are undefined. The concept is fluid. The confusion arises from the first absorption of sugar into our cultural bloodstream, when its uses were overlapping: a medicine, preserving agent and spice, as well as a decorative morsel and a symbol of wealth. The use of sugar as a general sweetener is a late development.

There are many words in current usage and in the speech and writing of times past that describe sweets, sweet dishes and sweet things. These need a degree of explanation before embarking on more particular accounts.

During the last two centuries, the word sweet has acquired two related but different meanings. It can be applied to sweets: dry, sugary confections bought from sweet shops. It has also come to mean sweet dishes, including jellies and fruit pies as well as suet puddings. In English, both usages date to early in the 1800s. Confusion over where sweets end and where puddings begin is not peculiar to Britain: the Arabic word *halwa* has similar connotations; and in Hindi, *mithai* indicates several different types of sweet, some of which are sugar confections and some of which are puddings.

The anomalies in our own language are due to the origin of sweets, or sweeties[1] (an older version), as diminutives of sweetmeat. This word, still not entirely obsolete, was in common use for over 400 years to the end of the nineteenth century. The suffix -meat has an archaic meaning of food in the widest sense (surviving in the phrase 'meat and drink'), so sweetmeat simply means a sweet food. Sweet stuff, as noted by Henry Mayhew in London in the 1840s, was a parallel term. Stuff was a generalized expression for almost any commodity, as in the word foodstuff. To the inhabitants of Tudor and Stuart England, sweetmeats were sugary foods in general, including pieces of flavoured candy and sugar-covered nuts and spices, products of medieval theories on the medicinal value of sugar, as well as dishes which used sugar as one ingredient amongst many, for structure, sweetness and an air of the exotic.

A word associated with sweet foods in English at this time was banquet.[2] The original meaning (and the sense now understood) was a large formal meal. Medieval feasts had provided several roles for sweetmeats. Apart from sweet dishes, sugar-work had a special part in the construction of large ornaments—sometimes edible, sometimes not—called subtleties.[3] Another role was as a *digestif*. A habit of serving sugared spices with wafers and spiced wine had developed; these were eaten at the *voidee*, the close of the meal after the table was cleared. By the late sixteenth century, this little afterthought had been expanded and it was this, in England, which evolved into a banquet consisting entirely of sweetmeats: biscuits, preserved fruit, sweet wines and sugar confectionery. Banqueters revelled in conceits, so some of the sugar-work was made to look like savoury food—marzipan hams, sugar paste bacon, or eggs made from jelly coloured white and yellow.

Banquets of sweetmeats might follow meals, or be separate afternoon or evening entertainments. They were intimate occasions: some large houses had a specially designed room or little folly tucked away for such indulgences; a few (Whitehall, for example) were mansions in their own right. They were also opportunities for displaying wealth and skill. Sugar and the other ingredients were expensive, and confectionery was a delicate task, whether produced by ladies for their own households, or bought from fashionable confectioners.

In the sense of a sugary feast, the word banquet became obsolete around the start of the eighteenth century, but the practice of putting sweetmeats on the table at the close of a meal continued to develop. This eventually became dessert (from the French, *desservir*, to clear the table). The word was in use in English by the end of the sixteenth century and it continued to mean a collection of sweet dishes and fruit after the separate sweetmeat banquet vanished.

By the early eighteenth century, under the influence of French confectioners, desserts had become very splendid. Dry sweetmeats were piled in elegant pyramids on stemmed dishes and epergnes disposed on elaborate damask cloths, the whole composition ornamented with figures and models, themselves often edible. Creams, jellies and compotes of preserved fruit added variety. Desserts were frivolous and self-indulgent. However, other sweet dishes continued to be served during the body of the meal itself, and it was a North American, not British, usage that introduced confusion in the late eighteenth century, by extending the range of foods presented at dessert to include tarts, pies and sweet puddings.

Of all the words associated with sweetmeats, pudding has probably the weakest link to sugar. Derived from the same root as the French *boudin*, it originally meant a mixture stuffed into an animal gut, as in black pudding, or hog's pudding. It could be sweet or savoury. The culinary method was extended in the seventeenth century to mixtures contained within cloths, which were cooked or boiled in the same manner as those in animal wrappers. Later still, it was accepted as a description of a mixture in a covered bowl or basin, that was boiled as if wrapped in cloth or bladder. The more general application to the whole sweet course appears to have evolved in the nineteenth century.

Puddings are still seen as 'proper' food, the final part of a structured meal. Puddings are not sweets; John Betjeman's poem, mocking

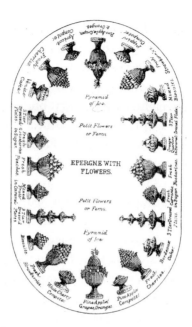

Figure 3. A summer dessert for 24 people, the frontispiece of William Jeanes, *Gunter's Modern Confectioner*, 1880 edition.

social aspirations, turns the conundrum neatly on its head, when the narrator asks about the last course, 'Is trifle sufficient for sweet?'[4] One thing is certain: a Stuart lady, whether or not she thought trifle (or dishes which predated it) as a sweetmeat proper for dessert, would have been vexed if that was all she had to put on a banquet table.

The battle between sweet, dessert and pudding still rages, with each usage vilified by one party or another for spurious gentility, inaccuracy, or the speaker's lack of understanding of antecedents—part of the linguistic class system chronicled by Alan Ross and Nancy Mitford. Restaurants have dodged the issue by calling the sweet course 'afters' or 'endings', much as they avoid the pitfall of false Frenchness by dubbing *hors d'œuvre* 'starters'. It underlines the fact that we have never, as a nation, managed an agreed set of terms to describe the progress of meal without borrowing from foreign vocabularies: perhaps because the very concept of courses was imported in the first place.

The word sweetmeat connects clearly enough to food and meals, but sugar's earliest links were with medicine. Medieval physicians thought it had intrinsically health-giving properties and knew it helped preserve the plant-derived essences on which they relied. Improving flavour was probably incidental. Sugar was combined with herbs, spices, flowers, gold and precious stones to make tonics and aphrodisiacs. The Latin word *conficere* was used to describe the act of putting together, making up or compounding their potions. From that were derived the English terms to confect and confection. Another one, comfit, came from the Latin in a more roundabout fashion, for its immediate root was the French *confit*. Used at first for fruits preserved in sugar, comfit soon defined sugar-covered spices (pills in other words). The regularity with which physicians deployed sugar in their armoury ensured the entry of these somewhat pharmaceutical words into general usage. By the end of the fifteenth century, confection had acquired the meaning of a sweetmeat.

In the early seventeenth century, the terms comfit-maker and confectioner both described people who made sweets. Confectioner and the collective noun, confectionery, have remained in the language. Advertisements and trade cards show that by the eighteenth century, confectioners made and sold a much wider range of goods than either mere medicines or what we call sweets: preserved and candied fruit, biscuits, macaroons, syrups, comfits, and more ephemeral sweet foods, such as ices, creams and jellies; often also pies and tarts (including savoury ones). They sold or rented dessert frames—devices for presenting large formal desserts in fashionable patterns—and sugar figures or 'images' for embellishing the table.

This broad definition of confectionery is echoed today in marketing and retail categories that group sweets with ice-creams and soft drinks, although the connection with flour-based baked goods is more tenuous. There is a practical reason for keeping the two skills apart: bread requires yeast, a substance the sugar confectioner does not want contaminating his premises and fermenting the preserves.

SEGUIN, Confectioner *from* **Paris,**
In the Minſter-Yard, YORK,

Makes and ſells all Sorts of dry and wet Sweetmeats, Apricots, Green Gages, Pears, Apples, &c.——Comfits of all Kinds, perfumed Ginger, Carrimum, Raſberries, Carraway, Images, and Sugar-Boxes.——All Sorts of Biſcuits and Macroons, as made in Paris.—— The true Paſte and Cakes of Mallows for Coughs ; Syrup and Paſte of Or-geat ; Syrups of Mallows, and Capilair of Orange Flower.——He makes Deſerts of all Kinds, either to ſell or lend ; beſides he makes Sealing Wax fine and common.——The whole in Wholeſale or Retale, at the moſt rea-ſonable Prices.

Figure 4. An advertisement from the *York Courant*, December 1764, which shows the range of goods then stocked by a confectioner, straddling the modern specializations of confectioner, pastrycook, sweet shop and pharmacist.

Yet in France, where the *pâtissier* deals mostly with very light and elaborate pastry, often heavily sugared, and the *boulanger* with breads and plainer confectionery, there are none the less plenty of shops which deal with bread, pastry, chocolate and sugar confectionery from the same premises.

Some medicines remained within the realm of the confectioner, who was expected to know about liquorice, pastes of marshmallow, and gum-based troches (pastilles or sweets for ailments such as coughs) while his trade was medically shadowed by the apothecary, whose stock included roses preserved in sugar, liquorice compounds, and syrups made from flowers or herbs. Confectioners and apothe-caries were respectable, but the itinerant quack physicians or mountebanks of the seventeenth and eighteenth centuries were not. These people, with the aid of much showmanship, sold cures, including sweet confections, to crowds in the street. Henry Mayhew recorded in 1851:

> perhaps the last mountebank in England, was [seen] about twenty years ago, in the vicinity of Yarmouth. He was selling 'cough drops' and infallible cures for asthma, and was dressed in a periwig and an embroidered coat, with ruffles at his wrist, a sword to his side, and was a representation, in shabby genteel, of the fine gentleman of the reign of Queen Anne.'[5]

By then, the more potent aspects of medicinal confectionery were transferring from apothecaries to the new profession of pharmacists.

Liquorice and marshmallow were on their way to losing their medical associations; mountebanks had vanished, and Mayhew could find only six street-traders who specialized in vending 'curative confectionaries'. In our own time, vestiges can be detected in cough sweets and pastilles sold by both sweet shops and pharmacies[6] and the original connection helps explain why the chemist in my home village included barley sugar sticks amongst his stock-in-trade.

There are numerous dialect words for sweets in English. 'Gi' us a spice,' we said in the village of my childhood, hoping for a fruit pastille or gum, an aniseed ball or a mint imperial. We never stopped to wonder why we used this word. It echoes the broader meaning of Old French *espice*. John Ayto explained the original meaning as 'a range of (mainly sweet) items used in cooking, but it was still far broader in application than its modern English descendant, *spice*: it could refer to jams and sweets, for example, to honey, sugar and milk.'[7] In twentieth-century Yorkshire dialect, it meant sweets of any kind, and if more specific links existed (for instance, with comfits, or the medieval classification of sugar as a spice), they have not been recorded. Another English dialect word for confectionery, more widely known, is goody, or goody-goody. This is similar to the French *bonbon*, expressing the notion that something which tastes good must be intrinsically good. *Bonbons* more or less coincide with items in the English category of sugar confectionery (although they are often more elegant). Many other terms have been recorded, such as comforters, sucks, suckers (or sookies)[8] and the lolly—now in common use for a sweet on a stick—thought to derive from an old word for tongue.

Some sweets, especially those designed to appeal to small children, are often repulsive to adult palates. So in France, *bonbon* is subverted to *bonbec* by children to indicate the 'rubbish' confectionery which adults hate (and call *la cochonnerie*).[9] An equivalent usage in the dialect of north-east England is kets or ketty (literally meaning rubbish or garbage).[10] Most of the sweets we bought as children, vividly coloured, highly flavoured and strangely shaped, would have been called *bonbecs* by our French counterparts. A fine tradition of modelling inedibles such as milk bottles, dinosaurs, mountain bikes, spiders, flies, and other creepy-crawlies out of fruit-flavoured gum flourishes. These are no stranger than the conceits beloved of Caroline nobles who decked their banquet tables with sugar models of gloves, buckles and shoes.

Of all the words in the sugar lexicon, candy probably has the most ancient derivation. Like sugar itself it can be traced through Arabic to Persian and Sanskrit antecedents. It could be regarded as the archetypal sweetmeat. Sugar that is hard, crystallized by evaporation of the boiling juice, is said to be candy. Sugar candy, broken off a loaf, was a standard form of household sugar in Europe until early this century.

The phrase 'sugar candy' was first recorded in English at the end of the fourteenth century. A hundred years later, it travelled to America with the earliest settlers where the word candy was adopted into North American English, developing a similar meaning to sweets on our side of the Atlantic, though without the wider notions of pudding. North Americans differentiate between several forms—hard candy (equivalent to English boiled-sugar sweets), soft candy, candy chews, cream candy, stick candy, and candy canes (striped rock in walking-stick shapes).

In Britain, the word candy in this generalized sense is rarely used. It survives only in dialect,[11] or with reference to specific confections, such as candied fruit. Even then, it is threatened by the use of 'crystallized' as a synonym. It is sad this useful and venerable word has passed from the wider British vocabulary.

CHAPTER III

Sucrose, sugar loaves and cassonade: facts about sugar

THE CONFECTIONERY industry would not exist without sugar. To the non-specialist, this seems a simple subject. When consumers speak of different 'sugars', they usually imply granulated, caster, icing or demerara. Food scientists, on the other hand, define these products as manifestations of a specific form of sugar which they call sucrose, extracted from either sugar-cane or sugar beet.

Manipulation of the distinctive chemistry of sucrose is the basis of the confectioner's craft. Chemists class sucrose as a disaccharide, which means it is made up of two simpler substances, both mono-saccharides, linked via a chemical bond. These are also classed as sugars and have their own names, glucose and fructose.[1] Sucrose, glucose and fructose are three representatives of a much larger group of substances, whose complexity varies from small, simple molecules to long, multi-linked chains. All are based on combinations of carbon, hydrogen and oxygen, and distinguished by the suffix -ose in their chemical names. It is these that chemists and food scientists have in mind when they speak of 'sugars' in the plural.

When considering the history of confectionery, it is useful to ask where the sugar came from, and what it was like. It has been imported to northern Europe from many different countries, and confectioners learnt that place of origin affected its properties. Types, qualities and prices varied as sugar production and refining techniques evolved.

Sugar-cane is thought to have been brought under cultivation in New Guinea and to have diffused to various Asian countries, incl-uding India, in prehistoric times. The development of refining, the

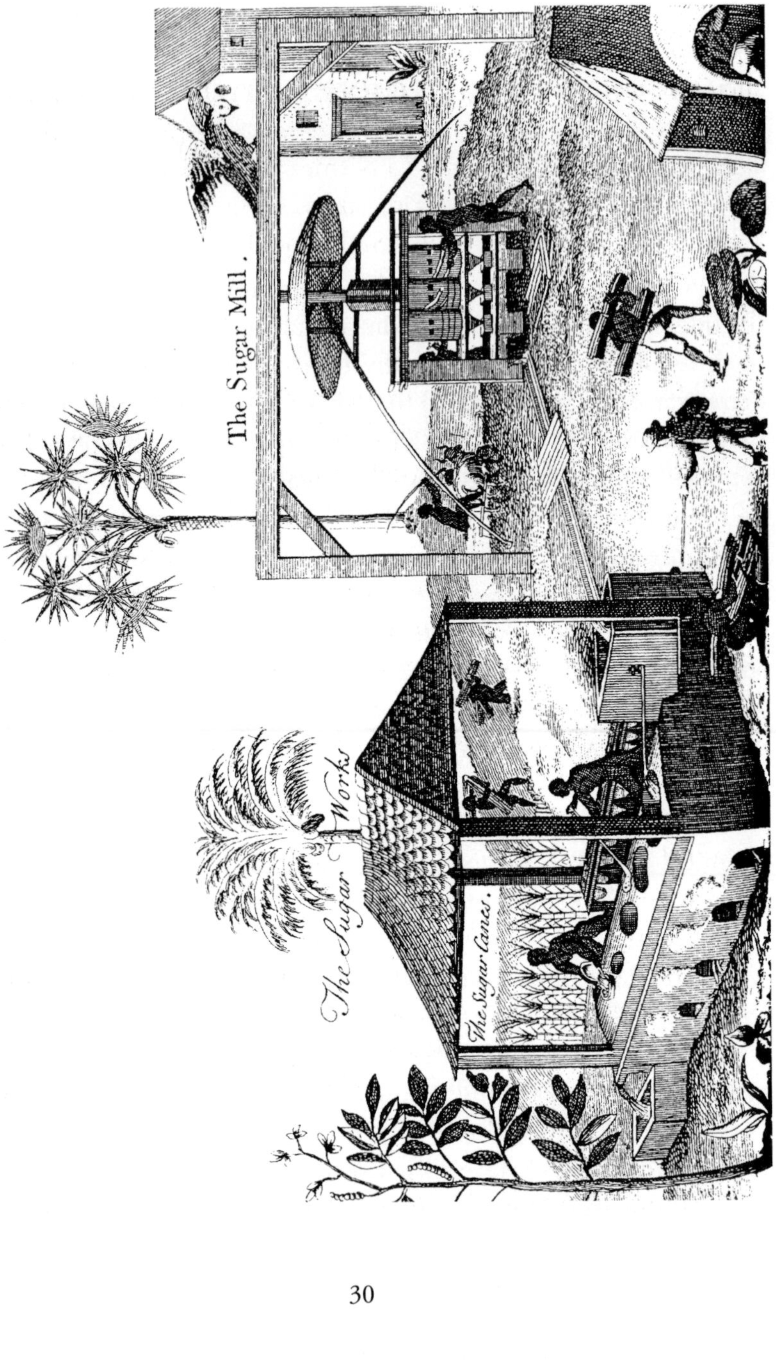

Figure 5. A sugar refinery on a plantation, illustration from Pomet, *A Complete History of Drugs* (1747).

forms—syrup or candy—taken by early types of refined sugar, and the extent of European knowledge of sugar before the Arab conquest are all matters for debate. It seems likely that if sugar was known in ancient Greece or Rome, it was only used medicinally. Whatever the answer to that puzzle, in the centuries since classical antiquity, sugar and Islam travelled together to permeate the Mediterranean world. The earliest known sources of sugar to modern Europeans were Moslem-controlled, especially Syria and Palestine. Sugar-cane was grown in the valley of the river Jordan, and it was here that Frankish crusaders first encountered it during the twelfth century.

In England, early records of imported sugar show that it came from Morocco, Cyprus and Alexandria. Barbary sugar (i.e. from north Africa) is another generic description.[2] Prices were unimaginably high. Absolute comparisons with modern prices are rather futile, because they take no account of the intervening switch from a subsistence to a money economy; but account rolls from Durham in 1422 show that a sugar loaf was valued at 8s 4d[3] (about 42p). This was a time when a dozen eggs might cost about a penny[4] (less than half of one post-decimal penny). Coarse sugar was slightly cheaper, and honey about a fifth of the price. Sugar of any sort was a luxury, treated as spice or medicine, not a basic kitchen ingredient. According to the historian of sugar, Noel Deerr, the best came from Egypt.

During this earliest period, the Italian cities of Venice and Genoa were the principal conduits of supply to northern Europe.[5] It is no surprise, therefore, that details about types of sugar come from an Italian source: the accounts of Francesco di Balducci Pegolotti, agent of a fourteenth-century Florentine banking house.[6] The best was *mucchera*, highest quality double-refined sugar made into small loaves (most of which was retained for the household of the Sultan of Egypt). Next was *bambillonia*, also in small loaves (the name derived from Babylon, a suburb of Cairo; 'cairene sugar' was an alternative name); and *cafetino* (probably so named because it was packed in palm leaves: in Arabic, *kaffa*), made both in small loaves of equal

31

Figure 6. The sugar-cane, illustration taken from Pomet, *A Complete History of Drugs* (1747).

quality to bambillonia, or larger, inferior loaves. *Musciatto* was less refined and made in large loaves of about three or four kilograms, easily broken up. The least valuable was *dommaschino* (which originally meant Damascus sugar), made into small loaves. Rose and violet sugars (flavoured with the appropriate flowers) were also mentioned, as were sugar candy and crystal sugar from disintegrated loaves. Of the sugar types listed by Pegolotti, 'Babilon' sugar, at least, was known in England.[7]

Other forms were also described in Britain in the late Middle Ages. One was called *phanid* or *fanid* (a word of Persian origin). This was only partly refined, was malleable and could be worked and shaped into ropes or cylinders. It gave English the now obsolete word *penydes* or *pennets* (a name for little sugar sticks, the ancestors of humbugs and seaside rock). *Zuker roch* or 'rock sugar' was also mentioned in English at the end of the thirteenth century, but it is not clear what was meant by this except that it was, presumably, hard.[8]

A characteristic of sugar production is that it has moved progressively westward. In the fifteenth century cultivation of cane expanded from the Mediterranean basin to the islands of Madeira, the Canaries and Sao Tomé. Development of sugar plantations on the western side of the Atlantic soon followed when the Portuguese began to grow sugar in Brazil. British interest began with development of plantations in the Caribbean from about the mid-seventeenth century onwards. 'Lisbon' sugar (the English name for a semi-refined sugar, which does not necessarily appear to have had anything to do with Lisbon) and that from the British possessions, especially Barbados and Jamaica, were important throughout the eighteenth century. Caribbean sugar remains so to the present day.

Some sugar reached Britain from eastern sources; this seems to have been used by confectioners in the early nineteenth century. William Gunter (a member of the family who ran one of the most famous and long-lasting of London confectioner's) said that 'East India sugars appear finer, in proportion to the price, but they do not contain so much saccharine matter, consequently they are less fit for wines and sweetmeats.'[9] Despite this, confectioners apparently continued using it. William Finemore, a journeyman confectioner in London,[10] wrote in his notebook, 'this sort of Sugar is most generally used for making of boiling Goods—viz—Sugar Sticks, Nelsons Balls, Bulls Eyes.'[11] 'East India' included places we do not consider to be part of the Indies, notably Mauritius. Sugar from there was produced by free labourers, as against slave-made sugar from the West Indies, a point used in its favour by the anti-slavery movement.

During the Napoleonic wars, a rival to cane sugar was developed in Europe: sugar beet. A method of extracting sugar from the juice of this plant had been discovered by the Russian chemist Andreas Siegmund Marggraf in the mid-eighteenth century. It took several decades for this to become commercially viable. Public interest was aroused when Marggraf's pupil, Franz Carl Achard presented a sugar-loaf made from beet in a Berlin refinery to the King of Prussia in 1799. However, it was Napoleon who saw the advantage to be gained from home-produced sugar and, from 1813 onwards, it was the French who really developed the industry. Beet became steadily more important as a source of supply and, by the First World War, Britain was importing sugar from eastern Europe.

33

EAST INDIA
SUGAR BASINS.

B. HENDERSON,
China-Warehouse,
RYE-LANE, PECKHAM.

Respectfully informs the Friends of Africa,
that she has on Sale an Assortment of *Sugar
Basins*, handsomely labelled in Gold Letters:
" *East India Sugar not made by Slaves.* "

A Family that uses 5lb. of Sugar per Week, will, by using
East India, instead of West India, for 21 Months, prevent the
Slavery, or Murder of one Fellow-Creature! Eight such Families
in 19½ Years, will prevent the Slavery, or Murder of 100 ! !"

Figure 7. An advertisement for anti-slavery sugar basins.

By this time, sugar had passed from luxury to bulk commodity. Its relative price had declined rapidly from the late seventeenth century as first the plantation system then industrial processing of beet sugar increased supplies and cheapened production. Needlessly high prices were maintained by a system of import duties, not abolished until 1874, that provided a revenue stream for the British government. None the less, the progressive cheapening of sugar was inescapable.

In the late twentieth century, the basic types of white sugar available in Britain are granulated, caster and icing sugar, diminishing in particle size from small crystals to powder. 'Lump sugar' is made from crystals similar to those in granulated sugar, packed together and moulded into cubes (lump sugar, in previous centuries, meant irregular pieces of sugar candy broken from loaves). In common with their predecessor, the triple-refined sugar cone, these all consist mostly of sucrose. Standardized white products of modern refining are 99.8 per cent pure sucrose; the various 'brown' sugars commonly available contain about 92 per cent.[12]

Two things allowed confectionery to go from being an adult status symbol to the target of children's pocket-money. First, confectioners developed increasing control over the idiosyncrasies of sucrose, leading to sugar confectionery as it is now understood. Secondly, there was the dramatic fall in relative prices.

The consequence is illustrated by the amount of sugar eaten. The total rose steadily as the price diminished: from an average of about 4lb per head per year in 1700 to about 13lb in 1800. In 1850, about 30lb per head per year were eaten and this more than doubled by the end of the century to 85lb.[13] Consumption continued to rise through the modern period (except during the two world wars).

These figures can only show general trends in the development of the collective sweet tooth; they do not directly illustrate the popularity of sweets. Initially, sugar was beyond the reach of all but the very wealthy: a few people ate quite a lot, the majority very little. The rise in consumption during the eighteenth century is mostly attributed to the rapid spread of tea-drinking in all income groups but greater ingestion of sugar confectionery must also have taken place.

By the beginning of the last century, sugar was used very widely. Some cheap confectionery was made by sweet-stuff makers and sold on the streets but as years passed, sweets were produced in ever-larger quantities by semi-industrial concerns who packed them in jars and tins for wider distribution by rail. The price of sugar had tumbled in relation to many other foods, bringing it within reach of the poorest households. It assumed its current role as general sweetener, comforter, and source of easily digested, quickly available energy. Only current worries about long-term, heavy sugar consumption introduced the concepts of empty calories (energy with no additional nutritive benefits) and sugar as 'bad for you'.

Separate figures for consumption of sugar- and chocolate-confectionery are now available. In Britain in the 1960s, the average for sugar-confectionery fell slightly from approximately 4oz per head per week (about 13lb, or almost 6kg a year) in 1960 to about 3.5oz (just over 5 kg a year) in 1965; these figures have remained roughly static up to the 1990s. Chocolate, in the meantime, has risen from approximately equal levels of consumption in 1960 to about 8.5kg per head

Figure 8. 'Suck, my darling, suck, your father says it's sugar!' A cartoon depicting sugar beet, encouraged by Napoleon as a way of beating the British continental blockade in the first years of the nineteenth century .

in 1989. When the two sets of figures are combined, they show the inhabitants of the UK buying more confectionery than almost any other country in the world.[14]

Although raw sugar was extracted from the cane at its place of cultivation, it was not usually refined until it had arrived in the country, or continent, of final consumption. The skill of refining moved westwards following the plant itself. The basic knowledge, including making cones or loaves for convenient transport and exchange, was known in the Islamic areas of sugar production around the Mediterranean. Venice and Bologna were important medieval European centres for refining, and as plantations moved to the New World, so refining became an activity of ports with easy access to the

Atlantic: first Antwerp and then Amsterdam were paramount. Much raw sugar from Madeira and Brazil was imported through Lisbon. By the seventeenth century, most other European countries had begun to refine their own supplies. The first English refinery was established in London in 1544. The trade gradually spread to other ports, especially on the western shore, such as Bristol, Liverpool and Greenock.

Sugar refining is a process which aims to extract as much purified sucrose as possible from the juice of cane or beet. Various grades are produced and waste syrup from the different stages of refining is reprocessed to extract more sucrose. From the sixteenth century onwards (and probably long before) triple-refined white sugar in loaves was esteemed the finest available. For these, the juice extracted from cane had undergone three labour-intensive boilings and clarifications with lime water and egg white or ox blood to remove impurities. Skimmed, strained, and properly concentrated, it was poured into conical moulds to set and drain. Unmoulded and dried, this was the sugar candy which Tobias Venner said was 'hard and of a resplendent white colour'.[15] Loaves or cones remained the standard form for best refined sugar well into the nineteenth century (three sugar loaves was often the sign used for a grocer's shop). They were notoriously hard, and had to be broken with a hammer or cut with special snips and ground with a mortar and pestle before use. This was the substance called for in recipes such as preserved rose petals, requiring the best powdered sugar.

Sugar candy was not necessarily white. Sugar refined once or twice also set hard. Venner recorded that sugar obtained from the first boiling of sugar-cane juice was 'grosse and of a red colour...somewhat tart in taste, by longer boiling it becometh hard, which we call Red Sugar Candie,' and that, 'when mixed with water and boiled again it became whitish and more acceptable to the taste and Stomacke. This kind of second Sugar we call common or kitchin Sugar.'[16] Even when double-refined, kitchen sugar must have been quite contaminated. Venner's near contemporary, Sir Kenelm Digby, reported that 12lb of 'best

Figure 9. A sugar refinery, from Diderot's *Encyclopédie*. The juice comes into a series of boiling kettles from the left. It is slaked with lime, then subjected to progressively greater heat until the syrup is thick enough to crystallize when cooled.

lump' kitchen sugar, would, after clarifying, be reduced to about 9lb.[17] This leaves one wondering what inferior sugar was like.

Other forms of partially refined sugar were available. Names for these varied over the years. In early fifteenth century England *blake* (black) sugar was cited; it is not clear if it really was black, or simply dark in contrast to the best white sugar. The centre of large sugar loaves, inadequately cured, was sometimes referred to as black sugar. References to loose and 'pot' sugar occur at about the same date. The latter was cheaper than loaves, and required more boiling for use in confectionery; the implications are that it was partially refined.[18] Black and loose sugar were, perhaps, terms roughly equivalent to the French *cassonade*. In the sixteenth century, Michel Nostradamus mentioned cassonade as a basic ingredient for some recipes. He said it was kept in chests, sometimes becoming black and unsightly. It apparently contained much extraneous matter: cassonade 'of reasonable good quality' had to be dissolved, boiled and strained carefully so there were no bits and pieces of cane or straw in it.[19] By 1611, Cotgrave, in his *Dictionary*, defined cassonade as 'powder sugar, especially suche as comes from Brasile.'[20]

In common with many terms used for sugar, the meaning of cassonade probably varied over time with reference to specific places of origin. During the late seventeenth century and the first part of the eighteenth, cassonade must have been understood in English. It was either left untranslated, or was merely annotated as in this instance from the English edition of Pierre Pomet's book on drugs: 'The *Cassonade*, or Powder Sugar, is much in Use among confectioners; above all, that of *Brasil*, by reason that it is less subject to candy; upon which Account the Confectioners value it the more.'[21]

At the time this was written, *cassonade gris* and *cassonade blanche* were both recorded as products of French-controlled West Indian sugar refineries.[22] Here, the term had come to mean a product which had been refined twice and 'clayed' (cleaned by covering the wide end of the loaf, still in the mould, with wet clay from which water percolated down, taking impurities with it). English confectioners, by this time, talked of 'Lisbon sugar', also a product which had been clayed. The technique actually gave three grades of sugar: the base of the cone closest to the clay being the finest, the centre portion yellow, and the tip, which retained most impurities, brown.[23] In modern French, *cassonade* is roughly equivalent to English light brown sugar.

Another unrefined sugar was 'muscavado'. This derives from the Spanish *moscabado* (sugar of the lowest quality). It was known in English from the mid-seventeenth century as a sugar type, but the sugar itself was little used by confectioners. Muscavado was originally obtained by simply evaporating sugar-cane juice and allowing the molasses to drain. Later it came to mean sugar which had undergone an initial refinement. Pomet said muscavado provided raw material

Figure 10. The final stage of refining, from Diderot's *Encyclopédie*. Once the sugar has crystallized, it is packed in conical earthenware forms, each with a bunghole at the apex to allow the molasses to drain. The cones are then 'clayed' by adding fuller's earth in suspension: water from this percolates through the sugar, removing more molasses.

for all other sugar types, including cassonade. He complained, 'there is some to be met with so moist, and with so much of the burnt Smell, that it is almost impossible to use it.'[24] Muscavado is now a general term for a moist dark-brown sugar: all methods for processing are carefully controlled, and a 'burnt smell' is no longer a problem. Until refined sugar became cheap in the nineteenth century, such coarser sugars and molasses were more affordable by the poor.

Until about the 1850s, confectioners did not rely on the product of refineries. They found it preferable to take in partially refined sugar and process it themselves. The state of unrefined sugar—full of impurities and left-over trash from the sugar-cane—meant clarification was essential. Instructions remained fairly standard throughout the early modern period. This example comes from Edward Lambert:

> Break into your preserving Pan the White of one Egg, put in four Quarts of Water, beat it up to a Froth with a Whisk; then put in twelve Pounds of Sugar, mixed together, and set it over the Fire; when it boils up, put in a little cold Water, which will cause it to sink; let it rise again, then put in a

little more Water; so do so four or five times, till the Scum appears thick on the Top; then remove it from the Fire and let it settle; then take off the Scum, and pass it through your straining Bag.

A practising confectioner, Lambert gave the reader the benefit of his experience in a note. 'If the Sugar doth not appear very fine, you must boil it again before you strain it; otherwise in boiling it to any Height, it will rise over the Pan, and give the Artist a great deal of Trouble.'[25] Anyone who attempts sugar boiling with unrefined sugar will discover this is still true.

Clarification methods were adapted to the relative impurity of the sugar. Jarrin described clarification of moist sugar (a fine-grained type) with charcoal and egg white, noting that the method gave good results for other sugars: 'As fine a syrup may be obtained from the common as from the double refined loaf-sugar if it be clarified in the same manner as the moist sugar.'[26]

He described and illustrated a boiler especially for the job. This must have been a necessity in any large workshop. Finemore observed that all the sugar needed for a day's boiling should be clarified at once. He suggested two hundredweight (101 kg) as an appropriate amount, and used ivory black (charcoal made from animal bone) as his filtering agent. Inevitably, some sugar was retained in the scum and straining bags during the process, and this was reclaimed:

The Scum that is left in the bags in which Ivory Black has been mixed must have water poured on it and rinsed thro' the bags to take out any sweetness that may be left in it—this water can be mixed with the scum from other Lump Sugar—adding Raw Sugar and boiling it and filtering through bags will make it fit for common boiling Goods such as Toffee Almond Rock & Hard Bake &c.[27]

Victorian confectioners began to see advantages in buying sugars which were thoroughly refined. William Gunter quoted a statement that, 'the coarsest [sugar] in quality, and consequently the cheapest in price, is far from being the cheapest in the end, as it is heavy, dirty, and of a very inferior degree of sweetness. That which is most refined is always the sweetest.'[28] He was quoting from 'Practical Economy' by

Figure 11. An eighteenth-century trade card showing the sugar cones that were often the mark of the grocer's calling. This one also depicts the honey bee and hive, the earliest source of sweetness to Europeans.

a Mr Colburn; the originator of the information appears to have been a sugar refiner, intent, perhaps, on emphasizing the utility of his own trade. No doubt many people—confectioners and cooks—continued to favour cheaper, partially refined sugars; but white sugar was becoming ever less expensive.

Technical advances such as vacuum pans (introduced in the 1830s) and the centrifuge (in the 1840s) made refining more efficient. By the end of the century, clarification, together with the mess of strainers and clarifying agents, had been transferred to sugar refiners. Confectioners could buy cheap supplies of pure sugar, needing only enough water to dissolve it. This was a great change. For centuries, they had relied principally on clarified syrup: relatively weak, based on sugar which contained a little molasses, and which had been heated quite a lot during clarification. These were all points which would have made the handling slightly different from syrups based on refined sugar.

In medieval Europe, apothecaries compounded remedies based on dark treacle, a by-product of sugar refining from Alexandria and other ancient centres of the trade. Treacle was originally a pharmaceutical term for a medicinal compound or salve. Particularly famous treacles from Genoa and Venice were regarded as sovereign remedies against venomous bites, poisons and malignant diseases. 'Common treacle', however, was plain molasses, sold off when supplies began to exceed the demand of apothecaries. It was probably much more palatable than the 'waste molasses' of present-day refineries, which has undergone more extreme processing.

The word molasses (derived from Latin *mellaccum*, meaning *must*, condensed grape juice),[29] came into English with reference to treacle produced by West Indian sugar plantations in the late seventeenth century.[30] Molasses or treacle now describe the by-products of sugar refining, semi-liquid combinations of sucrose, glucose and fructose, minerals, and water. That for human consumption is derived from earlier stages of refining as the final product is very strong flavoured. Pale treacle (known in Britain under the trade name Golden Syrup), is made by treating sucrose with acid at high temperatures, and was introduced in the 1880s.

The combination of different sugars contained in treacles and molasses was important in the development of confectionery because of the differing proportions of glucose and fructose. These, in turn, would affect the properties of the syrup when boiled. Treacles also played a more overt part in the development of some sweets, especially toffee and caramels, in which they are used to prevent formation of sucrose crystals.

Given its importance as a sweetener before the introduction of sugar, it is fair to ask why there has been little development of confectionery based on honey. It was free to anyone with enough skill to hive a swarm of bees in June and rob them in autumn. Yet honey is now rarely called for. Vestiges of honey-based sweetmeats can be detected. A few sixteenth-century recipes required it for preserving fruit, especially quinces (ancestor of marmalade, a technique which can be traced back to ancient Rome or Greece).[31] The alchemist Alexis of Piedmont[32] included methods for clarifying honey to conserve fruit among his secrets. Honey still has a limited use in some recipes, for instance the nougats, turrons and sesame halva from countries bordering the Mediterranean. It is also used in spiced biscuits such as German *Lebkuchen*.

There may have been more emphasis on honey in the past, but for the confectioner, it has disadvantages. Unlike sugar, it is not composed of equal amounts of glucose and fructose combined in sucrose crystals. Fructose predominates: typically, honey contains about 38 per cent fructose and 34 per cent glucose, plus water, small amounts of other sugars and traces of minerals. Unequal proportions of the two simple sugars do not combine readily to form sucrose; this is why both honey and molasses remain liquid at room temperature. Honey is also hygroscopic, since a property of fructose is that it attracts water. This means that honey-based confections become soft quite rapidly.

In addition, honey is brownish and has a distinctive taste; it does not show either the flavour or colour of ingredients such as fruit and flowers to their best advantage. This was particularly important when brilliance of colour was highly valued. Also, in Britain, there may have been economic factors involved in the decline of honey. Supplies probably waned after the dissolution of the monasteries in the 1530s (large scale bee-keeping is traditionally associated with monks). This coincided with a time when sugar was becoming more widely available, and the first plantations were being established in the New World. If honey was once important, this has been forgotten.

CHAPTER IV

Boiling and measuring:
the alchemy of sugar

HOW IS the raw material, sugar, made into sweets? The art of sugar boiling, by which confectioners work syrup through a series of transformations, is the key. In the past, the creation of fantastical, brilliantly coloured shapes from unpromising brown sugar must have seemed alchemy. Skills developed from a collection of formulae into a system of basic principles. This was the art and the mystery, defended initially as medical knowledge, then as trade secrets.

This chapter rehearses some essential practicalities about boiling sugar and its subsequent manipulation. It gives an account of what we know about past practice, contributing to a narrative history of sugar boiling: not a subject to enthuse the sweetest tooth. It can be pedantic in its attention to the terminology of recipes and adherence to chronological sequence, but it is a necessary prelude to any useful description of particular sweets.

Knowledge of the idiosyncrasies of sucrose chemistry gives a useful background to understanding early confections. The recipes often give little clue of what one can expect as a result: authors and their first readers must have been familiar with the various sweetmeats and did not need detailed descriptions. An encounter with recipes recorded in the early seventeenth century[1] left me wondering if the flowers in rock candy, preserves and pastes had any links at all with the sweets I knew. Marchpane, preserves of lettuce stalks, pastes of quinces, sugar plate and lemons cast hollow in sugar… where were the fruit drops, toffees and fudge of the village sweet shop? Where were the instructions on sugar boiling, now standard in every manual?

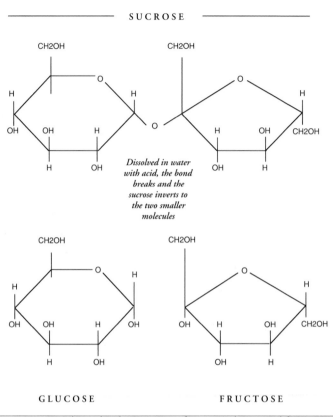

Figure 12. The molecular structure of sucrose, glucose and fructose.

To repeat a previous statement: refined sugar consists of sucrose, a disaccharide, made up of two monosaccharides, glucose and fructose, linked via a chemical bond. Sucrose dissolved in water is known to cooks and confectioners as syrup. In solution, a small proportion of the sucrose 'inverts', that is, the chemical bond hydrolyses (breaks), giving equal parts of the two simpler sugars, glucose and fructose. Adding a little acid, lemon juice for instance, enhances inversion, hydrolysing a higher proportion of sucrose. What happens when syrup cools depends on the confectioner's actions. The two mono-saccharides may recombine to become sucrose crystals (in other words, a solid—more or less firm), especially if the syrup is stirred. Or they can remain separate. The important point is the configuration of sucrose as a single unit which can be broken down into two smaller molecules which may, or may not, recombine.

Sugar boiling is a method of progressively concentrating syrup. It begins with refined sugar dissolved in water and heated through a series of agreed points. These are identified as temperature bands on a continuum, from syrup boiling a degree or so above 100°C (containing about 50 per cent sugar) up to 160°C, at which point the water has evaporated and the liquid in the boiling-pan is almost 100 per cent molten sugar.

Sugar syrup does different things at different temperatures. Each recipe for sweets or confections requires sugar cooked or boiled to a specific strength. A syrup composed of two-thirds sugar (sucrose) dissolved in one-third water is 'saturated' at room temperature, meaning that any more sugar added will not dissolve. If the syrup is heated, however, more sugar can be absorbed. It is then termed a supersaturated solution. Inversion also affects syrups. The component molecules of glucose and fructose are both more soluble than sucrose, so as the sugar inverts, yet more sucrose will dissolve into the syrup.

The more sugar contained in syrup, the higher the temperature at which it boils. Continued boiling increases concentration as water evaporates; simultaneously, the boiling point rises. The cycle continues until all the water has evaporated and the temperature rises above 160°C (the point at which sugar heated on its own liquefies, and above which it burns).

There are three methods of measuring the progress of syrup from one level to another. Two rely on instruments. The simplest is a special thermometer placed in the syrup during boiling. Temperature indicates, approximately, the concentration of sugar in the mixture, and is helpful to both novices and industrial confectioners. Alternatively, the density of syrup (how much water is left in the solution) can be measured using a saccharometer, but this technique is limited by syrup viscosity and is little used outside industry.

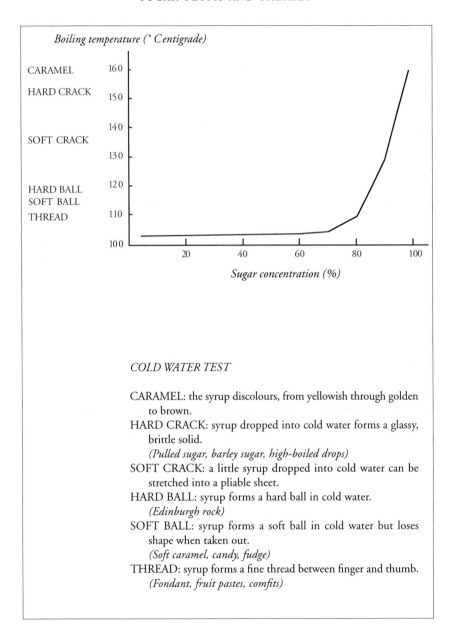

CARAMEL

HARD CRACK

SOFT CRACK

HARD BALL
SOFT BALL

THREAD

COLD WATER TEST

CARAMEL: the syrup discolours, from yellowish through golden
    to brown.
HARD CRACK: syrup dropped into cold water forms a glassy,
    brittle solid.
    (Pulled sugar, barley sugar, high-boiled drops)
SOFT CRACK: a little syrup dropped into cold water can be
    stretched into a pliable sheet.
HARD BALL: syrup forms a hard ball in cold water.
    (Edinburgh rock)
SOFT BALL: syrup forms a soft ball in cold water but loses
    shape when taken out.
    (Soft caramel, candy, fudge)
THREAD: syrup forms a fine thread between finger and thumb.
    (Fondant, fruit pastes, comfits)

Table 1. The relationship of sugar concentration, temperature and stages of boiling.

The third method relies on observation and manipulation of syrup samples dropped into cold water. In many ways, this is more accurate than temperature measurement because factors such as humidity and altitude have small but significant effects on boiling sugar and it is the texture of syrup, not its precise temperature, which matters. Since they require practice, the tests are of most use to craft confectioners; but they are accessible to novices, especially if readings taken from a sugar thermometer are used as a guide to when to begin testing. A summary of the relationship between temperature, concentration and tests is shown in the diagram.

These precise measurements are necessary because one confection depends for success on sugar boiled to within a whisker of burning so that it may solidify to a vibrant jewel of suckability, while others demand syrup (at a much lower temperature) be made to 'grain' into those most luxurious of textures, fudge or the soft, flower-scented centre to a chocolate. Graining, in the confectioner's vocabulary, describes the formation of crystals in a syrup, when fructose and glucose re-bond to form sucrose. It can happen spontaneously in syrups containing about 73 per cent sugar (boiling at about 106°C) or more. Fudge and fondant exploit graining. However, sucrose can remain in solution on cooling. At lower concentrations, liquid syrup is the result, but if it is boiled until most of the water has evaporated, then suddenly cooled, a translucent, glassy solid is produced. Consumers know the result as boiled sweets; food scientists call it non-crystalline sucrose. Historically, the preference of early confectioners for semi-refined sugar which they clarified themselves was possibly because some types were less liable to grain than pure sugar from refineries.[2]

******

The overall story of sweet-making and sugar work appears to be one of growing confidence, using increasingly concentrated syrups. As knowledge grew, vocabulary changed. Understanding the language is essential to interpreting old recipes. Equally, the language itself gives some indication of the level of technical sophistication of the original craftsmen. Especially important were the words which indicated concentration of sugar in syrup. Early practitioners referred to this as 'heights' of boiling, those in the eighteenth and nineteenth centuries to 'degrees' and, latterly, we talk of 'stages'. These terms refer to the same idea, which is to identify syrup consistencies appropriate for specific confections. Whilst there was general agreement in the craft over stages which were particularly useful, the art of confectioners lay in recognizing the optimum point for their own specialities.

A lack of written records before the sixteenth century, combined with the covert nature of early confectionery expertise, makes the beginnings of sugar boiling in Britain impossible to trace. Instead of laying the stages of boiling out for the uninitiated, early authors assumed a certain level of knowledge, making their recipes seem arcane. At the start of the sixteenth century, the little information available comes from manuscripts; shortly afterwards, material began to appear in printed books.

Recipes in the York manuscript[3] of 1500, described in the introduction, include instructions for clarifying sugar and making several confections which are variations on a formula (logical to the modern observer, but unusually well organized for this date). The basic recipe is 'sugere plate', which in this context meant a thin sheet of candied sugar.[4] To make it, a pound of clarified sugar was boiled until it reached a stage where 'ife it parte fro yr finger and yr thombe than it is soden ennogh.' This was for pot sugar; 'fine' sugar needed a little less boiling. The pan was taken off the fire, the syrup stirred until the colour changed from brown to yellow, then it was replaced and heated 'the maintenaunce of ave maria and whyle evermore steryng.' The recitation of the Ave Maria was a logical way to measure a short length of time when clocks were a rarity (it takes about 15–20 seconds). The sugar was poured onto a marble slab dusted with rice flour, and the 'thynner the plate is the fayrer it is.'

From this, several things can be deduced about sugar boiling at this period. First, a test for a stage of boiling is included. Experimentation (and mildly burnt fingers) indicates that 118–120°C may have been intended. The syrup was grained by stirring (the colour change being caused by formation of sucrose crystals). Different types of sugar had different qualities: pot sugar needed more boiling than fair sugar. Finally, thin plate was considered fairer or better. Some attempt at control was being made. Once sugar plate was mastered, it could be used as a basis for other confections; five are listed, flavoured variously with spices, honey and nuts.

Recipes for other sweetmeats are given, including spices 'in confyt' (covered with sugar); *madrian* (conserved ginger) and preserved fruits. They contain other tests for syrup, including, 'boyle it over the fyre tyll it reeche betwyx yr fynger and yr thombe.' This could be anything from modern thread stage up to as high as 114°C. Despite an apparent lack of precision, the recipes were intended to work. Details of tests and colour changes increase chances of success. They were probably trade secrets. For those in the know, the art of confectionery was well advanced. The author is anonymous, but the fact that the manuscript is bound in with medicinal formulae may imply that the confections were considered of benefit to health.

Later in the century, printed books containing confectionery recipes appeared. One which showed links between confectionery and the work of apothecaries was John Partridge's *Treasurie of Commodious Conceits and Hidden Secrets*[5] This contains a dedication addressed to a member of the Guild of Barbers and Surgeons in which the author speaks of making public 'hidden secrets'. Partridge probably took some of his information from Continental sources, such as Alexis of Piedmont's *Secrets*. Translated from French into English in 1558, the latter was an important source of sugar recipes in Britain at a time when the fashion for banquets of sweetmeats was developing rapidly.[6]

It was no accident that alchemists like Alexis of Piedmont and Nostradamus[7] recorded confectionery recipes. They valued sugar for its curative qualities as well as for its very desirability and it provided a medium for scientific experiment. It was transformed according to rules: grained, pulled out into ropes, cut, moulded and modelled. If things didn't work the first time, it could be dissolved back to syrup to try again. Sugar boiling must have seemed akin to magic.

When sugary foods were a means of conspicuous display, recipes were in demand. Early in the seventeenth century, several books appeared, notably *A Closet for Ladies and Gentlewomen*[8] and *Delightes for Ladies*.[9] These set a fashion in both publishing and sweet-making which ran for the whole century.

Charmingly written, these books speak of 'heights' of syrup including 'candy' height, 'sugar boiled to sugar again', and 'manus christi' height. Candy height was recognized 'when you may draw [syrup] in small threads between your finger and your thumb,'[10] according to the author W.M. in 1655. This is now the recognized test for thread stage. Recipes for two types of candy in the *Book of Fruits and Flowers*[11] instruct that the sugar is boiled until it will 'roule between your finger and your thumb,' a stage reached at the higher end of thread, now called soft ball.[12] The anonymous author of *A Closet for Ladies and Gentlewomen* also favoured candy recipes. In several of these, instructions are given to boil syrup, 'til it come to suger againe,' before adding ingredients such as flowers, and stirring until the sugar hardened (which meant that it had grained).

'Manus christi' height is especially confusing. Now meaningless, this term once indicated both a confection and a height of boiling.[13] Many recipes imply the former was made of grained sugar. When used to indicate a height of boiling, it is not clear what was intended. Recipes using this height, and instructions for sweetmeats of the same name, suggest that, around 1600, manus Christi height, candy height and sugar-boiled-to-sugar-again were approximate equivalents. Relating these three heights to temperature measured by thermometer is difficult. Seventeenth-century sugar varieties are not obtainable for trials; syrups boiled and re-boiled during clarification probably behaved differently to modern sugars in boiling, and instructions are too varied to show exactly what was expected.

A further complication is that stages overlap. Testing for thread can be carried out over several degrees of heat. The thread becomes longer as syrup approaches soft ball, eventually becoming strong enough to hold between fully extended forefinger and thumb. This is uncomfortably hot; most people put their fingers quickly into cold water and ease the sugar off—only to discover it can be rolled into a ball. The heat resistance of different individuals' fingers may have influenced tests. Other terms, such as 'the height of a perfect jelly', 'a proper height' and 'a good height', with no qualification, are now useless. Confectioners added to the confusion by describing syrups as being 'almost candy high' or 'almost as high as for manus christi'.

Generally, the heights seem to have indicated concentrations of syrup which boiled between about 110–120°C. This has sometimes puzzled later interpreters, accustomed to a system which frequently uses syrup boiled to 160°C. Some evidence for the use of hotter syrups comes from recipes for *penydes* (the antecedents of humbugs), as in the York manuscript's 'if it wax styffe and part lyghtly fro yr fyngers than it is ynow [enough],'[14] indicating a very hot syrup, possibly as hot as hard crack, 149°C. In 1651, the physician Nicholas Culpeper[15] gave a recipe for 'sugar penids' in which the sugar boiled until 'it rise up in great bubbles, and being chewed it stick not to your teeth.' This is an early method for testing sugar boiled to hard crack, the hottest degree of boiling. And John Partridge instructed that a little syrup be dropped onto a saucer, 'and if it will come from the saucer without cleaving it is enough,'[16] implying a relatively concentrated syrup. Both Partridge and Culpeper were concerned with the use of sugar in physic, as was probably the author of the York manuscript. These extreme heights were most useful to apothecaries.

A desire to protect professional secrets may obscure our knowledge of contemporary practice. Books intended (as many were) for ladies who took up sweetmeat making are unlikely to reflect trade secrets. They may also show a division of gender or social class. Recipes published by practising female confectioners[17] contain little evidence of high-boiled sugar. Today, the 'hot' end of a boiling room is dominated by men. Maybe women were not expected to handle very hot syrups; or perhaps the results were not considered elegant.

The most probable explanation for recipes apparently requiring temperatures lower than 120°C is that the sweets were expected to grain, or turn to candy, hardening in the process.[18] 'Candy' in recipe titles, and as a recognized height, suggests that spontaneous graining was anticipated. Few people made things as clear as Rebecca Price[19] in her manuscript recipes dated 1681 who recorded 'How to Boyle suger to a candy High':

> keepeing it stiring all the time, and when it comes to almost a candy high it will make a great noise in the boyeling and blader very much more than it did at first; and when it begins to be at a full candy high, it will grow very thike and make a broyeling noise like frying which when it doth so, it will immediately candy and turn all to suger againe.

Stirring is an excellent method for inducing crystallization. Most recipes leave one guessing if it was intended; few give explicit instructions to stir, or rub syrup against the side of the pan until it clouds—details which show that confectioners were aiming for candy.

There were many practical reasons for favouring candy. Graining made syrups set, so confectioners probably felt it unnecessary to waste fuel boiling it any further. There was the problem of controlling sugar at high temperatures: it progresses rapidly from clear syrup to one which has begun to colour and burn. Uncertain storage conditions may have played a part. Airtight packaging was not available, and grained sugar keeps relatively well in matchwood boxes between layers of paper, unlike high-boiled transparent sugar (leave the lid off a tin of boiled sweets for a few days—they become sticky, or start to grain spontaneously). Also, ingredients now commonly added to prevent graining, such as glucose or tartaric acid, were not fully developed until the nineteenth century.

From clarified syrup to the point at which the sugar grained readily, perhaps up to about 120°C, gave the basic limits of boiling temperatures for all but a few confections until the end of the seventeenth century. The term height at least suggests practitioners grasped that the phenomena concerned were relative to each other.

By about 1680, the heights of boiling had been placed in sequence. Some consensus had been reached over tests and progression from lower to higher temperatures was recognized. This more detailed knowledge is reflected in cookery manuscripts, such as that belonging to Margaret Savile, dated 1683.[20] After a method for clarifying, she tells how to test for candy height 'let itt boyle till itt draw betwixt your fingers in great flakes like your bird-lime.' For casting height: 'stirre itt sometimes with a stock or a spoone, & when you stirre itt swing your stick from you and when itt is att a casting heigth, your Sugar will flie from your stock, in great flakes of snow, or like Feathers flying in the aire.' Candy height is at the upper end of the modern thread stage, about 114–115°C, and casting height a degree or two higher.

A similar, more detailed sequence appears in the manuscript known as *Martha Washington's Cookery Booke*.[21] Clarification is followed by 'thin surrup', 'full sirrup' and manus christi height, when syrup 'will draw betwixt yr fingers like a small thrid', and progresses through to casting height, giving tests identical to those of Margaret Savile.

This system was shortly replaced by one of degrees based on French terms. They came to dominate sugar boiling during the eighteenth century. Transmission of knowledge from France is a consistent theme in British confectionery from the Restoration onwards. The aristocrats who spent the years of the Commonwealth (1653–9) in exile must have enjoyed the products of French confectioners and brought their recipes back to England. During the ensuing decades, several important works on confectionery were translated from French into English. Later, at the end of the next century, the trade benefited from the presence of French craftsmen who worked in shops or wealthy households.

French-speaking confectioners were able to study *Le Maître d'Hôtel* (1659) or *Le Parfait Confiturier* (1667). Eventually the information they contained was translated by Giles Rose and published in 1682 as

BISHOP, 1850	TEST FOR SYRUP	SKUSE, c. 1890
Caramel	It should snap clean when bitten.	Crack 310°–315°F (154°–157°C)
Cassé	The bullet should crumble, and on biting sticks to the teeth.	
Gros boulet	The ball, or bullet, will be harder when cold.	Ball 250°–255°F (121°–124°C)
Petit boulet	Dip your fingers in cold water, then into the sugar instantly, and again into the water, when the sugar will roll into a ball which should be supple when cold.	
Grand plume	Take the sugar in the skimmer, give it a shake, and if the sparks are large, and adhere together on the rising, it is at the right point.	Feather 240°–245°F (116°–118°C)
Petit plume	The sparks should be larger and stronger.	
Soufflé	Take a skimmer full of sugar and blow through it, and small sparks of sugar will fly from the other side.	
Grand queue de cochon	The streak or tail is now larger.	
Petit queue de cochon	Take some sugar up on the skimmer and drop it on the rest, when it should form a slanting streak on the surface.	
Grand perlé	Little raised balls are formed on the surface of the sugar.	
Petit perlé	The thread may be drawn as far as the span can open without breaking.	Thread 230°–235°F (110°–113°C)
Lissé	The thread will draw a little further.	
Petit lissé	Take a drop of syrup on the thumb and touch it with the forefinger, if on opening them it draws to a fine thread and in breaking forms two drops on each finger, it is at the right point.	Smooth 215°–220°F (101°–105°C)

Table 2. The fully codified stages of sugar boiling and their empirical tests are shown in the left and centre columns, as given by F. Bishop in 1850, just before the introduction of the thermometer. The stages recognized by Skuse 40 years later and his observations of their temperatures are in the right-hand column.

the confectionery section of *A Perfect School for Instructions for Officers of the Mouth*.[22] In this, tests for degrees of sugar boiling were grouped together, listed in order of increasing temperature, and placed as a preface to the confectionery recipes. Now the accepted model, this must have been a true innovation in a printed book.

Rose lists four degrees of sugar boiling in French and English. *À lisse*, or smooth, was the lowest, when a little syrup would stand in a rounded drop on the thumb nail. At *gros pearle*, the syrup was strong enough to hold threads between forefinger and thumb when fully opened. *Soufle*, 'to be blown away,' could be told by taking a skimmer with holes, dipping it into the boiling syrup and blowing through the holes 'and if your Sugar be boyl'd enough it will fly away like dryed leaves but if it run you must boyl it again…or instead of a Scummer put in a Spartle [stirring stick], and if your Sugar be boyl'd it will fly away in the Air.'[23] Finally, *casse* or break, could be detected by dropping a sample of syrup into cold water; if it hardened to become brittle, then it was at the correct height. In the recipes, a fifth stage is introduced, sugar boiled *à la plume* or feather, which is said to be 'beyond a candy height'[24] (the concept of codification, one feels, was not quite fully grasped).

The test for *soufle* is unmistakable; it takes place at about 114–115°C and continues over a limited temperature range. Rose also relates *soufle* directly to English candy height, as do instructions from his anonymous contemporary[25] who advised blowing through a skimmer to see if the sugar formed 'little bladders' as a test for candy height. The alternative, using a spurtle, is similar to that for 'casting height' used by Rebecca Price and the Martha Washington manuscript. A few years later, this was specifically equated with *plume* or feather in work by François Massialot.[26]

The five terms—*lisse* or smooth, pearl, blow, feather, and *casse* or break—remained standard during the eighteenth and nineteenth centuries. They were split into 'lower' and 'higher', which then became regarded as degrees in their own right. The term *caramel* was

Figure 13. The title page of *Le Cannameliste Français* (The French Confectioner), by J. Gilliers (1750). The lower half shows a perspective of a workshop, with charcoal stoves for sugar-boiling.

added. Confusingly for the modern reader, this indicated the degree just before the sugar begins to colour. It is now regarded as the hard crack stage.

Such attention to detail implies that confectionery became very accomplished during the eighteenth century but, despite this, written instructions were often inconsistent and blasé. Recipes were plagiarized, inadequately copied, or suffered from a problem which still afflicts manuals: the person who wrote the instructions already knew what to do. It is not surprising that the degrees of boiling were still not fully understood. Early in the century, Massialot observed,

> The common People only judge the Sugar to be sufficiently boil'd, when the Drops that are put upon a Plate grow thick, as it were a Jelly, and cease to run, any longer: indeed this way of Boiling may be sufficient for certain Jellies of Fruit and *Compotes*; but no great Progress would be made in the Art of Preserving if nothing else were known…and even the most skilful Confectioners know nothing otherwise, after the Feathered Boiling.[27]

Confectioners remained circumspect about boiling sugar higher than feather. In 1726, John Nott remarked that low temperatures were 'not enough for the whole Art of Confectioning.' Obliquely, he offered an explanation as to why high temperatures were little used. Care was needed, and when sugar was 'boil'd to its utmost *caramel* Height…take it off the Fire immediately, or else it will be burnt, and fit for no Use at all.'[28] When syrup is heated to higher degrees, the remaining water boils off quickly, and the temperature rises fast. Unless heating is checked at exactly the right moment, the sugar browns. Confectioners favoured heavy copper pans which retain heat well; even off the fire, syrups would go on cooking. It was (and still is) easy to end up with a carbonised mixture and a spoilt pan. Many eighteenth-century confectioners instructed readers not to allow sugar to colour at all during boiling, saying that if it did, it was ruined. From their point of view it probably was. Even slightly burnt sugar has begun to break down and cannot be re-boiled. The economical use of scrap was important when sugar was such an expensive commodity.

Figure 14. A confectioner's workroom, from Diderot's *Encyclopédie* (1763–72)

Higher degrees came into use gradually. In the sixteenth century, only apothecaries were confident with them. In the next, Rose translated one recipe which required sugar boiled to *casse* or break. In the eighteenth, sugar boiled to the highest degree, *grand casse*, or *caramel*, had a limited use. Massialot said that caramel was proper for 'Barley-sugar and certain small Sugar-works call'd by that name.'[29]

His compatriot J. Gilliers, writing in 1751, described caramel as sugar boiled to *casse*. It was coloured, and used for figures to decorate the table. Other confectioners used caramel for decorative purposes and do not seem to have made many boiled-sugar sweets of the type now familiar. Only at the beginning of the next century did Jarrin make it clear that he included browned sugar in the term caramel.

By then, confectioners recognized twelve or thirteen degrees of sugar boiling such as were recorded by a craftsman and author who styled himself 'an ingenious foreigner', known only to posterity as Borella.[30] A full list was given in a book written 50 years later by Frederick Bishop,[31] just about the time thermometers were coming into use. His system, together with the stages recognized at the end of the century by E. Skuse[32] and the equivalents he gave in degrees Fahrenheit, are laid out in table 2 on page 56.

Instruments developed by scientists wishing to make accurate observations had a considerable effect on confectionery skills during the Victorian period. The two which became important to the sugar boiler were the hydrometer (for measuring specific gravity of liquids) and the thermometer. The concepts behind both of these had been understood for a long time but accurate, standardized measurement, and instruments robust and inexpensive enough for everyday use, were a different matter. A scale for measuring specific gravity was proposed in 1768 by the French chemist Antoine Baumé,[33] using a hydrometer. This instrument consists of a weighted hollow bulb and a stem bearing a graduated scale which floats upright in liquids, allowing readings to be taken. By the late eighteenth century a type specifically used for sugar solutions had been developed. This became known as a saccharometer.

Confectioners in Britain began using the instrument during the first half of the nineteenth century. In the 1830s, Jarrin updated his *Italian Confectioner* with information on the use of the 'syrup weigher' (saccharometer). This, he said, was generally used after clarifying sugar for ascertaining the strength of sugar solutions. He remarks:

> The advantages of the syrup weigher are immense, not only as a matter of economy, but as a guide to the workman, who cannot work with certainty, without knowing the degrees of boiling or heating, and which can only be learned by practice. For example, Le Lissé…the syrup weigher will mark 25°; Le Perlé, 30°; Le Soufflet, 34°; Strong, at 36°, which is made use of for candy.[34]

About twenty years later William Jeanes commented of saccharometers that 'these instruments may be purchased at any respectable optician's,'[35] which implies their use was by then widely accepted. He also mentions a Fahrenheit or Réaumur's thermometer, but this was to monitor the low temperature of stoves used for candying and drying sweetmeats, not for boiling syrups.

It took another three decades for sugar-boiling thermometers to become widespread. The problems of manufacturing instruments to

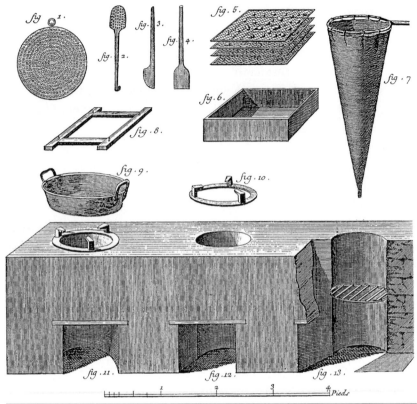

Figure 15. A confectioner's furnace, from Diderot's *Encyclopédie* (1763–72). It shows a conical strainer, frames, trays and paddles such as are being used in the illustration of the confectioner's workroom, figure 14, page 60.

withstand the high temperatures probably had something to do with this. Sugar in syrup has to be fully dissolved and at a temperature close to boiling before a thermometer can be placed in it. As late as 1910, May Whyte recommended the confectioner, 'Dip your thermometer *quickly* in and out of the boiling sugar several times until the mercury runs up to 150° or 160° [Fahrenheit; about 65–70°C]; then put it in, leaning it against the side of the pan.'[36] Careful handling was obviously needed; dipping prevented the glass thermometer breaking under the shock of the hot liquid.

Figure 16. Saccharometers, taken from John Kirkland, *The Modern Baker, Confectioner & Caterer* (1907).

Despite such problems, thermometers had become essential. Around 1890, Skuse instructed readers that they should supply themselves with sugar thermometers.

> The cost of this is very soon repaid by the saving of material and time as well as anxiety. While the sugar is undergoing the process of boiling, it is almost impossible for a learner to determine the exact degree which the sugar has attained without its aid, and even the journeyman finds it so useful that you will find very few indeed who boil sugar without it; in fact many of the large shops will not allow a sugar boiler to work without one.[37]

In theory, confectioners would never have to burn their hands on hot sugar again. In practice, instruments, cheap sugar and machines developed from the mid-nineteenth century onwards led to large-scale production. Technical aspects become increasingly important as confectionery moved from craft to industry. This made it cheap and widely available, but obscured the magic.

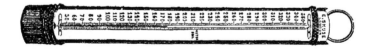

Figure 17. Sugar thermometer; from Skuse, *Confectioners Handbook* (c. 1890).

Figure 18. Patterns of Coleman Patent Rubber Candy Moulds, made by the Voorhees Rubber Manufacturing Co. in Jersey City, USA and advertised in a catalogue dated 1912. The selected moulds would be made up into rubber sheets for mass production. Similar shapes were cast in plaster for starch-moulding.

CHAPTER V

Candy complexities

SUGAR CANDY is crystallized sugar. Candy was known almost 2,000 years ago. The *OED* traces the word through Arabic to the Persian *qand,* for the crystallized juice of the sugar-cane, thence eastwards to India. The ultimate origin is thought to be Sanskrit *khanda*, meaning sugar in crystalline pieces. The modern definition is still close to the latter. For a substance to retain an ancient name in such a widespread form is witness to its value. This long history suggests that much early sugar confectionery probably was literally candy. The earliest records of candy in English are in the phrase 'sugar candy', paralleled in the French *sucre candi*, Spanish *azucar cande,* and equivalents in Portuguese, Italian, and medieval Latin.

Candy, in the confectioner's world, describes refined sugar that has been dissolved in water, boiled to a certain point and then allowed or encouraged to re-crystallize (in technical parlance, to grain) so that the confection sets as a more or less hard mass. Candied sweets include tablet, fudge, sugar mice, Kendal Mint Cake and all those cream fondant fillings of chocolates.

For North Americans, the term candy covers almost the same ground as sweets in Britain and means all sorts of things which aren't candy in the technical sense.

There are one or two special uses of the word which have survived here, such as candied fruit. Soaked in syrup until enough sugar has penetrated by osmosis to the middle of the fruit to preserve it, the 'candy' part comes right at the end when the pieces are dipped in a lightly grained syrup. This hardens to form a shell of candy around each one, and is probably what Charles Dickens described when he mentioned 'the candied fruits so caked and spotted with sugar as to make the coldest lookers-on feel faint and subsequently bilious.'[1] Even these are disappearing, replaced by 'crystallized' finishes (which usually means preserved fruit rolled in granulated sugar) or 'glacée' coatings (dipped in syrup which remains shiny when cool).

Another specialized use of the word is in the term rock candy. This is composed of large, semi-transparent crystals grown slowly over a period of days on sticks or strings suspended in warm sugar solution. These are huge versions of the crystals which form from sugar-cane juice boiled down to a syrupy consistency, which are the stuff of sugar loaves. It is not always clear from early recipes which sort of candy they refer to.

******

For generations, confectioners have been aware that crystals form easily in syrup concentrated beyond a certain point. Stir too much whilst it is hot and the sugar will start to grain. This appears first as a faint trace of cloudiness in transparent syrup and gradually increases until it becomes opaque. If the confectioner is really unlucky, the whole lot suddenly becomes crystals of sugar again: sugar boiled to sugar, as in the seventeenth-century expression. Sugar boilers have been attempting to control this process of graining ever since, developing techniques for forming and controlling crystals in syrup.

Only in the past century has sugar chemistry provided an explanation. Sucrose, ordinary sugar, dissolved in water and heated, inverts to a solution of glucose and fructose, the two smaller component sugars. As long as energy is being put into the mixture—as long as it is being heated—the two remain separate. When heating stops and the syrup begins to cool, the glucose and fructose can recombine, becoming molecules of sucrose which grow into larger crystals. This is graining. It can happen spontaneously, triggered by rough handling, or when undissolved sugar crystals remain from before boiling commenced (in which case it is a rapid process). Alternatively, graining can be deliberately encouraged by stirring the mixture.

Sweets made by this method are boiled to relatively low temperatures, about 112–118°C. If allowed to cool undisturbed, these syrups have a relatively high water content and a sticky consistency when cold; but beating encourages the whole mass to re-crystallize. In a simple mixture of sugar dissolved in water, the size of crystal which develops depends on the concentration of the syrup, the temperature at which graining takes place, and how much it is stirred as it cools. An alternative method for forming crystals, the one now usually used by the confectionery industry, is to 'seed' the mixture by adding pre-prepared sugar crystals of the desired size; this produces a uniform and reproducible texture with a minimum of problems.

The skills of creating and controlling grain have been a secret weapon in the armoury of the British confectioner for centuries. Early recipes include many candied mixtures of sugar with perfumes and flowers, poured out and cut into squares or diamonds. Grained sugar was also used for casting, poured into plaster of Paris moulds shaped like lemons or pears or oranges, or any other shape which lay within the imagination and skill of the confectioner. These were the precursors of still-popular sugar mice and pigs and some seaside novelties.

Many of these early candies were elegant and interesting. In the York manuscript,[2] six varieties are listed: *sugar plate* (plain candy), *gobett ryall*, coloured with tournesoll,[3] flavoured with ginger and mace, and cut into 'gobetts' (small pieces), and *garyofilate*, coloured with saffron and flavoured with cloves (in Latin, *caryophyllata*). *Paste ryall* contained honey, egg white, ginger and mace; it was poured into boxes and stuck with cloves. If the honey was omitted and the sweet cut in gobbets, it became *manus Christi*. The sixth sort, *penande*, was mixed with pine nuts, cloves and mace:

To make penande:
Take a lb of clene claryfyed sugere and pute it in a panne and sette it on the fyre… and whan it is sothen sette it fro the fyre and put therto di lb of pynes clene pyked and stere all togedere with a spatour to thei begynne to wax colde and parte and then put thereto IIII ounce of claryfyed hony and stere all togedere and set it on the fyre agayne the mantanance of II pater noster.

> Whylle, evermore steryng with the spatour and set it fro the fyre and put
> thereto zinzeber and macez eche di unce and put it in cofynes and zyf ze
> wyll make them in gobetts kutt them as ze have done zour gobetts before.

This makes an excellent confection, rather sweet, but one which will
please anyone who likes the characteristic flavour of pine nuts,
although in my experiments, by the time the sugar separated from the
nuts, graining had gone too far and produced dry, uneven sandy
lumps and broken pine nuts. See the modern version at the end of
this chapter for instructions.

It is not clear why sixteenth-century confectioners added the
honey. This is an isolated instance of its use in candy. It may have
reflected earlier practices, an attempt to glue the mixture together or
to soften the texture. Honey helps to prevent graining and in theory
would produce a smoother, more unctuous confection. However,
there is little evidence for its deliberate use in this way until the nineteenth century. It could also have had supposed medicinal qualities or
perhaps, simply, the flavour was appreciated.

Many texts from the sixteenth and seventeenth centuries include a
recipe for a confection called manus Christi, literally 'the hand of
Christ'. The name has never been adequately explained.[4] It appears
very curious in a country accustomed to a secularized way of life
loosely based on the Protestant version of Christianity. Four centuries
ago, religion was more deeply woven into everyday life, and the name
would not have seemed so odd. Sweetmeats are still closely entwined
with religion for the Catholic church in southern Europe, where
production of special confections and drinks is associated with
monasteries and nunneries, for whom it provides income.

Many recipes for manus Christi lack detail about the processes
involved. From a twentieth-century perspective, it is easy to make the
assumption that a clear sugar drop, like a modern boiled sweet, was
intended (in some cases, such as Plat's 'wholesome and comfortable
manus christi' for which a recipe appeared in 1653, perhaps it was).[5]
It seems much more likely that a candy-type sweetmeat was generally

desired. In the York manuscript, manus Christi occurs as a candied mixture of sugar and egg white, flavoured with spices. By about 1600, it consisted of highly refined sugar boiled with flavourings, usually rosewater, and mixed with gold leaf. Some versions were expensively perfumed with musk or ambergris, and included ground-up pearls; others used oils of spices such as mace. This recipe, from *A Closet for Ladies and Gentlewomen,* is clearer than most:

> *To make Manus Christi.*
> Take halfe a pound of refined Suger, and some Rose water, and boyle them together, till it come to sugar againe, then stirre it about while it be somewhat cold, then take your leaf gould, and mingle with it, then cast it according to art, That is, in round gobbetts, and so keep them.[6]

'Somewhat cold' is a relative term, as the sugar grains and becomes stiff whilst still quite hot. Seventeenth-century sugar must have recrystallized less easily than modern refined sugar. Whatever was intended, the recipe can be made to work, and produces a delicate, beautifully white confection.

By the early eighteenth century, manus Christi had become a cordial of sugar and rosewater or violets, given to people who were in weak health. Soon afterwards it vanished from the repertoire. Or did it? Perhaps it was just the name which went, as the English consistently showed a taste, first for candy or sugar paste, and later for fondant, flavoured with rosewater or violets.

Sugar was considered to have health benefits; it was also useful for preserving decoctions of herbs and other physic such as flowers and roots. It made bitter herbs more palatable and, formed into candy, allowed the slow release of soothing essences for sore throats and coughs. Recipes of this kind were probably the ancestors of several sweets which have survived as regional specialities: cough candy, Kendal Mint Cake, and Scottish tablet. Cough candy, as sold by confectioners and herbalists in northern England is a chestnut-brown, fudge-like confection, flavoured strongly with medicinal ingredients (traditionally horehound and coltsfoot, but now often commercially produced essences). It has a long precedent, and is a survivor of many other candied medicaments, most of which have vanished. Cures for other ailments were sometimes administered in candy, as a recipe from *A Queens Delight* shows:

> Sugar of Wormwood, Mint, Anniseed, or any other of that kinde. Take double refined sugar, and do but wet it in fair water, or Rose-water and boil it to a candy, when it is almost boiled take it off and stir it till it be cold; then drop in three or four drops of the Oyls of whatsoever you will make, and stir it well, then drop it on a board, being before fitted with sugar.[7]

The qualities of mint as a digestive, and the alternatives (wormwood, a vermifuge, and aniseed, which eases flatulence) suggest the recipe was intended to comfort the digestion.

The recipe is an early published example of the use of mint in sweetmeats in Britain. This flavour, now a distinctive feature of Polos, mint imperials, spearmint gum, Glacier Mints and many others, appears to have become popular in the middle of the last century. A factor may have been ready availability of good-quality mint oil from Mitcham in Surrey, at a time when sugar confectionery was rapidly commercializing. Mint oil was reliable, probably relatively cheap, and a strong flavour which was easy to handle, by small- as well as large-scale confectioners. Candied peppermint was one of several simple mint-flavoured confections given in a small, provincial book on sugar boiling published by S.W. Stavely of Nottingham in the 1820s.[8] Mint-flavoured candy is still made by a similar process to the seventeenth-century recipe given above (but without the rosewater) and sold under the name of Kendal Mint Cake. Why this confection should survive as a speciality of a small town in north-west England is not clear. The first record of an association between product and town occurs in the mid-nineteenth century.

A little further north, another type of candy survives. This is Scottish tablet, which is similar to a crisp version of fudge—brown, sugary, with a characteristic flavour derived from sugar and milk cooked together. A version was known in the eighteenth century when Lady Grisell Baillie recorded purchases of 'Taiblet for the bairns' in her household book between 1692–1733.[9] Recipes for tablets flavoured with orange, rose, cinnamon and ginger were published in Glasgow by Mrs McLintock in 1736. These are simple candy recipes, made only with sugar, water and flavourings. This is her recipe:

Orange Tablets with the Grate:
Grate the Oranges, take 2 lib. of sugar, and a mutchkin of water, then clarify it with the White of 2 Eggs, and set it on a slow Fire, and boil it till it be almost candyed, then put in the Grate of the Oranges, and take your white paper, rub it with fresh Butter, pour it on your Paper, and cut in little pieces.[10]

This is a candy similar to those from the previous century. The word tablet has medicinal overtones, as in the commonly accepted meaning of a small flat disc containing some drug or health-giving substance. Medicinal or not, this recipe tastes good.

In tablet now made in Scotland, both orange and ginger are still found amongst the flavourings, but milk has become essential to the definition. Probably a nineteenth-century addition, it was one which had become universal by the time F. Marian McNeill was writing *The Scots Kitchen*. In her recipe for tablet, milk (or thin cream) replaced water for dissolving the sugar. In other respects it is similar to that from two centuries earlier, down to the proportions—two pounds of sugar and three teacupfuls of liquid, plus flavouring. Once boiling has finished, she recommends,

now put the pan into a basin of cold water and stir rapidly with a spoon. It [the sugar mixture] soon begins to solidify round the edge, and this must be scraped off repeatedly. Keep stirring until the mass is sufficiently grained, and then pour it immediately onto a buttered slab. If too highly grained, it will not pour out flat; if too thin, it will be sticky. Only practice makes perfection.[11]

The instructions convey something of the difficulties involved. The process of graining in hot syrup can be surprisingly swift, the mixture going from a slightly thickened texture to a stiff mass of uneven sugar crystals in seconds. Achieving a confection which is hard enough to set, but soft enough to spread whilst warm and look tidy when cold, is not easy, but as many Scottish children learn, the mass can be put back in the pan and briefly re-boiled for another attempt.

The addition of dairy produce was a development which contributed more than just flavour. Milk, cream and butter contain proteins and fats: large, complex molecules, whose chemistry is very different to that of sucrose. These physically intrude between sugar crystals, preventing them from growing beyond a certain size. This is exploited by fudge, a confection which relies on similar ingredients and principles to tablet, but is richer, softer and requires a slightly lower temperature. On first tasting, the similarities seem overwhelming, both in flavour (derived from a reaction between sugar and the protein in dairy produce during cooking) and general texture. It is easy to assume that they share a common origin; but the derivation of the name fudge and the origins of the sweet are both obscure. Fudge as now understood seems to have travelled east to Britain from North America. Anecdotal evidence links it to women's colleges in the late nineteenth century,[12] and most early recipes include chocolate. It is possible that Scottish migrants took the idea of milk-based tablet to North America. Whether these were influenced by fudge-like mixtures of brown sugar and nuts from the Creole cuisine of the southern states is unclear.[13]

Fudge appears to have been taken up by confectioners and large companies some years later. Skuse, who actively collected formulae, including North American ones, did not give one for fudge in the early editions of his *Confectioners Handbook*, but recipes first appear in British books in the first decade of this century. One was given just after the First World War by Louisa Thorpe:

Chocolate Fudge
8 oz loaf sugar, 8 oz butter, 8 oz unsweetened chocolate, 1 pint milk, vanilla essence to taste, 4 oz chopped walnuts if desired.
Put the ingredients into a saucepan and boil them all gently together, keeping them stirred very slowly; cook the mixture until it will form a soft ball when a little of it is dropped in cold water and rolled between the fingers. When

the boiling is complete, put the mixture aside in the saucepan until it is nearly set, then work it with the hand into a paste. Roll with a rolling pin and cut into squares.[14]

This mixture needs careful, slow cooking and thorough stirring, or it will curdle or catch on the base of the pan and scorch. The results are worth the trouble.

******

An important development for confectioners had been the discovery in the eighteenth century, by the scientist Andreas Marggraf, that glucose could be produced by boiling starch with dilute sulphuric acid. This opened a line of research that eventually led to the industrial manufacture of glucose syrup. This is one of a number of added ingredients, called in the trade 'doctors', that can alter or delay the process of graining. These chemists' creations gave confectioners Faustian control over their raw material and became central to the growth of large-scale manufacture of confectionery from refined sugar as well as encouraging the invention of modern sweet types. I give more information about 'doctors' in the following chapter.

In the mid-nineteenth century, old-fashioned, hard-textured sugar candy developed a new, softer variation. This was fondant (the word derives from French *fondre*, to melt, describing the texture) whose best known manifestation is now 'cream' or 'creme' fillings in chocolates. Like candy, the process is one of graining sugar syrup boiled to 115°C, or a little lower. The difference is that for fondant, syrup is allowed to cool before stirring, producing a small, fine textured grain of sucrose crystals suspended in a syrup in which the rest of the sugar remains inverted. By the time Skuse was writing, confectioners had discovered that fondant texture could be achieved more reliably by adding glucose. This interferes further with graining, giving minute crystals suspended in syrup, with a characteristic soft, melting texture.

Like many sweet creations, fondant could be moulded at the whim of the confectioner; and this was made easier by the development of a

73

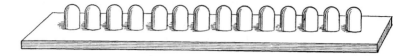

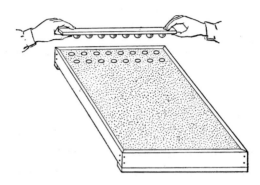

Figure 18. A plain moulding strip (above) and a starch tray being moulded. From John Kirkland, *The Modern Baker, Confectioner & Caterer* (1907).

Figure 19. Starch-moulding. From the left: the tray being filled and the starch smoothed; the moulds being pressed; the moulds being filled from a fondant funnel. From Skuse, *The Confectioners Handbook* (c. 1890).

technique called starch-moulding. Jarrin seems to have been the first person to describe this in English. In 1836 he discussed how to make a frame filled with dry starch, levelled and then printed with special shapes:

> You should have wooden or plaster moulds, or they may be made in brass, or ivory, or lead; they should represent the desired object exactly, such as baskets, vases, flowers, scissars, buckles; in short, any thing that may be wished.[15]

He instructed that the impressions be filled with syrup, making drops which were probably close to old-fashioned candy in texture. A few years later, William Finemore recorded in his notebook that barley sugar drops, ginger and rhubarb candy, and 'raspberries de gum' could all be moulded in starch. 'Orange cream'—which was almost a fondant—he shaped in tin hoops.

In principle starch moulding is simple. A shallow tray is filled with well-dried powdered starch (cornflour works in a domestic situation, although industry now demands starches especially modified for the purpose), and impressions made in the surface using objects to hand—a marble or a shell, for instance—or specially-made shapes. Warm fondant or syrup is poured into the hollows and left to set. The starch has a dehydrating effect, drawing moisture from the sugar, encouraging a firm crust to form. Then the shapes are sieved out and dusted off, ready for dipping in chocolate, or submerging in sugar syrup for a layer of fine sugar crystals to grow on them.

Fondant is relatively simple to make, and lends itself to many variations in colour and flavour. In the 1890s, various handbooks suggested it as a dainty suitable for making by ladies wishing to earn a little income, both in Britain and North America. Catherine Owen drew a picture of 'French cream candies' as made at home in North America from white of egg and raw sugar. She declared, 'none of these as usually made, however pleasant for an evening's amusement or acceptable for home consumption…could enter the market as saleable articles.' As well as being simple to make and readily exploited for

Figure 20. A fondant funnel. The molten fondant is agitated and the flow controlled by the plunger.

cash, she recommended fondant as a means of self-expression: 'The making of real French cream candies will allow the utmost scope for artistic taste, and the woman who has some knowledge of mixing colours will be the most likely to produce beautiful results. As a rule, all the high colours should be avoided.'[16] Presenting confectionery as a creative pastime which allowed the practitioner to show off expertise and good taste echoed the seventeenth-century ideals of gentlewomen who could make banqueting conceits.

Fondant is now rarely seen without a coating of chocolate, and is no longer considered an exciting novelty. It can be bought in blocks from specialist suppliers by people who require small amounts. Any recipe which is going to be useful has to have something special about it. The one for maple fondant given at the end of this chapter is adapted from a recipe in *How to make Candy* by Walter W. Chenoweth.[17]

Exploitation of fondant and starch-moulding led to a fin-de-siècle flourish of pastel confectionery in myriad shapes and colours. About 1900, Skuse commented of 'Fondant Cream Work' that, 'this department has developed more rapidly and more extensively than perhaps any other in the business, if we except chocolate, and even then, fondant cream has been of great assistance to the coca bean.'[18]

Ironically, it was fondant which acted as a midwife to chocolate—now the dominating confection. Since 1866, the Bristol company of Joseph Fry and Sons had been selling their Chocolate Cream Bar, filled with fondant. This was an enormous success (and remains popular). Much fondant is still eaten, but it is now thought of almost exclusively in the context of chocolates; and other sugar-candy-based confections have become curiosities.

Figure 21. Plaster moulds for fondant or jellies. These shapes could be pressed into a tray of starch to make the individual sweetmeats.

RECIPES

PENANDE

250g granulated sugar • 150ml water • 125g pine nuts
60g pale honey (about a tablespoonful)
a good pinch each of mace and cloves
Equipment: marble slab or metal tray covered with silicone-coated paper.

Put the sugar and water in a pan and stir over a low heat until every crystal has melted. Turn up the heat and boil to hard ball, 120°C. Remove from the heat and add the pine nuts. Stir carefully for about a minute; the sugar will begin to look slightly opaque, a little stiffer, and lose its shine, and the nuts make a faint rustling noise as they are stirred. Immediately add the honey and spices. Return briefly to the heat, just enough to bring the mixture back to a more liquid state. Stir to mix the honey evenly, and then pour onto the slab or tray in an even layer. Within about 5 minutes, it should be possible to mark into squares or fingers about 2cm wide. If it is still soft, leave a few hours, by which time it should grain and stiffen enough to mark out. Leave overnight, break into pieces, and pack in an airtight box. With care, an evenly grained version can be made. It is better to stop stirring whilst the syrup is still moderately liquid.

MANUS CHRISTI, OR ROSEWATER CANDY

250g granulated sugar or sugar lumps • 100ml rose water
a piece of gold leaf about 2cm square (optional)
Equipment: marble slab or metal tray covered with silicone-coated paper.

'Lump' sugar, which is often referred to in old recipes, originally meant chunks of candy broken from a highly refined sugar cone. Technically, the modern equivalent is granulated or caster sugar, not 'sugar lumps' or cubes which are simply a different presentation of crystals. However, I did test this recipe using sugar cubes and the result was a confection of beautiful delicacy and whiteness. Put the rosewater and sugar in a small pan and stir to dissolve the sugar. Make sure the lumps are fully dissolved. As the sugar comes to the boil, it may froth; watch that it doesn't boil over. The foam will soon subside. Then increase the heat, and boil to soft ball, 114°C. Remove from the heat and stir with a wooden spoon. Initially, a lot of bubbles will form, but these will vanish and the mixture begin to look slightly cloudy. Stop when the syrup becomes so opaque that it is difficult to see the bottom of the pan. Drop the mixture in small rounds onto the paper. Work fast, as it stiffens very quickly. Leave to set, lift off and pack carefully in an airtight box.

If you use gold leaf, either pull it into little pieces and stir it into the sugar after graining or, for a very pretty effect, when the sugar drops have set, take a clean damp paintbrush and just moisten the top of each round enough for a fragment of gold leaf to stick.

MRS McLINTOCK'S ORANGE TABLETS

250g granulated sugar • 150ml water
finely grated zest of 1 orange
Equipment: marble slab or metal tray covered with silicone-coated paper.

Heat the water and the sugar together in a small pan. Stir at first to dissolve all sugar crystals, then increase the heat and boil to just above soft ball, about 118–119°C. Remove from the heat, add the orange zest, and stir quite vigorously for about 2 minutes. The sugar will foam for a moment, and then subside. When the mixture begins to look opaque and feel a little heavier as it is stirred, pour immediately onto the slab or tray lined with paper. Mark into squares or lozenges straight away, leave overnight. Snap into pieces the next day.

LOUISA THORPE'S CHOCOLATE FUDGE

500g granulated sugar • 250g butter
250g bitter chocolate (at least 60% cocoa solids) • 600ml milk
vanilla essence to taste • 125g chopped walnuts (optional)
Equipment: a tin 20cm square, lined with greaseproof paper.

Doubling the quantity of sugar suggested in the original recipe on page 72 makes the mixture a little easier to handle. Put everything except the vanilla and walnuts into a large saucepan over low heat. Allow the butter and chocolate to melt and bring to a gentle boil, stirring. Cook over a moderate flame, stirring constantly, and boil gently until a little of the mixture forms a soft ball when it is dropped into cold water. Add the vanilla (and the walnuts if used). Leave to cool in the saucepan for about 20 minutes, then stir until it stiffens. Pour or press into the lined tin and leave to set before cutting into squares.

MAPLE-FLAVOURED FONDANT

600g granulated sugar • 250ml maple syrup • 125 ml water

In a saucepan, mix the sugar, syrup and water. Heat gently, stirring, until all the sugar crystals have dissolved. Turn up the heat and bring to the boil. Cook until it reaches 113°C or will just begin to form a soft ball in cold water. Pour into a shallow bowl, put in the thermometer, and allow to cool undisturbed to 45°C. Remove the thermometer and then stir the syrup with a wooden spoon until it becomes opaque and the texture resembles cream cheese. Gather together in a ball and knead by hand until smooth. Store overnight in a jar or a bowl covered with plastic film .

I consider this is best divided into small pieces, each decorated with half a pecan. If you want to do this, allow about 250g pecan halves for this quantity of fondant.

CHAPTER VI

Written in sugar: pulled sweets and seaside rock

PULLED sugar forms a large category of sweets, among the favourites of childhood. They were often the subject of marathon sucking competitions: rolled around the mouth, periodically withdrawn to see how progress was going, sucked again until bedtime. The group embraces lettered seaside rock and twists as well as that acme of oral satisfaction, the humbug.

These sweets need sugar boiled beyond the candy stage, poured onto a flat surface and rested a moment while an outer skin is allowed to form. Then it can be cautiously worked and folded with the hands. As it is manipulated, it turns an opaque white. The 'pulling' of the definition is undertaken by repeatedly stretching the mass of worked sugar, often looping it over a hook and pulling it out to thinner strands. The mixture need not necessarily be left neutral and white: it can be coloured with dyes, flavoured, or otherwise toyed with.

As with almost every other object on display in the sweet shop, the humbug or the stick of rock have a long and sometimes tortuous history; but each stage is connected and a chain of circumstance may be forged that links medieval Arabia to the beach at Bridlington on a sunny bank holiday

Like much to do with confectionery, pulled sugar probably came west into Europe during the Moslem expansion in the seventh century AD. The English words pennet and penide have both been obsolete for a hundred years, although they survived for longer in northern dialect. They described humbug-like sweets or barley sugar, often with medicinal implications. Penide (pennet has the same

Figure 22. Hooks for pulling sugar, from an American catalogue of confectioners' requisites of the 1930s.

Figure 23. Pulling sugar over a hook. Illustration taken from Garret, *The Encyclopaedia of Practical Cookery* (*c.* 1890).

etymology) is an anglicized version of the medieval Latin *penidium*. This word comes from Arabic *al-fanid*, an expression recorded in thirteenth-century Moslem Spain, meaning pulled sugar shaped into rings and discs.[1] The Arabs probably borrowed the word from the Persian *fanid* or *phanita*, which seems to have meant a kind of paste of worked sugar (sugar which has been pulled is still sometimes described as a paste). *Al-fanid* was also absorbed into Spanish, as *alfeñique*, and Portuguese, as *alfenim*, meaning boiled sugar pulled until white. Alphenic, a version occasionally used in pharmaceutical English during the seventeenth and eighteenth centuries, was said to mean 'white barley sugar' or white sugar candy.[2]

Pennets were known to the seventeenth-century physician Culpeper, who observed of 'sugar penids', 'I remember country people were wont to take them for coughs.'[3] He was recording a tradition in the use of sugar sticks that was probably ancient. His implication, to which we will return, was also that this sweet was linked to provincial habits and considered of dubious value.

Sugar was thought to be good for colds, and this was due to early ideas about physiology. Medieval physicians subscribed to a holistic system, including notions of hot and cold. This fixed the place of sweetmeats within European diet and pharmacopoeia: sugar was considered moderately hot, but not as hot as honey. These ideas had nothing to do with physical temperature, but were based on a concept of pathology established in the second century AD by the physician Galen. Taking ideas from Hippocrates (fifth century BC) and Pythagoras (sixth century BC), he thought people could be divided into categories based on their 'humours'—sanguine, choleric, melancholic or phlegmatic—according to disposition and appearance. Each humour had its particular combination of qualities, described in terms of hot, moist, cold or dry. As long as these were in balance in the body, the patient remained healthy, but if one got out of hand, disease resulted. It was also held that foods had similar qualities, so the appropriate action was to administer food and drugs which had the correct characteristics of hot or cold, dry or moist needed to restore the balance.

The concept of sugar as medicine probably came from the traditions of Moslem physicians. They came from a culture which knew and used sugar, and they transmitted the humoral system to Dark Age Europe through points of contact such as Sicily and Andalusia. Physicians working within Galenic theory stated that sugar was hot, and therefore suitable for treating conditions caused by excessive cold; its effects could be moderated by adding ingredients such as roses and violets which had cooling qualities.

That sugar was an expensive and exotic luxury, used medicinally by the subtle and learned Arabs, probably helped reinforce medieval European ideas of its intrinsic goodness. There were plenty of ailments in northern Europe for which sugar was considered suitable treatment— coughs, colds, chest infections, agues. The Church allowed that sugar was medicinal (St Thomas Aquinas himself apparently considered and pronounced on the subject), which meant it could be legitimately nibbled during Lent, probably adding to its appeal.

It is no coincidence that our earliest information about pulled-sugar sweets in Britain, using the very word penides that travelled all the way from the Orient, comes from compilations of medicinal formulae, not elegant books on fine confectionery. A description of pulling sugar was written down about 1500 in the York manuscript, under the title *To make penydes*. Unclarified sugar is boiled until if you can 'assaye it betwyx your fynger and your thombe and it waxe styffe and parte lythtly fro your fyngers,' it is sufficiently boiled. (Don't try this test—a temperature of something between 130° and 150°C is intended.) It should not be stirred much whilst boiling. Meanwhile, the confectioner should oil a marble slab, and his hands, with 'swete mete oyle' in preparation for working. When the correct stage is reached, the sugar is poured straight from the fire onto the marble slab. When it has cooled a little, it is worked with both hands by drawing it on 'a hoke of yrone tyll it be fayre and whyte.' Then it is drawn out to the thickness of a thumb, cut with 'fayre schers' into pieces an inch long, and 'pute them in a warm place and than the warmnes schall pute awaye the toughnesse.' A final instruction warns against trying to make this confection in humid or wet weather.

The art of pulling sugar was evidently well understood 500 years ago. A high temperature (one wonders how many novice confectioners burnt their fingers), minimal stirring (avoiding anything leading to re-crystallization), and working syrup until white are still features of pulled-sugar recipes. Many pulled sweets are still cut in pieces about an inch long; working with sugar in humid weather is still considered a thankless task by confectioners. The curious instruction to take away the toughness means that the sweets underwent a maturing process, which encouraged them to grain and soften. The final result was probably reminiscent of a piece of rock which has been exposed to the air for a few weeks.

This recipe is significant in the early history of pulled sugar. By the nineteenth century *penydes*, or *penides*, were called pennets (perhaps confused with the idea of little pieces, so becoming the 'pellets' amongst William Finemore's pulled-sugar recipes). This name became obsolete shortly afterwards, replaced by humbug. We consider the latter, striped in two colours, to be a typically 'Victorian' confection, and fail to recognize that it is just one link in a long tradition.[4]

In the centuries between *al-fanid* and seaside rock, a poorly-defined category of confectionery called barley sugar evolved. That now sold in both England and France (where it is called *sucre d'orge*), has nothing to do with barley and consists of transparent yellow drops or sticks—despite the seventeenth-century definition of alphenic as 'white barley sugar'.

The French physician Pierre Pomet gave a description of barley sugar. He said that it:

> is made of either white Sugar or brown; the first sort is boil'd 'till the sugar becomes brittle, and will easily break after it is cold …cast it upon a Marble … and afterwards work it to a paste, in any Figure you fancy. The other

sort, improperly call'd Barley-Sugar, is made of Cassonade, or coarse Powder Sugar, clarified and boil'd to a Toughness that will work up with your Hands to any Shape, and is commonly made up in little twisted Sticks.[5]

He noted the second form was difficult to make, and had to be boiled to exactly the right temperature. When made, it 'ought to be a fine Amber colour, dry, new made, and such as does not stick to the teeth: Some Confectioners, to make it a fine Colour, stain it with Saffron.'

Confectioners in the early nineteenth century often stated that formerly barley sugar had been prepared with a decoction of barley. One or two surviving recipes do include this, such as one given by William Salmon in 1692:

Saccarum Penidium, Sugar Penids
They are prepared of sugar dissolved by a gentle fire in Barley water, and the whites of eggs diligently beaten together, and clarified twice by boiling: then strain it through a Cloth, and boil it gently again till it rises up in great Bubbles, and being chewed, sticks not to your Teeth; then pour it upon a Marble anointed with Oil of Almonds (letting first the Bubbles sink after it is removed from the fire) bring back the outsides of it to the middle, till it looks like Larch Rosin: after that, your hands being rubbed with white Starch, you may draw it into threads, either short or long, thick or thin: and as it best likes you, let it be hardened in what form you please.[6]

It is now easier to use white granulated sugar to make this. Clarifying brown sugar with egg white before boiling may be authentic, but adds substantially to the time involved in making the sweets.

It is quite easy to overcook barley sugar made with barley water, caramelizing the sugar in the process. The result (provided it hasn't been caramelized to the point of burning) is very pleasant, with a deep orange-gold colour and a glassy appearance—just like modern barley sugar, in fact, although using water with barley starch gives it an attractive, slightly malty, toasty taste. When overcooked, it is impossible to pull, as it hardens too fast on cooling and the starch gives it a curious elastic quality. The idea of barley sugar made from pulled sugar probably lasted longest in the provinces. In the 1820s, James Wallace included one recipe, which no longer required barley:

Barley Sugar Twist
Put six pounds of loaf sugar in a pan with a pint and a half of water, boil it
gradually, when it is boiled enough it will snap like glass...after which it
must be powdered on a marble stone, then take a part of it and pull it on a
long staple made for that purpose, until it becomes as white as snow; when
done, twist it over the other which is on the stone, make it up for twist, or
cut it into short lengths, or into any other shape you may fancy. It may all
be pulled if you choose, and you may colour it either red, yellow or any
other colour...[7]

Wallace's contemporary, S.W. Stavely, contented himself with calling
this 'twist' and indicated that the two types for which he gave recipes
were not pulled.[8] These show, perhaps, the last remnants of medicinal
pulled barley sugar, at the point when the definition was changing.
From the 1830s, barley sugar was the familiar clear sweet known
today whilst pulled-sugar twist lost any associations with barley and
was incorporated into the seaside rock tradition.

It is not obvious what Wallace intended by the phrase 'powdered
on a marble stone'. It could be a misspelling or misprint for pouring.
'Powdering' food in general meant sprinkling it with something (for
instance, spices and salt in 'powdered beef'). Powdering in the context
of sugar work could have meant sprinkling starch on the stone prior
to working, or it could have meant sprinkling powder sugar over the
syrup. At first glance, the latter does not make sense, because adding
powder sugar would encourage the syrup to grain; but some
confections require this. Edinburgh rock, a regional variation on
pulled sugar, provides an example, as recorded by F. Marian McNeill.
Using loaf sugar dissolved in water, with a pinch of cream of tartar,
she instructed:

boil without stirring until it reaches 250°F in cold weather or 260°F in
hot—that is, until it forms a lump in cold water...pour onto a buttered
marble slab...as it begins to cool, turn the ends and edges inwards with a
buttered knife. When cool enough to handle, dust it with powdered sugar,
take it up and pull gently (being careful not to twist it) until it is dull. Cut
in pieces with a pair of scissors. Place the rock in a warm room and let it
remain there for at least twenty-four hours.[9]

The recipe is balanced between preventing and encouraging recrystallization. Cream of tartar (which is mildly acid) is added to inhibit graining, whilst dusting the syrup with powdered sugar seeds the mixture with small, evenly sized crystals. Of the flavours used for Edinburgh rock, rose and ginger probably go back the furthest, and both were originally associated with medicinal confections.

Popularization of Edinburgh rock is attributed to the early nineteenth-century confectioner, Alexander Ferguson. An 'accidental discovery' story is often quoted—that a batch of rock was forgotten, and when rediscovered, it was found to have mellowed. Since it was known in the sixteenth century that pulled sugar softened in a warm room, this seems unlikely (preventing grain is more of a problem). Without modern packaging, it is difficult to store pulled sugar so that it doesn't grain, and it is much more stable once it has done so. Ferguson may have used an archaic method for finishing the rock, the 'accidental' story evolving as a later rationalization when others had ceased to practise it. Alternatively, he may have revived the method when it was becoming obsolete; or he may have improved it technically, using a lower boiling point or by adding cream of tartar—an ingredient finding new applications in confectionery at just this time.

Recipes of that period for pulled sugar, whether from smart London confectioners or from the provinces, have one thing in common: the presence of ingredients which the casual observer might think were added as flavours, but have other, occult, functions. Confectioners referred to them collectively as 'doctors'. Two were cream of tartar or tartaric acid and vinegar (which Stavely added to paradise twist, stating that it 'will cause it to give you more time to make it up').[10] William Finemore recommended lemon juice or tartaric acid, and Jarrin, in his recipe for French ribbon, instructed, 'Take clarified sugar, boil it to a crack, add to it, an instant before it is done, a quantity of white honey about the size of a filbert, or some lemon juice.'[11]

These show the addition of an ingredient at the end of boiling which alters the chemistry of the mixture. Jarrin's suggestions show an empirical understanding of alternatives: alter the proportions of the monosaccharides (honey contains more fructose than glucose) or encourage sucrose to remain inverted after boiling is complete by adding an acid such as lemon juice or vinegar. Either way, such 'doctors' 'cut the grain' or 'greased the sugar', preventing it graining, important when working syrup intensively, as there is always a risk that it will recrystallize and need boiling again. The deliberate and widespread use of these substances was important, encouraging the development of humbugs, bulls eyes and many boiled sweets now considered 'traditional' but which, in fact, did not become commonplace until this relatively late sophistication of the sugar-boiler's technique.

The spread of knowledge about 'doctors' gave increasing confidence and creativity to confectioners working with pulled sugar. There is no question that skill was well developed. Provincials such as S.W. Stavely[12] and James Wallace[13] both published recipes for pulled-sugar sweets such as twist, bulls eyes and barley sugar. It was a substance which became ever more popular. Common twist was made from raw sugar, half pulled, half clear, flavoured with peppermint, whilst 'paradise' twist was made from loaf sugar, half pulled and half clear, and then streaked with red, similar to candy canes still made in North America. The colour was added to the unpulled sugar, just as red colouring is used in rock-making by seaside confectioners today. Bulls eyes, said Wallace, were coloured twist which was cut into shorter lengths. An early version of these may survive in 'Berwick Cockles', a speciality of Berwick-upon-Tweed, a fawn sweetmeat with thin red stripes.[14] The red and white combination is probably early.

William Finemore also detailed many pulled-sugar recipes, several of which showed the influence of the Napoleonic Wars on confectionery fashions. Finemore was from Devonport, a major naval centre; desire for identification with national heroes must have been particularly strong amongst small boys in the area. 'Wellington Sticks'

Figure 24. The lollipop:this example is pulled sugar in a twist. The derivation of the word is linked to the northern dialect 'lolly', meaning tongue.

were striped red, blue and yellow; 'Buonapart's ribs' were striped sweets cut in sticks and flattened. 'Gibraltar rock'[†] and 'North Pole' were very complex, made from sugar which was divided into batches, some coloured red and some plain, some pulled and some left clear, assembled in patterns, pulled out and cut; the resulting sticks were then put together in a bundle, cased with more sugar and pulled out again. He lists nearly two dozen different pulled-sugar sweets: bulls eyes in yellow or pink with clear stripes, lemon or mint rock, Nelsons Balls, pink or white 'pellets' and artful pieces of pulled, patterned sugar, requiring skills which could have just as easily been used to make letters.

In confectionery for the table, for a more refined market than the sweet stall, recipes for pulled sugar were less common. In 1820, Jarrin told how to make 'French Ribbon', elegantly worked in four colours. Some years later, William Jeanes gave instructions for 'celery sugar', pulled sugar made to look like a head of celery: 'Three or four pieces are placed on a dish with some rock sugar, and French Ribbon round it. This is generally used as a dessert dish.'[15]

That the form was perhaps resolutely proletarian—as it would be in its final glorious efflorescence by the seaside—is illustrated by this account of the humbug in the Victorian countryside:

> [It was] common in old dames windows 50 years ago. The kind which I recollect was made by a very old woman. She boiled treacle and sugar to a thick paste, and then rolled it on a baking-spittle [a board] into a straight stick. She then cut the humbugs off the end with a pair of scissors, cutting the stick across alternately, so as to leave, when hardened, four sharp corners to every humbug. The woman sold them at two for one halfpenny. She also made walking sticks out of the same material, and round balls called 'bulls eyes'.[16]

The final element of the conversion of pulled sugar from pennets into seaside rock is a strong flavouring of mint. When pulled-sugar pennets were considered medicinal, in the seventeenth century, their

† Were they so proud of British ownership of the rock of Gibraltar that it eventually gave its name (rock) to this whole *genus* of sweet?

Figure 25. The humbug, acme of pulled-sugar sweets.

potency seems to have been thought due to form, as much as to any particular taste or content. This is illustrated by their occasional use as ingredients in cures made from complex mixtures including liquorice, herbs, and other types of sugar. By the nineteenth century, flavours were used. According to Mayhew, in London during the 1850s:

> The flavouring—or 'scent' as I heard it in the trade—now most in demand is peppermint. Gibraltar rock and Wellington pillars used to be flavoured with ginger, but these 'sweeties' are exploded.[17]

Wallace and Stavely both instruct their readers to flavour pulled sugar with mint and William Finemore quoted a selection—mint, lemon, clove, ginger. Modern pulled-sugar sweets almost always have some flavouring; fruit essences are added for those who want a change.

Pulled sugar, then, is deeply embedded in popular perception as a good thing. The method was well established by the nineteenth century when, from making small, plain sticks of sugar, confectioners began to elaborate and experiment with flavours and colours, adding a gloss of novelty and fashion.

These were the elements required for making rock, which is white pulled sugar and red boiled sugar, shaped into sticks. The other strand to this particular amalgam was the habit of combining mottoes and sweetmeats.[18] One thing which was lacking was widespread literacy amongst consumers. The situation altered, however, as a result of legislation in the 1830s which required all children to undergo a minimum of schooling.

Henry Mayhew, observing street-life in London, recorded the sweet-stuff sellers and their wares. Amongst these he described sticks of pulled-sugar rock, made from syrup which had been boiled to a high temperature, and then worked whilst hot by stretching it over an iron hook, folding, and pulling again and again until it turned opaque and white. It was he said, 'variously flavoured and coloured', and sold in several forms. He continued:

> The man who has the best trade in London streets, is one who, about two years ago, introduced—after much study, I was told—short sentences into his 'sticks'. He boasts of his secret. When snapped asunder, in any part, the stick presents a sort of coloured inscription. The four I saw were: 'Do you love me?' The next was of less touching character 'Do you love sprats?' The others were, 'Lord Mayor's Day', and 'Sir Robert Peel'. This man's profits are twice those of my respectable informant's.[19]

There was obviously a market for this novelty and many sugar-boilers were keen to learn the secret. Forty years later, E. Skuse lamented despairingly:

> Had it not been for the great number of letters I have received from customers in reference to this class of goods I would certainly have passed over motto rock. I feel myself quite unable to give you instructions clear enough to begin this, the most laborious task a sugar boiler has to undertake.[20]

Anyone who has visited the English seaside will recognize 'motto rock' as Blackpool rock, Brighton rock, or souvenir rock from any one of a thousand resorts, shocking pink outside, white within, and bearing the name of the town in red sugar letters through the middle.

At the end of the twentieth century, the technique for making lettered rock has scarcely changed since it was first developed. Describing it is still not easy. Briefly, the process, which relies heavily on hand work, is that rock is made in batches from sugar and glucose dissolved in water and boiled together to 150°C (hard crack). This is poured onto a cold surface. As soon as the sugar cools and forms a skin, the boilers start dividing it, which has to be done carefully as the sugar is very hot and can burn the skin badly. They turn the shiny lumps of 'toffee', as they call the viscous syrup, sides to middle, adding flavours, and colouring some pieces. A proportion of the sugar is 'pulled'—repeatedly stretched and folded whilst hot—becoming white in the process. This, which formerly required much manual labour in front of the iron hook, is one step in rock-making which has been successfully mechanized.

The various pieces of sugar, still warm, are worked by hand into narrow oblongs and long cylinders. The initial aim is to compose the desired pattern by putting the pieces together longitudinally, for instance using a white cylinder wrapped in a thin layer of red to form a letter 'O', and then assembling the shapes so that the cross-section reveals the correct sequence of letters or patterns. White pulled sugar usually forms the matrix, filling in between letters or providing a background for pictures.

At this stage, construction of the message or pattern is rather like the building-up of a Battenberg cake: the cook is working in one plane—the horizontal—but aiming at the pattern being translated into the vertical. It would be impossibly pernickety work if the confectioner had to construct his letters and messages to the same size as the finished product. Somehow, therefore, a means of tidy shrinkage had to be devised.

The end result of the preliminary layering and arrangement is a large multi-coloured lump, one end of which is deliberately tapered. This thinner end is introduced to a batch roller, which is a pair of heated rollers placed at an angle to each other. These rollers progressively squeeze and compact the sweet-stuff so that from this machine, slender 'strings' of rock are spun out. The pattern, proportionately reduced in size, extends through these. When cold, they are cut into the familiar short lengths and packed.

When the manufacture is laborious, and sugar an unfashionable medium, why do confectioners still produce rock, and why do people buy it? What hold does it have on our collective unconscious? Perhaps it is simple affection for a folk art, a 'Victorian favourite'. The presence of rock and humbugs at the British seaside, where confectioners' shops provide repositories for many ideas which featured in sugar banquets of the seventeenth century, suggests they once had more status. But although some of the elaborate shapes made from pulled sugar (such as 'bacon and eggs') echo ideas from that century, there are no recipes of banquet conceits which would result in anything approximating to a bull's eye, let alone rock.

The name 'rock' leads to more confusion. To nineteenth-century confectioners, rock could mean pulled sugar, as in the modern definition, but it could also mean rock candy, large crystals grown on sticks in sugar solutions, or 'rock sugar', made from royal icing foamed by the addition of hot syrup.

Rock, as a souvenir of the seaside resort, was an equivalent of a modern Disneyland badge. It said, 'I can afford a holiday, been there, done that'. Less obviously, it represents a memory of pulled-sugar sweets produced by the magic skills of the apothecary or confectioner: as an exotic luxury for easing all sorts of winter ailments. Perhaps pennets, made from coarse, unclarified sugar, were always a little less expensive than other sweets; they were, at least, available in rural communities when Culpeper remembered them. The skill of making pulled sugar appears to have become part of the repertoire of provincial and journeymen confectioners, and of women for whom few other opportunities of generating income existed. The implication is that even children in poor and remote villages were likely to have access to these, though not exposed to more elegant and courtly confections. Combined with developments in the confectioner's skill, and popular literacy in the nineteenth century, this led to the novelty of motto rock, exploited for its potential in communicating all sorts of messages from the personal to the political, and still flourishing.

RECIPES

It is best to have help pulling and shaping sugar, because once it has reached the right consistency, it cools and stiffens suddenly, and there is not really enough time for one person to shape and roll it properly unless they are very practised.

Always handle hot sugar with caution. If it becomes too stiff to work easily, heat it at the open door of a warm oven (about 160°C, Gas 3).

WILLIAM SALMON'S BARLEY SUGAR MADE WITH BARLEY

50g pearl barley • 600ml water • 500g granulated sugar
*Equipment: a marble slab, a metal scraper and kitchen scissors, all oiled
lightly with almond oil; extra oil for your hands.*

Mix the barley and water in a small pan, cover and simmer gently for about 90 minutes (check every so often to see that it doesn't boil dry). Strain, reserving the barley water. Make it up to 300ml with some extra water if necessary. Allow it to settle for a few minutes and ladle off the clear barley water for dissolving the sugar, discarding the starchiest part. Mix the sugar and barley water together, stirring to make every crystal dissolve, and bring to the boil. It foams, so boiling has to be relatively gentle. Cook to hard crack, testing by dropping a little syrup in cold water.[21] Immediately remove the pan from the heat and pour the sugar onto the oiled slab. After a minute or two, use the scraper to flip the edges of the sugar mass to the middle. Oil your hands and use your fingertips to cautiously ease the mass out into a long strip, fold in half and ease out once more. Repeat until pale and opaque, then pull into a rope about a finger's width, and use the oiled scissors to cut it into short lengths. Store in an airtight box.

EDINBURGH ROCK

500g granulated sugar • 300ml water • a good pinch of cream of tartar
icing sugar for dusting • colours and flavours to taste
*Equipment: a marble slab and metal scraper, both buttered or oiled with
almond oil; extra butter or oil for your hands; a lightly oiled tray.*

Dissolve the sugar in the water and heat gently; add the cream of tartar
as it comes to the boil. Boil to hard ball, 123–126°C. Pour carefully
onto the slab. At this point, the batch can be split if you want to make
more than one flavour of rock. Drop a few drops of colour and flavour
onto the sugar. When the edges harden, flip them to the middle. Allow
it to continue cooling for 4 or 5 minutes.

Dust the surface lightly with icing sugar: a good pinch, lightly
rubbed over the top with your fingers is ample. Push the sugar into a
lump with the scraper. Oil your hands and begin to work it into a short
stubby cylinder. Be careful at first, as the sugar will still be liquid inside.
Pat it into a roll between your hands, fold, and pat out again, working it
gently. Keep working; it will become opaque and less sticky as it cools.

When almost cold but still malleable, the sugar should be looking
dull and opaque, and have lost most of its stickiness. Don't stop
working, because it will harden and grain. Work it into sticks about a
finger's thickness and 10cm long and put on the oiled tray. Leave in a
warm place overnight, which should be ample time for the texture to
soften and become chalky.

If you are making rock in sympathetic colours and flavours, Marian
McNeill recommends lemon or vanilla for white; raspberry or rose in
pink; ginger for fawn; and orange or tangerine flavour in yellow rock.

Figure 26. Patterns for fruit or acid drops that could be bought from Thomas Mills & Brother, Inc. of Philadelphia in the 1930s.

CHAPTER VII

Sweet acidity: fruit drops and fruit preserved

UNSEASONAL fruit which has never been near a tree is a recurring theme in confectionery. A whole dessert of perfect orchard produce and berries could be shaped from marzipan or cast sugar, artfully coloured and piled in baskets as if fresh from the garden. At a sweet-meat banquet, this conceit was as valued for its artifice as the originals were esteemed for freshness and beauty. The epitome of that banquet experience is the fruit drop, whose allure lies in the massing of shapes and the sparkling colour, intense and glowing like gemstones.

There are two notable things about fruit drops (and acid drops, and other boiled sweets). They are transparent and they have gone quite quickly from being a technical novelty to something banal. Clear sugar sweets are now so ubiquitous that they seem a logical outcome of sugar-boiling but they represent centuries of progressive technique, control, and ingenuity in the use of flavours and colours. In 1932, Fred Steel wrote: 'To the confectioner who is not interested in chocolate covering, the sweet of greatest interest is, without doubt, the hard-boiled drop. There is in this class of goods ample scope for the confectioner to display his skill.'[1] Hard-boiled drops have now been relegated to the niche of 'old time favourites'.

The discovery that tartaric acid prevented the sugar from graining at high temperatures eased the sugar-boiler's trials when making transparent boiled sweets. In his tradesman's handbook, Skuse spelt out the problem and its solution:

Refined sugars, whether lump or crystallized, when boiled to any degree above the 'ball,' or 250 [°F; 121°C] by the thermometer, are grainy, and would, if turned out of the pan, become a solid lump of hard candied sugar. To prevent this the grain must be cut by the addition of cream of tartar, which in its action will cause the sugar to be pliable while hot, and transparent when cold.[2]

A growing understanding of graining and the role of acids and simple sugars led to the development of boiled sugar drops and eventual industrial production.

Hard-boiled drops are see-through because the sugar has not crystallized. Cold and hard to touch, apparently solid, their molecular structure is that of a liquid.[3] When sugar is dissolved in water to make syrup, it becomes transparent (it is the light-reflecting property of sucrose crystals which makes dry sugar appear opaque), and the sucrose inverts to the smaller, simpler molecules of glucose and fructose. Boiling concentrates the syrup beyond the point at which glucose and fructose normally re-combine as sucrose crystals; adding tartaric acid enhances the effect of inversion, making it harder for the two to re-combine. Then the mixture is suddenly cooled: traditionally it is poured onto cold marble. This preserves the amorphous molecular structure of syrup. The sugar remains inverted, becoming a 'super-cooled liquid'. Effectively, the result is a syrup consisting of about 98 per cent sugar dissolved in two per cent water.

Not that confectioners were aware of this; they just knew if they followed the rules, the result would be beautiful, translucent, gem-like confections. It was all part of the semi-magical world of sugar-work. From the 1680s, when Giles Rose translated the term *casse*, until the early nineteenth century, confectioners remained circumspect about high-temperature boiling, although they did have one advantage over the modern sugar-boiler in beginning with clarified syrup. This meant all sugar was properly dissolved. When the starting point is granulated sugar and water, the confectioner must ensure every crystal of sugar is dissolved before it begins to boil.

This recipe, translated by Giles Rose, might have produced something approaching a modern high-boiled drop:

To make Carmalet
Boyl your sugar to that height, call'd breaking or casse, being boyl'd take it
from the Fire, and perfume it with a little Amber, and so put it out in little
rounds, upon a plate or dish.[4]

The explicit instruction to boil sugar to *casse* (about 149°C) suggests
that the author really did intend a transparent sugar drop—although
my own version grained after a few days. 'Amber' means ambergris, a
substance much used in seventeenth-century confectionery.

By the middle of the next century, the French had developed the
art of boiling sugar to a high temperature and had begun to develop
methods to prevent graining. J. Gilliers understood this when he
wrote:

*Caramel: Lorsque votre sucre sera à cassé, mettez-y la couleur telle que vous
jugerez à propos avec quatre ou cinq gouttes de jus de citrons, suivant la quantité
que vous aurez de sucre, pour empêcher qu'il ne graine; vous l'essayez comme au
cassé, et lorsque vous verrez qu'il se cassera net comme le verre, il sera au caramel.*[5]

[Caramel: Once your sugar has reached cassé add the amount of colour you
think appropriate along with four or five drops of lemon juice, according to
the amount of sugar, to prevent it from graining; test as for cassé, and once
it breaks as clean as glass, it is at caramel.]

Caramel (which, remember, to eighteenth-century confectioners was
not browned sugar, but sugar boiled until just before it begins to
colour),[6] must have been considered quite special. Gilliers used it for
making figures. Arms, legs, draperies and so forth were cast separately
by pouring the caramel into special moulds, stuck together with more
caramel after unmoulding. As table decorations, they looked like
figures made of coloured glass.

Gilliers described grain as a confectioner's expression for little glob-
ules of sugar, the size of a grain of corn, in a preserve or sugar cooked
to caramel. He recognized various causes, amongst which were over-
cooking preserves, insufficient lemon juice, or badly clarified sugar.
Graisser was the term he used for sugar cooked to caramel with lemon
juice added. Shortly afterwards, this appeared in English as 'greasing'

the sugar. It was not long before it was clear that confectioners in England knew about preventing grain, as shown by Jarrin's recipe for transparent barley sugar:

> When the sugar is near the crack, add to it two or three drops of lemon juice to prevent its graining, or a little vinegar or alum dissolved in water; any acid will grease sugar.[7]

The idea of sugar being 'greasy' now seems strange, but fat or greasy were both adjectives used to describe particular qualities of sugars, presumably ones which were less likely to crystallize.

'Doctors' were useful to confectioners who wanted to make transparent drops. These, it will be recalled, were any substance which greased the sugar or 'cut the grain', preventing crystallization. Adding them to boiled sugar meant that it could be boiled in large quantities and worked without fear of re-graining. Acids of various types, butter or cream, and honey all worked; so did molasses. Doctors are still intensively used in the confectionery industry, although they are now more likely to be called interfering agents.

Acids had been combined with sugar for centuries: naturally occurring ones were added inadvertently with fruit juices used for flavourings and others were added for special effects. Some juices worked well as doctors even when the effect was not desired. Jarrin warned readers to be careful with barberry, raspberry and pineapple juices because they would grease the sugar. Lemon juice was considered most effective and convenient, perhaps because it had little flavouring effect. William Finemore recommended that a glass container should be marked with graduations of a teaspoonful on the sides specially for adding the appropriate amount of lemon juice. Tartaric acid was widely used, as well as less palatable substances such as vitriol.[8] The best confectioners were careful over their choice of doctor. Skuse remarked:

> Several other acids have been used with more or less success, such as pyroligneous acid, sulphuric acid, vinegar &c, but experience has taught me that cream of tartar is the best, safest, and most to be relied on.[9]

Tartaric acid and cream of tartar had the advantage over lemon juice that they were available as a powder. Stored in a dry place, they kept almost indefinitely. Under the older name of *argil*, tartar had been known as a crystalline deposit on the inside of wine-barrels. The original reason for adding it to confectionery remains a mystery. It may have been considered good for one's health, or it may have entered the sweet-making process on the back of another ingredient: it was often used in formulae for making cochineal colour.

Butter and cream (and other fats, such as palm or coconut oil) are another category of doctor; they work because the molecules of protein and fat involved are very different to those of sugar. They were not used for transparent sweets but were important in toffee making. Toffee boilers also used molasses which, with honey and glucose, form a third group.

For many confectioners, glucose remained an unknown quantity into the 1890s, when Skuse was obliged to explain:

> I have had several letters enquiring what 'glucose' was…glucose is a beautiful white and clear syrup extracted from wheat starch, being a chemical conversion of the sugar found in it. Some sugar boilers use it in boiling sugar for drops, &c.[10]

Honey, molasses and glucose syrup work by contributing more of one simple sugar than the other, and unequal quantities of glucose and fructose do not readily re-crystallize as sucrose. The net effect is similar to using an acid doctor. The discovery in the mid-eighteenth century by Andreas Marggraf that glucose could be produced by boiling starch with dilute sulphuric acid opened a line of research eventually leading to the industrial manufacture of glucose syrup. Modern boiled sweets depend for their translucency, texture and keeping-qualities on a balance of sugar, glucose syrup, and acids, boiled for carefully calculated times.

Experiments with these substances in high-boiled sugar generated a new confection, acid drops. William Finemore recorded two recipes in his notebook, probably some time around 1840:

Figure 27. The orris root, *Iris florentina*, from Pomet's *Complete History of Drugs* (1747). It was used mainly as a flavouring agent, the root considered to have a smell like that of violets or raspberries when dried and powdered.

Lemon Acid Drops
4 lb Lump Sugar—pint of Water—boil to the Ball—add 2/4 Teaspoonsfull of Lemon Juice—boil to the crack—pour it on a very clean and well oiled marble Slab then add to the Sugar 1 oz of Tartaric Acid and a little Essence of Lemon mould it well to mix in the Acid—put it into a tin—Oiled—before the Fire to keep it hot—cut off pieces as you want it roll it on a marble slab dusted with powdered Sugar cut with Scissors into small pieces and rolled quite round on a Penbric[11] Slab—and flattened—then put into powdered Sugar

Rose Acid Drops
Same as Lemon Acid Drops coloured with Cochineal Colour—and flavoured with Otto [attar] of Rose.

Rose acid drops are more interesting in flavour than ordinary lemon: it is a shame that confectioners and consumers lost the taste for them.

Acid drops are rarely seen in Britain now, although their Scottish equivalents, 'soor plums,' survive. This probably means 'sour sweets' ('plum' as in the expression sugar-plum), although Scottish confectioners claim they commemorate an incident some time in the past when English marauders foraging plums for supplies were worsted by the Scots.

In the eighteenth century, confectioners making boiled sugar relied heavily on flavours which had long been in use, including flowers (rose, violet, orange flower, carnation) and spices (cinnamon, clove, ginger). Acid was used occasionally, probably for supposed medicinal value or visual and flavouring effect. An instance is Culpeper's suggestion to add vitriol to violet cordial to redden it and sharpen the taste. The range of fruit flavours open to confectioners was limited. Jarrin and his West End colleagues could afford to buy pineapples and other fruit and employ journeymen to extract the juice, but even they must have encountered problems such as the instability of some flavours at high temperatures.

For the less ambitious, options were limited. Stavely suggested only peppermint, lemon essence, ginger and horehound for the small provincial confectioner making candy and pulled sugar. William Finemore's notes also show only a few flavours in use with boiled sugar. Apart from tartaric acid and otto [attar] of rose, he mentions

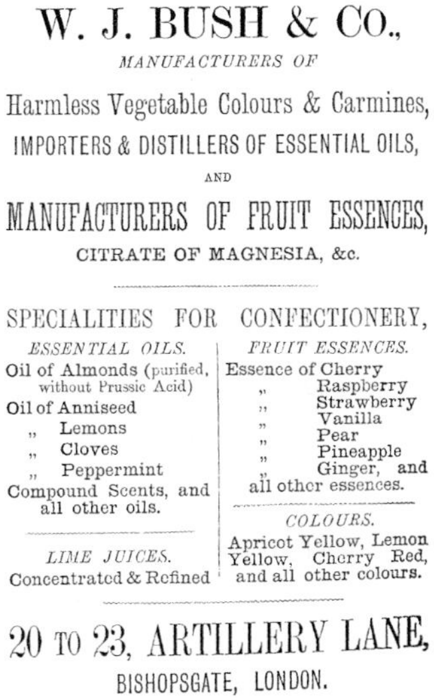

Figure 28. An early twentieth-century trade advertisement for essences, flavourings and colours especially for use in high-boiled sweets.

W. J. BUSH & CO.,

MANUFACTURERS OF

Harmless Vegetable Colours & Carmines,

IMPORTERS & DISTILLERS OF ESSENTIAL OILS,

AND

MANUFACTURERS OF FRUIT ESSENCES,

CITRATE OF MAGNESIA, &c.

SPECIALITIES FOR CONFECTIONERY,

ESSENTIAL OILS.	*FRUIT ESSENCES.*
Oil of Almonds (purified, without Prussic Acid)	Essence of Cherry
Oil of Anniseed	,, Raspberry
,, Lemons	,, Strawberry
,, Cloves	,, Vanilla
,, Peppermint	,, Pear
Compound Scents, and all other oils.	,, Pineapple
	,, Ginger, and all other essences.

COLOURS.

LIME JUICES.	Apricot Yellow, Lemon Yellow, Cherry Red, and all other colours.
Concentrated & Refined	

20 TO 23, ARTILLERY LANE,

BISHOPSGATE, LONDON.

105

Figure 29. A hand-turned machine for producing moulded fruit drops. Illustrated in a catalogue of confectioners' requisites and machinery issued by Thomas Mills & Brother, Inc. of Philadelphia in the 1930s. The patterns and designs shown here were established at least 50 years previously.

Figure 30. A roller suitable for fitting in the machine illustrated above. From the same catalogue.

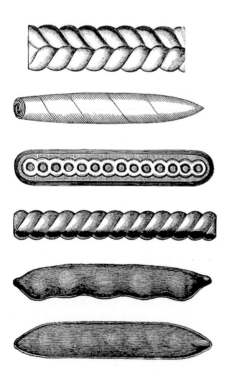

Figure 31. Roller patterns for long fruit or acid drops that could be purchased from the same manufacturer as above.

mint oil, ginger, clove oil, essence of lemon and 'raspberry'. The latter was actually orris root and tartaric acid in red-coloured sugar.

Rose was a flavour with a very long precedent. The combination of it with acid shows a transition in taste: the sensation of sharp and sweet combined with familiar floweriness. Rose acid was described as a 'transparent sweet' by Henry Mayhew, suggesting this was still a novelty in 1850. Acidity and texture continued to be exploited, but flavours changed and the range expanded, swinging away from flowers and spices. This was partly due to developments in applied chemistry, displayed with many other achievements at the Great Exhibition of 1851. One advance, breathlessly reported by the *Illustrated London News,* was the synthesis of artificial flavourings:

> In one department, lozenges from the pine-apple, jargonelle pears, and various other fruits have been sent. Mr Langdale has furnished oils of cognac, pears, pine-apples and grapes, which so exactly taste and smell of those fruits, that few would be able to distinguish them. These preparations are, to our mind, the most extraordinary productions of modern chemistry; for the fruits themselves have nothing to do with the matter, and they are simply made from the refuse of distilleries. We hear that they are now extensively employed.[12]

Another development which contributed both to the industrialization of confectionery and to the popularity of drops was a new method for handling hot sugar. This was noted by William Finemore: 'instead of cutting [the boiled sugar drops] with Scissors—the method now used in London to form them into Drops is by a Machine.' The 'machine' was a pair of drop rollers with a pattern engraved on each, hung so that, when turned, they revolved against each other, registering the patterns together. They cut high-boiled sugar neatly, quickly and evenly into drops, doing away with any laborious handwork and problems of temperature control. Drop rollers had the added advantage that any pattern could be engraved. Equipment catalogues from a few decades later show patterns for everything from fruit to frogs, seashells to shamrocks. Sparkling in brilliant colours and luxuriously flavoured with essences, artificial or otherwise, these sweets suddenly meant that everyone could taste fruit at any time of the year.

For a few decades, high-boiled drops were probably seen as an affordable substitute for fruit, at least by the poor. They combined sophisticated sugar work, bright colour, fancy shapes and flavours which only the rich were usually privileged to taste. The twentieth-century view is that sweets are decidedly inferior: given the choice between a ripe dessert pear and a pear drop there is little contest. Consider the differences. A perfectly ripe pear is that late twentieth-century oxymoron—a healthy, low calorie, virtuous treat. It is soft, juicy, perfumed and generally delicious, turns bad in a few days, and the season is short. What about the pear drop? It is small, approximately pear shaped, any colour the confectioner fancies but usually half red, half yellow. Dry and hard, pear drops have little smell until someone else is eating them, when they produce a strong aroma reminiscent of pear, with the addition of a curious and intense sweet-ness which catches at the top of the nose. They keep forever (several months, anyway). As sweets, they have acquired many negative implications to do with calorie content and dental caries.

Now imagine you are a child of a poor family in an industrial town of the 1860s. Pears, during the few short weeks when they appeared in the greengrocers, were expensive, smelt delicious. There are no pears on the market stalls at present (not much fresh fruit of any sort at this time of year), but the sweet-stuff seller has a new line of bright red and yellow sugar drops which, he says, taste just like the preserved Jargonelle pears that the quality eat, so you buy a few with a penny earned for running an errand and are soon enjoying the flavour.

Of the contradictions behind fruit drops, the altered status of sugar is the one now most apparent. Expensive, it was valued by the rich; once cheap, sugar was fantasy land for the poor. It represented dreams whose only limitation was the skill and imagination of the confectioner. Objects wrought in transparent sugar were diverse: classical statues, pineapples, pistols, fish… whatever the confectioner thought would appeal to the customers. If real fruit wasn't available, or was too expensive, it could always be modelled using syrup cast in moulds or bits of fruit paste. In the twentieth century the dogma is 'fresh fruit good; sugar confectionery bad' and 'natural is best, artifice is wrong'. Yet artifice has always lain behind getting any out-of-season or exotic fruit to the table. Now it goes into transport and packaging, not the use of sugar as a preservative. In the past, the taste of preserved fruit represented luxury, and the growing control confectioners had over making transparent, flavoured sugar shapes was an admirable novelty. Pears and pear drops, fruit and fruit drops—the sweets were models of the real thing, a glimpse of possibilities.

******

Acid drops and fruit drops were the saccharine distillate of the art of preserving fruit. While almost the product of the laboratory, it represented a real desire to offer the sweet acidity of fruit itself to palates reluctant to accept the imperative of summer bounty succeeded by winter's pale dearth. Preserved fruit had been a status symbol for centuries. Before canning, freezing and air freight, sugar was the only medium of conservation available.

Most books on sugar work devoted much space to the subject; some give the impression that confectioners did little else. Almost two-thirds of Mrs Mary Eales's *Receipts*[13] for instance, is occupied by instruction on preserving. Originally, the technique was used for more than merely keeping the fruit from rotting. Fresh fruit was regarded as suspect by physicians, who thought it mostly 'cold' in humoral terms. In the seventeenth century, Tobias Venner thought quinces, peaches and apricots cold and dry, apples and pears cold and moist with a 'crude and windie moisture', but that marmalade cotiniate (quince paste with sugar) was 'verie delectable to the taste and stomack'. Preserving with sugar (which was moderately hot) made delicious sweetmeats that tempered the coldness of the fruit.

Figure 32. Figure moulds for clear sugar 'toys', from Thomas Mills & Brother, Inc. of Philadelphia in the 1930s. Each figure would have weighed abour one-third of an ounce, 10–15 grams.

Fruit sweetmeats, including a few using honey, can be traced back to the earliest collections of recipes.[14] The confectioner faced with a glut of fruit had three options: preserve it whole (in syrup or candied); cook to a homogenous paste; extract the juice and boil it with sugar to make a jelly. In skilful hands, all three were exploited for decorative, beautifully coloured and flavoured sweetmeats.

Preserving whole involved a serious attempt to conserve the integrity of fruits so that they appeared as natural as possible. All recipes for preserves or 'suckets' began by cooking fruit gently, and then steeping in syrup over several days. The syrup was concentrated by boiling a little more each day (if a concentrated syrup is used initially, the fruit toughens and shrivels). Finally, fruit and syrup were transferred to gallipots[15] or glasses and sealed with bladder or paper until needed. Drained, the preserves could be sprinkled with fine sugar, or candied by dipping them in sugar boiled to candy height so encasing each piece in a sugar shell. The method uses syrups boiled to relatively low temperatures. Candied fruits are still made with varying degrees of skill in France, Italy, Spain, Portugal and their former colonies. The quantities of sugar required, as well as the time and expertise, make these expensive and luxurious sweetmeats even now.

The other options of making pastes or jellies destroyed the form of the fruit but allowed more freedom with colour, texture and shape. Many sweetmeats took the colour of the fruit from which they were made: pale, pinky beiges from apples or pears, the warm oranges of peaches or apricots, deep pinks and reds from berries. Confectioners also learnt to manipulate colour in some fruit. Rapid open boiling of quinces produced a pale, orange-red paste, or 'quince paste white' (white was a relative term); slow, close-covered simmering made a deeper colour, 'quince paste red'.

Fruit for paste is cooked to a homogenous mass, then boiled with an equal weight of sugar until it sets when cold. Getting this right was a matter of experience. Quinces were popular[16] because their high pectin content meant paste made from them set reliably. For fancy work such as 'jumballs' (knots), paste had to be quite dry, so that it became slightly elastic and strong enough to be worked by rolling into lengths. Alternatively, paste was simply cut in lozenges or other shapes. Coated with powder sugar, it would have been not unlike a soft version of a fruit pastille. Apple paste was sometimes coloured and shaped to counterfeit fruit such as cherries; adding a stalk to each piece completed the effect.

Making fruit jellies began in the same way as paste, but involved straining the cooked fruit to extract the juice. Again, quinces were the archetypal fruit for the method. Both pastes and jellies could be elaborately moulded or 'printed' with motifs, as in Sir Hugh Plat's recipe:

Quidini of Quinces
Take the kernells out of eight great Quinces, and boile them in a quart of spring water, till it come to a pinte, then put into it a quarter of a pinte of Rosewater and one pound of fine Sugar, and so let it boile till you see it come to bee of a deepe colour: then take a drop, and drop it on the bottome of a sawcer, and if it stand, take it off, then let it run through a jelly bagge into a bason upon a chafing dish of coles to keep it warm, then take a spoone, and fill your boxes as full as you please... and if you please, printe it in mouldes.[17]

'Quidini' was one rendition of the French *cotignac*, a word which gave English speakers enormous trouble—spellings include quod-iniacke, quiddeniock, quiddony, quiddany and condomacke. A clear, bright, carnelian coloured jelly, *cotignac* is still a speciality of the French town of Orléans. It is sold in large rounds, printed with moulds depicting subjects such as Joan of Arc. Smaller quantities are run into little wooden chip boxes, exactly like seventeenth-century sweetmeat boxes.

Getting pastes and jellies to setting consistency without spoiling the flavour by overboiling must have been problematic with many fruits. Confectioners boosted the pectin content of some fruit by adding juice from cooked apples or gooseberries. Another method for encouraging setting was to make 'clear cakes,' as told by Eliza Smith:

> Take your gooseberries, or other fruit, and put them in an earthen pot, stopt very close, and put them in a kettle of water, and let them boil till they break … run them through a cloth; take the weight of the liquor in sugar; boil the sugar candy high; then put in your juice, and let it stand over a few embers to dry till it is thick like a jelly … pour it into clear cake glasses and dry them with a little fire.[18]

Clear cake glasses were shallow moulds. Filled, they were placed in a confectioner's stove at very gentle heat (the 'little fire') until the top had candied to make a sugar crust. Then the jelly was turned out onto plates or glasses, cut in fancy shapes and put back to candy on the other side. The method required skill and patience, as well as a suitable place to candy the jelly. Many people must have resorted to simpler fruit pastes, such as another recipe given by Plat for conserve of damsons. After the damsons had been scalded and then cooked to pulp, they were sieved to get rid of the skins and stones.

> [T]hen set the pulpe over the fire againe, and put thereto a good quantitie of red wine, and boile them wel to a stiffenesse…and when they be almost sufficiently boyled, put in a convenient proportion of sugar: stir all well together and put it in your gally pots.[19]

The use of gallipots suggests that a consistency between a jam and a paste was anticipated, although, with care, it can be boiled to a solid paste.

By the end of the eighteenth century, confectioners made many types of preserves to be served in pyramids or compôtes for desserts. This decorative, status-bound aspect of their skill probably made a major contribution towards the way other people felt about fruit drops when they appeared in the mid-nineteenth century. Such preserves were part of a grand tradition encompassing eye-catching colours and shapes, notions of exotic imports (many were brought from southern Europe), reminders of palaces where skilled gardeners produced abundant fruit for preserving, and of smart London confectioners to effect the transformation. They helped fix in the public mind an ideal of jewel-like, sparkling masses of fruit confectionery as a luxury.

RECIPES

CARMALET

250g granulated sugar • 150ml water
a drop of vanilla essence
Equipment:a marble slab or metal tray oiled with sweet almond oil.

For an authentic seventeenth-century flavour, if you can obtain a little ambergris to use in place of the vanilla, a scrap the size of a rice grain will be plenty.

Put the sugar and water in a small pan and heat gently, stirring to dissolve all crystals. Increase the heat and boil to the upper end of hard crack, about 154°C. Immediately remove the pan from the fire and quench it by dipping the base quickly in a bowl of cold water. Add the ambergris or vanilla, and allow to melt into the mixture. Quickly drop the syrup in small rounds on the oiled slab or tray and leave to cool.

Figure 33. The fruit bonbon: the fruit paste centre relies on a centuries-old technique, whilst the crunchy casing is similar to high-boiled sugar used in fruit drops.

ROSE-FLAVOURED ACID DROPS

500g granulated sugar • 200ml water
5ml (a teaspoonful) lemon juice • 10g tartaric acid
2 -3 drops rose oil • 2 -3 drops red food colour • icing sugar
*Eqipment: a marble slab or large metal tray; a metal scraper; a pair of
kitchen scissors, all lightly oiled with almond oil.*

It is an advantage to have help when shaping these sweets, as the sugar cools and stiffens quite rapidly. Dissolve the sugar in the water. When every crystal has vanished, increase the heat and boil to hard ball, 121°C. Add the lemon juice and continue to boil to hard crack (149°C). Immediately remove from the heat and dip the base of the pan in cold water to halt cooking. Carefully pour the hot sugar in a pool on the slab or tray (watch it doesn't run off the edge). Immediately sprinkle over the tartaric acid, and drop the rose oil and food colour onto it. As it cools, a skin forms on the surface. Take the scraper, and flip the edges of the mass to the middle. Repeat this action several times, until the colour has dispersed through the mixture.

As soon as the mass of sugar is cool enough to handle, make it into a long stick about a finger's thickness. Use the scissors to cut off pieces a little under an inch long and roll them into balls. Drop into icing sugar and, when cool, store in an airtight bottle with some of the sugar.

Always handle hot sugar with caution. If it becomes too stiff to work easily, heat it at the open door of a warm oven (about 160°C, Gas 3).

SIR HUGH PLAT'S QUIDINI MADE WITH PIPPINS

1kg apples • 1 litre water • 100ml rosewater • 500g granulated sugar
Equipment: a jelly bag for straining; suitable shallow containers—glass or pottery dishes, or, if you can obtain them, shallow matchwood boxes.

Wash the fruit and remove any blemishes; cut into quarters or eighths, depending on size; discard the pips. Put in a pan with the litre of water and cook gently, stirring occasionally. As the fruit disintegrates quite fast and the chances of it sticking increase, stir more as it thickens. Add the sugar and rosewater. When reduced to a well-cooked pulp, take the pan off the heat and run the contents through a jelly bag into a clean pan. It is better not to let it drip too long, because there is a small risk of the pectin beginning to set—about 60–90 minutes should be enough. The remaining purée can be sieved and mixed with cream or custard for a fool. Bring the syrup back to a gentle boil, skim and allow to reduce a little. Check for setting by dropping a little on a cold saucer and when it makes a very firm jelly, run into the dishes or boxes to a depth of about 1 cm.

Apples of the pippin type (for example, Cox) make an acceptable quidini, although quinces work better. If quinces are available, substitute them for the apples. Remember that they take much longer to soften and do not collapse to a purée as apples do, and that they also contain very strong pectin, so the chances of the juice setting after it drips through the bag are increased. Seventeenth-century confectioners also suggest using plums and raspberries, but these do not set as reliably. I find the colour produced by quinces and apples during cooking unpredictable: generally, the longer and slower they are cooked, the deeper and redder they become.

CONSERVE OF DAMSONS

500g damsons (other plums, such as Victoria, also work quite well)
150 ml red wine
about 500g granulated sugar, plus extra for dusting
Equipment: a tin 20 cm square, lined with silicone-coated paper.

Wash the damsons and put in a pan with the wine. Cook gently until they have disintegrated. Push through a sieve or a mouli-légumes, discarding stones and skin. Weigh the pulp and measure (in a separate bowl) an equal amount of sugar. Return the pulp to a clean pan and stir it over medium heat for 5–10 minutes to dry it a little. Add the sugar, stir well to dissolve, and cook fairly briskly. Stir constantly until the paste thickens and a wooden spoon leaves a trail when drawn across the bottom of the pan. Remove from the heat and pour into the lined tin, shaking gently to level the paste. Leave overnight to cool.

Next day, dredge a board or tray with granulated sugar and turn the paste onto it. Peel off the paper, and sugar the top of the paste as well. Cut into lozenges, toss in sugar and store in a box with sheets of paper between the layers.

Other stone fruit such as apricots and peaches also make good paste, but use white wine with these.

Figure 34. Illustration of a comfit-making workshop, from Diderot's *Encyclopédie* (1763–72). The pearling pot can be seen suspended on the rope between the two balancing pans in the foreground. The workman at the back of the room is using a pan tilted over a barrel, a technique for making *nonpareils*.

CHAPTER VIII

Lost meanings: comfits

Alice had no idea what to do, and in despair she put her hand into her pocket and pulled out a box of comfits (luckily the salt water had not got into it), and handed them round as prizes. There was exactly one a-piece all round.[1]

I WAS puzzled by this scene in *Alice's Adventures in Wonderland*. What were comfits, and why did people have boxes of them in their pockets? A comfit, said my mother, was a kind of sweet. The next day in the corner shop, I read all the labels but couldn't see any comfits. They were there all the time, of course; I just didn't know what to look for. A comfit is a little something, traditionally a spice or a nut, covered in a layer of hard sugar. Shiny red aniseed balls, pastel sugared almonds and smooth white mint imperials are all good examples. As children in the 1960s, we knew them only by their trade names.

Although we didn't recognize them as a generic group, comfits were important in our lives as symbolic markers of time passing. Silver or gold balls decorated Christmas cakes. Multicoloured hundreds and thousands bled dye onto the white-iced fairy cakes at birthday parties, until someone made an innovation and used Smarties instead (thereby replacing one very old type of comfit with an updated version of a not-quite-so-old one). When school broke up for the spring holidays, speckled sugar eggs appeared in the paper baskets which we'd left out for the Easter bunny. Relations and friends returned from seaside trips with jars of 'beach pebbles', resembling stones in colour, shape and hardness, but sweets all the same. The more lurid and vibrant species—liquorice torpedoes, gobstoppers and jelly beans—we bought for ourselves.

Comfit derives from the word confect, so these could be considered the original confections, some of the most venerable items in the
history of sweets in Europe. A remote origin is sometimes claimed for
them, as honey based confectionery pre-dating the use of sugar. John
Ayto says of dragée:

> The word appears to come ultimately from Greek *tragemata*, 'sweets', plural
> of *tragema*, which was derived from the verb *trogein*, 'gnaw'. These Greek
> sweets consisted typically of aromatic seeds, such as aniseed or fennel, coated
> in honey, and this was the association the word *tragemata* carried with it
> into Latin, and thence into Old French as *dragie*. This was borrowed into
> English in the fourteenth century as *drege*, by which time sugar had replaced
> the honey as the outer coating. *Comfit* soon replaced *dredge* as the English
> term for such sweets, but in the nineteenth century English re-borrowed
> the French word, which by then had become *dragée*.[2]

Dragée has failed to catch on in general usage and comfit, as a
collective term, has virtually disappeared, leaving no word to satisfactorily fill the gap. Sugar-plum, another name for comfits (in use
from the seventeenth to the nineteenth centuries), has also become
archaic. The confectioners' expression 'panned sweets' (referring to the
large pans used for making comfits) is too technical, prosaic and
clumsy. Perhaps this is a sign that they have run their collective course
and finally lost meaning as indicators of status and sophistication.
Also, the subject of comfits was always a little more complicated than
the definition implies. The earliest meaning included any sweetmeat
preserved with sugar, such as citron or orange peel.

For about a hundred years, until perhaps the 1950s, one type of
comfit was a source of fascination to children: that leviathan of the
sweet shop counter, the gobstopper. Roald Dahl captured this in his
autobiography:

> Gobstoppers, costing a penny each, were enormous hard round balls the
> size of small tomatoes. One Gobstopper would provide about an hour's
> worth of non-stop sucking and if you took it out of your mouth and inspected
> it every five minutes or so, you would find it had changed colour. There was
> something fascinating about the way it went from pink to blue to green to

yellow. We used to wonder how in the world the Gobstopper Factory managed to achieve this magic. 'How *does* it happen?' we would ask each other. 'How *can* they make it keep changing colour?'

'It's your spit that does it,' young Thwaites proclaimed.[3]

'They,' the manufacturers, simply exploited the peculiarities of the method. Gobstoppers, like all comfits, are made by engrossing centres (in this specific case, sugar crystals) in successive layers of sugar. The centres are placed in a heated revolving pan and syrup added in a series of charges. The pan turns, simultaneously tumbling the centres in syrup and drying them, so each acquires a thin layer of sugar. The process is repeated over and over again until the comfits have built up to the desired size. A well-proportioned gobstopper requires up to a thousand coats.

Producing coloured layers is just a matter of using a different colour in each batch of syrup as engrossing proceeds. Flavours can be added if desired. As a principle, comfit-making has always been simple. In practice, it was one of the most difficult and tedious methods in craft confectionery, requiring specialized equipment, careful heat control, and experience. Using traditional methods, it takes several days to make and finish a batch of sugar almonds.

Instructions on comfit-making were rarely published. It was seen as a specialized craft, beyond the housewife or amateur. Initially, it was probably a secret belonging to apothecaries; pills are still sugared to make bitter drugs easier to swallow. The few early recipes give real detail about quantities, implements and methods, indicating that a need for precision was recognized.

Early in the seventeenth century, Sir Hugh Plat gave instructions on covering 'all kinds of seeds, fruits or spices with sugar'. A grasp of two important points in comfit-making—keeping the centres in motion and controlling the heat—are both implied in the list of equipment required:

First of all you must have a deepe bottomed bason of fine cleane brass or latton,[4] with two eares of Iron to hang it with two severall cordes over a bason or earthen pan with hote coales. You must also have a broade pan to

put ashes in, and hot coales upon them. You must have a cleane latton
bason to melt your Sugar in, or a faire brazen skillet. You must have a fine
brasen ladle, to let run the Sugar upon the seedes.[5]

Suspending a shallow basin on cords from the ceiling meant that the
confectioner could shake it with one hand, and stir the seeds with the
other, keeping them in constant motion. It also meant they could be
kept at an appropriate height above the heat source, warm enough to
dry the sugar gently, but not hot enough to burn it.

The hanging basin later became known as a 'balancing pan'. An
alternative, known by the early sixteenth century, was a pan placed
over a small furnace; the seeds were stirred with one hand and the pan
turned with the other 'for cause of more het on the one syde more
than on the other tyll they [the seeds] be hotte and drye.'[6] Both types
of pan were illustrated in Diderot's *Encyclopédie*; the second type, by
then, was shown fixed in the top of a wooden tub or barrel. In 1820,
Jarrin remarked that a flattish pan or basin, over a barrel, was used to
make fine *nonpareils* as well as comfits.

Comfit-making requires a subtle understanding of the concentration of sugar solutions. Slight variations give different finishes. Two
types of finish were generally recognized: smooth and textured (described as rough, crisp, or pearled). Plat noted these differences. For
ordinary comfits, he instructed his readers to take the whitest, finest
and hardest sugar, beaten to a fine powder, three pounds of which
were dissolved in a pint[7] of water, and boiled gently 'until it will
stream from the ladle like turpentine, with a long stream and not
drop.' The sugar was not boiled any more, but kept hot over a
chafing-dish. For making smooth, round comfits, Plat noted that a
slightly hotter boiling was used at the start, and a lighter, less
concentrated syrup towards the end. Raising the temperature of the
syrup to concentrate it a little more, and pouring sugar from some
distance above the pan gave comfits an irregular surface:

> For crispe and ragged comfits, make your sugar of a high decoction…and
> let fall a foote high or more from the ladle, and the hoter you cast in your
> sugar, the more ragged will your comfits be.[8]

This difference had been known for at least a century previously. In the York manuscript, instructions for 'annez in confit' (aniseed comfits), to be worked until they were as 'gret as peasen' (the size of peas), required a relatively light syrup. The author warned that, 'the hyyer decoction of the suger makes it roug and Ragged,'[9] and gave separate instructions for textured comfits, such as 'canell in confyte frysed' (made from cinnamon cut in short slivers). 'Frysed' probably meant 'frizzed', in the sense of having an irregular, wavy or bumpy texture.[10] By the late seventeenth century, irregular comfits were described as 'pearled,' perhaps indicating the visual effect of a bobbly surface. The term came into English from French, together with the sugar-boiling degree of 'pearl', between about 103–107°C (just below modern thread stage). Smooth comfits were achieved using a syrup boiled to the degree of *lisse* (literally, smooth), a lower temperature of about 102°C. It is not clear if the comfits took their name from the degrees, or vice-versa.

To make rough comfits, the syrup had to be poured onto the seeds from well above the pan. For this a pearling pot or beading funnel was used. Like much to do with confectionery, it had a long precedent; this description was recorded in the York manuscript:

> zyfe ze have no man to helpe zu in the poryng make zu instrument above zor panne in this maner. A lytell pewter balle the gretnes of a pynte made lyke a round ladyll in the mydds of the ladyll make a lytell round hole and in the hole a pynne of yron and put the sugere in your balle and whan you wyll lat it ryne pull out the pinne and in this maner shall ze make all fresyd confections.[11]

Although it is clear that the author saw this as a device to help the confectioner working alone (controlling the temperature of the sugar syrup, pouring it, and manoeuvring the pan were easier with two people), it is recognizable as a pearling pot. The arrangement of a hanging funnel, with a pin to control the syrup flow, over the suspended balancing-pan remained the standard apparatus for making comfits until the development of steam-heated revolving pans in the second half of the nineteenth century.

Figure 35. The equipment necessary for comfit-making, from Diderot's *Encyclopédie* (1763–72): a balancing pan over a charcoal brazier, and pearling pot to dispense the syrup.

Of various other methods for covering spices or nuts with sugar, none really produced the same effect. Pralines, of almonds or pistachios, were stirred in a pan with melted sugar, at a much higher temperature: very delicious, but not the same as comfits. Other methods involved making the centres sticky, and then rolling them in powder sugar (or sugar and starch). Such was François Massialot's recipe for fennel [seed] which, 'may be serv'd up to the table iced, after it has been soaked in Orange-flower Water and the White of an egg, and then roll'd in Powder-sugar.'[12] This iced fennel was coloured and dried. Aniseed could be treated in the same way.

Variety in shape and size was another attraction of comfits. Slivers of cinnamon bark were made into 'long' comfits or, as they were known in early eighteenth-century Scotland, 'bandstrings'.[13] These were usually given a pearled surface. Strips of candied orange or lemon peel could be used in the same way. Most spices produced round comfits, but ginger was diced before panning. Almonds or hazelnuts made larger, more oval shapes.

The size of comfits varied considerably. Plat considered that relatively small comfits were 'fairer' or better. A quarter of a pound of anis or coriander seeds and two pounds of sugar made comfits 'great enough' but half a pound to a pound more of sugar made them 'faire and large'. A quarter-pound of coriander seeds and three pounds of sugar produced 'great, huge and big comfits' (probably almost as big as gobstoppers), whilst half a pound of aniseed or a quarter-pound of fennel seeds and two pounds of sugar produced 'fine small comfits'. Plat called these 'biskets' (confusingly, for the modern reader, because 'bisket' also meant relatively large flour-based affairs in the modern sense of sponge fingers and rusks).

Grains of sugar were used as centres for very small biskets. Plat recorded that a dram of sugar powder took an ounce of sugar in syrup to make the 'biskets somewhat faire, and somewhat greater than poppie seeds'. Alternatively, cinnamon powder was panned with as much sugar syrup as needed 'until they [the comfits] bee as greate as poppie seedes'. Such comfits could be made round and plain, or crisp. The modern name for tiny comfits, a little bigger than poppy seeds, is hundreds and thousands. An alternative, much used throughout the eighteenth century, was the French *nonpareil*, 'unequalled', although Pomet dismissively remarked that these were 'nothing more than Orrice-Powder, cover'd with Sugar'.[14]

Whiteness was considered desirable in comfits. Whilst paleness was probably prized for its own sake, it also showed the comfits had been properly dried and would keep well. In the early sixteenth century, the confectioner was instructed not to box comfits whilst they were hot, but to stir them in the pan until cold, otherwise they would not change colour—that is, become whiter as the sugar dried out. Plat recommended alternative methods:

> When your comfits bee made, set your dishes with your comfits upon papers in them before the heat of the fire, or in the hot sun, or in an Oven after the bread is drawne, by the space of an houre or two, and this will make them very white.[15]

Comfits were (and still are) coloured by adding dyes to the final coats of syrup. Red is the earliest mentioned; the modern red aniseed ball has a pedigree which stretches back to the fourteenth century at least, when *anise vermeil*, red anis, was recorded in France. Turnsole (a violet or purple colouring) and sanders (powdered sandalwood) were used to make sixteenth-century comfits red; the larger 'frysed' coriander ones could be made 'lyke strawberys' by finishing them with three red coats followed by a white one[16] In the seventeenth century, Plat stipulated *brasell*[17] or turnsole for colouring red comfits, beet leaf juice for green ones, and saffron for yellow. Or, for a display of wealth combined with the magical properties of an elixir of life, you could 'lay golde or silver on your comfits,'[18] creating the ancestors of the silver dragées, the little cake decorations still sold for children's party cakes.

If mixtures of colours were desired, as in hundreds and thousands, the comfits were mixed after they were coloured. As Jarrin explained about nonpareils in the early nineteenth century, the almost-finished sweets were divided into batches. Some, he said, should be left plain:

> the quantity of white nonpareils being double that of any other colour, this being necessary to set off other colours to advantage.[19]

The remaining batches were panned separately with coloured syrups as required. Nonpareils were useful for adding colour to all sorts of other confections, and cooks were often instructed to sprinkle them on the top of creams or tarts. They were also used to add colour to the new, rather dull-looking chocolate. This was shaped into drops, or made into ovals enclosing nuts and then covered in comfits, as shown in Eliza Acton's recipe for chocolate almonds:

> When the chocolate has been softened…enclose singly in small portions of it some almonds previously *well* dried, or even slightly coloured in the oven, after having been blanched. Roll them very smooth in the hand, and cover them with the comfits…Filberts and pistachio-nuts may be substituted for the almonds with good effect; but they also must be perfectly dry.[20]

Chocolate drops, without nuts but sprinkled with hundreds and thousands, are still a children's line. Eventually, chocolate itself provided a centre for panning, and resulted in one of the most popular of British brands—Smarties—introduced in 1937.

The ingredients used for centres had several functions. At the most basic level, they provided something for the syrup to adhere to. Fine, powdered sugar provided minute grains which did this as well as anything else. But often another powder was used: cinnamon, orris and ginger were all mentioned. These had the double function of forming centres and making the sweets aromatic. Sometimes comfits were made from sugar with musk added for a really luxurious perfume. Many were based on whole spices. Aniseed, coriander, caraway, fennel, ginger, clove, mace, cubebs, cinnamon slivers and 'greynes' (cardamom) were listed as possible centres at the start of the sixteenth century.[21] They were considered good for the digestion; they were also expensive. Coating with sugar moderated the flavour, enhanced their medicinal properties and added to their status as consumer goods. Many of these spices have disappeared from the English repertoire, although cinnamon is still used in North America, where another has been added to the list: the heat of an 'Atomic Fireball' is provided by an extract of chilli.

Apart from seeds and spices, Plat describes a paste made from grated bread, cinnamon, ginger, saffron, sugar and borage water, heated together and mixed, made into 'balles or other formes', then dried and used as centres. He also mentions orange rinds cut into strips and almonds. Sugared nuts, though, are more often encountered as the influence of later French confectioners makes itself felt. Almonds and pistachios were centres used in recipes translated by Giles Rose, as were cucumber seeds, *citrouil* (water melon or pumpkin) seeds, 'million' (melon) seeds, pounded and preserved apricot (perhaps the distant ancestor of the modern jelly bean, also a panned sweet or comfit), and preserved lemon pulp. In fact, as Rose said, 'you may take farther notice that you may make Dragees of all sorts of dry conserves and the paste of fruit of all sorts.'[22]

Pierre Pomet wrote in his *History of Drugs*:

127

> There are infinite Variety of Flowers, Seeds, Berries, Kernels, Plums, and the like, which are, by the Confectioners, cover'd with Sugar, and bear the Name of Sugar-Plums, which would be endless to set down and are too frivolous for a work of this nature.[23]

It should be remembered that Pomet had been 'chief Druggist to the late French King Lewis XIV,' and perhaps felt these things to be beneath him. Despite their supposed medicinal attributes, one gains the impression that frivolity and conspicuous extravagance had long been the chief object of comfits. A dish of comfits said, 'this is a festival,' combined with overt messages about the wealth, power and status. Comfits are shown quite frequently in paintings of still life or domestic scenes from this period;[24] perhaps as indicators of sophistication, as a photographer might now accessorize an interior with exotic fruit.

Comfits came into their own at parties. As *espices de chambre* (digestive sweetmeats for the table, as opposed to the *espices de cuisine,* used in cookery), they were served at the end of late-medieval meals. Several types, including *anis vermeil* and *dragée blanche,* are listed amongst items to be bought for feasts in a work on household management from fourteenth-century Paris.[25] For those who could afford them, comfits became part of all festivities. Sir Hugh Plat mentioned them in the context of several celebratory confections, especially marchpane (a large flat cake of marzipan). He directed that this should be iced with rosewater and sugar and, 'sticke long comfits upright in it, cast biskets and carrowaies in it, and so serve it; gild it before you serve it.'[26]

The habit of making festive marchpanes with icing and comfits continued. Shortly afterwards, in the English kitchen, this became the topping for fruit cakes, giving the now familiar form which distinguishes Christmas and wedding cakes: symbols of sweetness and status at our most important celebrations.

Comfits are now little used on wedding cakes, but the custom did not die out entirely. Like so many things to do with sweets, it became mostly for children, and may be the origin of the habit of decorating party buns with icing and hundreds and thousands. From the artfully sculpted and iced marchpane to fairy cakes turned out by the dozen may seem a slither down the social scale, but it shows that even the humblest denizen of the tea-table may have a complex history.[27]

Sweetmeats, including comfits, make good missiles. There are hints that the food at banquets ended up being flung about, rather than eaten. 'Let it hail kissing-comfits,' says Falstaff in *The Merry Wives of Windsor*; and John Evelyn recorded a banquet at which 'the banqueting stuff [was] flung about the room profusely'.[28] Hurling the comfits about seemed to become less popular in England during the eighteenth century, but carried on in Italy, where Goethe witnessed the Roman carnival:

> Now and then a masked fair lady mischievously flings some sugar-coated almonds at her passing friend to attract his attention...But real sugared confetti is expensive, so a cheaper substitute must be provided for this kind of petty warfare, and there are traders who specialize in plaster bonbons...No one is safe from attack, everyone is on the defensive, so now and then, from high spirits or necessity, a duel, a skirmish or a battle ensues. Pedestrians, coachmen, spectators alternately attack others and defend themselves.[29]

Eventually the plaster imitations of sweets were replaced by small pieces of paper cut in fancy shapes, and these have found their way back into British tradition as confetti .

The portability of comfits led to a gentler custom of handing them out as gifts. In 1702, Massialot mentioned placing on the banquet table little baskets of dry sweetmeats decorated with ribbons: one for each guest, to be taken home and shared with the family. It is echoed by the gift of 'favours', little bags of sugared almonds, to wedding guests in southern Europe.[30] Not just wedding guests: different colours of almond indicate different celebrations, a christening, an engagement, an anniversary (although some—for instance graduations—may be inspired by modern marketing rather than long tradition). Favours could be more personal; William Gunter noted of nonpareils:

These, mixed up with other comfits, play a most important part in the ceremonies of New Year's Day, in France and Italy. Every Beau is expected to present to *all* his lady acquaintance, a packet of *Drâgets*, saluting her at the same time, as his reward.[31]

However, the notion has probably always had as much to do with expressing the collective wealth of a family and the perceived value of acquaintances as with tokens of individual affection.

As objects of display, comfits had to be put in some container. Elegant *drageoirs*, *bonbonnières* and other precious dishes soon evolved to show them off. Alternatively, a vessel might be edible. In a recipe for modelling fruit or nuts in two halves using marchpane or sugar paste, Plat suggested that 'you may convey comfits within, before you close the sides'.[32]

His contemporary, the anonymous author of *A Closet for Ladies and Gentlewomen* also provided instructions, 'To make a Walnut, that when you cracke it, you shall find Biskets and Carrawayes in it, or a prettie Posey written.'[33]

In 1820, Jarrin recorded an elaboration of this idea. The container, a comfit shaped like an egg, was edible, but the filling might not be:

Egg Comfits:
Have the two halves of an egg made in box-wood; take some gum paste, roll it out quite thin, and put into the casts, make it lay close, cut off with a knife the outside edges quite smooth, let them dry...They are usually filled with imitations of all sorts of fruits—In Paris they put in a number of nick-nacks, little almanacks, smelling bottles with essences, and even things of value, for presents. Join the two halves with some of the same paste, moistened with a little water and gum arabic.

These eggs were covered with syrup in the comfit pan, which, considering the fragility of sugar paste, must have been a delicate operation. It is still perfectly feasible to make such eggs, although no-one but the most dedicated of experimental confectioners would ever attempt to pan them. The underlying concept has survived, but removed to an entirely different branch of confectionery, to enjoy enormous success as the chocolate Easter egg.

Sir Hugh Plat instructed when making comfits, 'put no kinde of starch or Amylum to your sugar'.[34] From the eighteenth century onwards (and probably long before) most confectioners added starch or a solution of gum arabic. The best practice was the judicious use of gum solution in the early stages of covering almonds and some kinds of fruit. This helped fill small surface irregularities, and provided a seal, giving a finer finish and preventing oil seeping from nuts into the sugar coat and discolouring it. Some confectioners were less particular. In 1830, Stavely's instructions were:

Comfits
Take one pound of raw sugar, and make it into syrup with water; then take one pound of coriander seeds, and dip them in the syrup; then put the seeds into a sieve with a little flour, shake them well in it, and then set them to dry. Keep steeping them in the syrup, adding flour, and drying them till they are of the size you want them to be.[35]

Such crude techniques and adulteration were common. In 1820, Frederick Accum found that, 'the white comfits, called sugar pease, are chiefly composed of a mixture of sugar, starch and Cornish clay (a species of very white pipe clay).'[36]

In 1839 the editors of the *Magazine of Domestic Economy* were not pleased with the comfits they generally found on sale. Not only were the colours derived from dubious, and sometimes actively harmful substances, the comfits themselves were generally of poor quality:

Caraway comfits...those of the cheaper sort are made in a single day. They contain a very small proportion of sugar, and a large one of starch...Scotch comfits...These are the larger and finer sort of caraway comfits. Here the starch must be less and the quantity of sugar greater...Cardamum sugar-plums ...These comfits, which from the form of the seed are always round, generally contain little sugar and much starch, though in our opinion this ought to be reversed[37]

Scandals over the composition of confectionery and other foods were a matter for public concern.

In the late nineteenth century, comfit-making was rapidly indust-rialized. The balancing pan was replaced by revolving, steam-jacketed pans (still used; they look like large concrete mixers), and the sugar

OSCILLATING STEAM COMFIT PAN.

Manufacturer of Improved Revolving Oscillating Steam Comfit Pans, Marmalade, Jujube and Coltsfoot Rock Machines, Double Cased Syrup and Jam Pans, Sugar Mills, and every description of Confectioners' Machines.

Figure 36. A steam comfit pan, taking the work out of the balancing pan. From a late nineteenth-century trade advertisement.

was melted in steam pans with a regulated temperature. Skuse remarked:

> Formerly a good workman would require to do his best to make 1/2 cwt [25.5 kg] of well finished comfits per day; at the present time a skilled workman could superintend nearly a dozen steam pans, which would produce three or four tons per week.[38]

The arrangement was both easier and safer than the balancing pan and the dangerous charcoal braziers used until then. Another innovation was the development of ventilation systems, blowing hot or cold air across the comfits as they tumbled, helping to dry the sugar.

As with many other sweets, mass-production and cheapness banished the magic. They have become slicker, from techniques for glazing the surface with edible waxes. They have become more yielding, as 'soft panning' evolved, using glucose syrup in place of the sugar syrup required for old-fashioned hard comfits, and relying as much on air currents as on heating to dry the sweets. Jelly beans are the best example: developed in the USA, these spread eastwards to Europe, together with chewing gum (the varieties of this which have crisp little sugar shells are also panned). Of all the comfits once considered so special, only sugar almonds seem to be anything more than trivialities.

RECIPES

MASSIALOT'S ICED FENNEL

2 teaspoons fennel seed • 1 teaspoon orange flower water
1 teaspoon egg white • a drop of green food colouring
100 g icing sugar.

Mix the fennel seed, orange flower water, egg white and colour, and leave to stand for about two hours. Put half the icing sugar onto a large plate, and add the fennel mixture. Rub it in with your fingers as if mixing fat and flour for pastry, so that each seed is coated with sugar. Add a little more sugar, distribute the seeds across it, and leave to stand for about an hour. Then repeat the rubbing-in process, adding more sugar if necessary. Leave them in sugar overnight to dry thoroughly, then pick out the coated seeds and store them in a dry place.

This is a very simple method. Although the results are not really comfits, it is probably the most accessible recipe for anyone wishing to attempt sweets of this type. True comfits require perseverance, dedication, and equipment difficult to manage in a small modern kitchen.

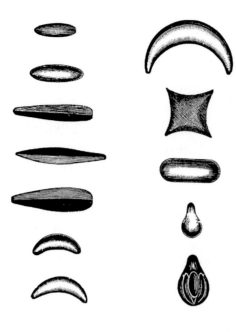

Figure 37. Moulds for the soft centres of American panned sweets, illustrated in the catalogue of Thomas Mills & Brother, Inc. of Philadelphia, 1930s.

ELIZA ACTON'S CHOCOLATE ALMONDS

125g dark chocolate • 60g whole almonds, blanched
hundreds and thousands (allow about 125g)

Toast the almonds until golden brown (7–10 minutes in a moderate oven, 180°C, Gas 4). Put aside to cool. Put a couple of tablespoons of hundreds and thousands into a cup or a shallow bowl.

Break the chocolate into pieces and put it into a bowl over a pan of simmering water. Stir as the chocolate begins to melt. When it is half melted, remove the bowl from the heat, and keep stirring. You want it just soft enough to cover the almonds, not completely liquid.

Coat the almonds by dropping them into the chocolate and turning until covered. Using a fork, transfer to the hundreds and thousands. Shake gently until the chocolate is completely coated with the hundreds and thousands. Then pick out the nut on another fork and set aside to harden. Repeat until all the chocolate is used.

Blanched pistachio nuts or skinned, toasted hazelnuts can be used instead of the almonds.

JARRIN'S SUGAR EGGS

Sugar paste (use home-made or bought petal paste)
colours for the paste (optional)
icing sugar for rolling out
For filling
marzipan fruit, silver or gold balls, hundreds and thousands, chocolate
covered coffee beans, sugar almonds, etc.
*Equipment: plastic moulds of the type sold for making small chocolate
Easter eggs*

For details of buying petal paste and colours, see the appendix. A recipe for making sugar paste is given on page 151, as 'sugar plate'. If you want coloured eggs, knead some powder colour into the paste before starting. Roll out the paste on a surface sprinkled with icing sugar. Thickness, to some extent, will depend on the size. About 3mm is appropriate for ones the size of a hen's egg. Line both halves of an egg mould with the paste, trim, and carefully turn onto a wire rack. Allow to dry for 24 hours. Reserve the paste trimmings; wrap them in plastic film so that they don't dry out.

To assemble, select the items for filling as required, and place in one half of the moulded shell. Work some of the paste trimmings with a little water and carefully use it to join the two halves of shell together. Leave to set and decorate with ribbons, flowers and so forth, as you please.

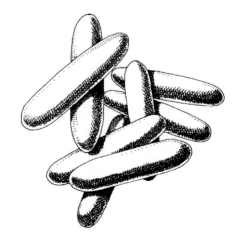

Figure 38. Liquorice 'torpedoes' – survivors of the 'long comfit' tradition.

135

Figure 39. A table set up for drying flowers and ornaments made from sugar paste. From Guglielmo Jarrin, *The Italian Confectioner* (1820).

Figure 40. Making paste flowers. The figure on the right is rolling and cutting the paste, the craftsman in the centre is building the flowers petal by petal. From J. Gilliers, *Le Cannameliste Français* (1751).

136

CHAPTER IX

Consuming wealth and eating words: sugar paste

ANYONE attending a wedding in Britain for much of the twentieth century would have admired a cake covered with royal icing piped stiffly into formal patterns. During the 1980s, tastes suddenly changed and in came soft icing, rolled out in sheets, draped, frilled and laced like cloth, then sprigged with flowers which looked real but were made with great artifice from a mixture of sugar, water and gum arabic. These blooms were one of the oldest and simplest sweet confections—sugar paste, or *pastillage*.

There are few ideas in confectionery which are absolutely new, so it is no great surprise to find John Murrell instructing his readers in 1617 to make roses from sugar paste.[1] At the start of the eighteenth century Massialot described how to make flowers from gum paste and slivers of preserved fruit, and in 1751 Gilliers illustrated a confectioner delicately shaping sugar flowers. Some years later, Jarrin showed flowers moulded in wooden forms, cut with appropriately shaped tin cutters, and modelled with ivory tools.

The popularity of sugar paste itself has waxed and waned as fashions in confectionery went from elaborate to simple and back again. As a medium for modelling figures and buildings, it probably went into medieval subtleties. It was used for Elizabethan and Jacobean conceits for the banqueting table and provided ornaments for Georgian desserts. In 1820, Jarrin remarked that sculptural sugar work generally had gone out of fashion. A decade or two later, Antonin Carême, one of the most influential nineteenth-century confectioners, revived the art. Sugar paste, gum paste, pulled and

Figure 41. A lozenge box lid from the nineteenth century.

spun sugar were exploited throughout the Victorian era for elaborate *pièces montées*. Then, once again, such table decorations were regarded with a mixture of derision and awe, only to re-emerge in a baroque flourish of edible floristry on wedding cakes of the 1980s.

Sugar has long conveyed messages of status and love with more or less subtlety. Sometimes it said things loud and clear, often to the extent of spelling it out for anyone who could read. Right at the end of the nineteenth century, an American confectionery manufacturer advertised a large gum-paste centrepiece for a wedding cake. This was described as 'consisting of a horseshoe framed by flowers. Below the horseshoe stands a blacksmith forging two rings, which represent marriage. Behind him, on the horseshoe, is the word *constancy*.'[2]

It is not clear if this centrepiece was intended to be eaten: probably not. The encyclopaedist Theodore Garret made a distinction between edible sugar paste and inedible gum paste. He considered the latter to have great value: 'To the artistic confectioner Gum Paste has much the same meaning as clay and marble combined have to the sculptor....there is no form of decorative construction that cannot be undertaken and successfully carried out by those who understand the

Figure 42. A gum press. Illustrated in Guglielmo Jarrin, *The Italian Confectioner* (1820).

manner of its application.[3] But it had one great drawback. This, said Garret, was the mistaken notion that ornaments made with gum paste were *edible*.

The consumer was not necessarily aware of this. The trouble was that both sugar paste and gum paste might mean the same thing—an edible mixture of sugar and gum. Alternatively, a confectioner might consider that the terms represented opposite ends of a spectrum, the sugar end being edible, and the gum paste, compounded with starch, plaster of Paris and various suspect colourings, most unpalatable. Confectioners loved modelling with both, and consumers were left to discover edibility by trial and error. Perhaps it was this confusion which led to the general neglect of paste during the modern period.

Apothecaries, meanwhile, found sugar paste useful for delivering (with reasonable accuracy) measured quantities of drugs and tonics. This was a more subtle role, less prone to reversals in taste. Paste eased conversation by soothing sore throats and sweetening the breath. So even if the confectioner found his sugar models *passés*, the apothecary found a consistent demand for troches and lozenges. This dual role, as a sometimes edible ornamental medium and a utilitarian base for tablets, means that sugar paste has been in constant use since the sixteenth century and probably earlier.

Methods for making it have changed little. No boiling of syrup is involved; it is a simple mixture of powdered sugar kneaded with soaked gum arabic or gum tragacanth (often misspelt as dragant, or corrupted to dragon) to bind it into a malleable mass. The two gums, both derived from trees (*Acacia* and *Astralagus* species respectively), have long been used in sweet-making. Apothecaries found them useful when incorporating medicines into tablets, because they slowly released drugs when sucked. More frivolous confectioners concentrated on the ability of gum to bind sugar into pastes which could be modelled like clay, dried, and kept indefinitely.

Both gums are collected by hand from trees which grow in a wide area across the Sahel, into the Middle East and India. As natural, unrefined products, their quality varies; the colour ranges from almost colourless to amber and they often have scraps of twig or sand sticking to them. Gums (and resins and latexes), said Harold McGee, 'are among the more common, more visible, and more mysterious of plant products. They...are composed of long carbohydrate molecules with a limited capacity of holding water and are produced in the walls of certain plant cells: when tissue is broken, the gum flows in to fill the injury, drying to a hard mass when it reaches the air.'[4] The pieces have a hard, tough texture, and are irregular in shape and size, from about as big as an orange downwards. For confectionery, gum is broken up into small particles before use. Confectioners have always preferred the paler grades, and emphasized the necessity for straining after soaking; they would wring the solution through a cloth.

Gums do not sound a particularly attractive proposition, but their 'limited capacity of holding water' is a useful attribute. It means that they can be partially redissolved, mixed into paste, and then dried again. In principle, their use is easy. They are soaked in water for about twelve hours to soften and dissolve as much as possible, then strained and mixed with sugar. The finer the sugar powder, the whiter the result. Egg white, lemon juice and rosewater were also added in the past. In practice, as ever, there are nuances of quality, especially in the texture, malleability and evenness of colour in the finished paste, the knowledge of which separates experts from amateurs.

Some gum-based sweets made remain recognizably close to the original opaque confections once made from sugar paste. But a second strand, exploiting gums as transparent setting agents for sugar syrup, was evident by the early nineteenth century. Precedents came from fruit sweets, such as pastes, cotignac and 'clear cakes'[5] which relied on pectin and sugar to make them set. Jellies, their texture probably less fragile than modern jelly desserts but not as stiff as jelly sweets, were also made from gelatine, extracted by boiling calf's feet and then allowing the liquid to reduce until syrupy.

By 1820, when Jarrin gave this recipe, clear gum and sugar sweets were being made under the name of *jujubes*:

Jujube Paste
1 pound of Gum Senegal,[6] half a pound of Sugar, Orange Flower Water.
Take a pound of gum senegal, pound and dissolve it in orange flower water
…put it on a slow fire to reduce, and keep stirring it; when it is of the
consistence of paste, clarify half a pound of loaf sugar, boil it to a *blow*, and
add it to your paste …dry it to a good consistence; run it into moulds of tin
about a quarter inch thick, and place them in a stove. When dry, take out
the paste and cut it into small pieces, or any shapes you please.

Jujube paste, he added, 'is in great vogue in France, and on the
continent as a medicine for coughs and colds.'[7] The texture must have
been very stiff. Some observers were not complimentary, William
Gunter remarking that jujubes reminded him of edible india-rubber.
Jujubes were apparently popular as cough-cures throughout the nineteenth century but a wide range of other clear fruit-flavoured
confections evolved as well.

The earliest versions of sugar paste were opaque, and prized for
their whiteness. In the past, gums do not appear to have been
treasured for any immediately apparent virtue (although there is the
ever-present possibility that they were thought of as medicine). They
were probably more valued for what they could do when combined
with sugar. Creating models was the most remarkable manifestation
of this, and some items were useful as well as decorative. One of the
earliest known detailed sugar paste recipes in English is for making:

plate of sugre, whereof a man maye make all manner of fruites, and other
fyne thinges with theyr forme, as platters, dishes, glasses, cuppes, and such
like thinges, wherewith you may furnishe at table; and when you have doen,
eate them up. A pleasant thing for them that sit at table.[8]

This recipe, given in the translation of the alchemist Alexis of
Piedmont in 1562, required 'gum dragant', a piece the size of a bean,
steeped in rosewater, a walnut shell full of lemon juice and some egg
white mixed with sugar in a mortar, which was kneaded with more
powdered fine sugar to make a paste. This was rolled out and
moulded into tableware. The word 'plate', at this time, could simply
mean a thin rigid sheet of something, and 'sugar plate' was a term

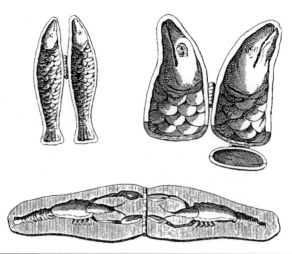

Figure 43. Moulds for sugar paste objects, illustrated in Diderot's *Encyclopédie* (1763–72).

which had been used in English since the fourteenth century.[9] But this recipe shaped it into plate in a more complex sense as well, in imitation of vessels for food. A good display of these, especially when made from precious metal, was an overt sign of wealth. Given that sugar was still not cheap, fragile platters and cups of paste, broken and consumed when the meal was over, were a remarkable piece of conspicuous consumption. It was the sixteenth-century equivalent of lighting cigars with banknotes.

The idea of edible tableware must have been considered amusing and stylish for some decades. It was lightweight, thin and elegantly white, especially in comparison to the heavy earthenware pottery with dark glazes that was common in Britain. Even imported majolica and delft, though pale and patterned, were relatively thick. It was only when Chinese porcelain was imported and imitated in large quantities in the eighteenth century that something with the delicacy of sugar plate became available in more lasting form. So, for a while, confectioners and rich ladies giving sugar banquets must have continued to make their sugar plate.

The basic recipe stayed essentially unchanged, but the details were refined. Sir Hugh Plat, in his instructions for 'the making of Sugar-plate, and casting thereof in carved moulds,' demanded the whitest refined sugar and a small proportion of the best starch, mixed with gum dragant. This, he said, 'must first bee well picked, leaving out the drosse,' before it was steeped in rosewater and strained through canvas. All ingredients were mixed up with some egg white and then rolled out and shaped in wooden moulds dusted with powdered sugar. For making 'sawcers, dishes, boawls, &c' the sheets of paste were pressed into the required vessels, trimmed, and allowed to dry partially, then unmoulded and the edges gilded with gold leaf stuck down with white of egg.[10]

Sugar plate could be coloured and scented with flowers. By using the results judiciously, it could be made to resemble fine marble (yet another sign of substance), as in this recipe from *A Queens Delight*:

> *To make paste of flowers the colour of marble, tasting of the natural flowers*
> Take every sort of pleasing Flowers, as Violets, Cowslips, Gilly-flowers, Roses or Marigolds, and beat them in a Mortar, each flower by it self with sugar, till the sugar become the colour of the flower, then put in a little Gum Dragon steept in water into it, and beat it into a perfect paste; and when you have half a dozen colours, every flower will take of his nature, then rowl the paste therein, and lay one piece upon another, in mingling sort, so rowl your Paste in small rowls, as big and as long as your finger, then cut it off the bigness of a small Nut, overthwart, and so rowl them thin, that you may see a knife through them, so dry them before the fire till they be dry.[11]

This is a very simple idea which can easily be made, although modern tastes might veer towards fruit flavours. It provided yet another conceit, imitating the expensive and inedible with something deliciously consumable. Flavoured pastes might also be left unmixed and cut into little diamond shapes, or moulded in imitation of something else. Paste coloured and flavoured with cinnamon and ginger, according to the author of *A Closet for Ladies and Gentlewomen*, was rolled out thin and 'then you may turne it upon stickes made of peeces of arrowes, and make them hollow like Cynamon stickes.'[12]

Figure 44. The Polo, descendant of the conversation lozenge as well as the apothecary's tablet.

Many ornamental but less obviously edible items were made with paste. Murrell listed 'Shooes, Slippers, Keyes, Knives, Gloves &c'. Larger, more elaborate ornaments in the tradition of subtleties were also possible. Robert May spoke with regret of models of a castle, a ship, and a stag with an arrow in its side (although these were all made from a baked paste, probably a type of coarse pastry), and implied that such frivolities were no longer considered amusing.

The eighteenth century saw a flowering of ornaments and table decorations carefully cut, sculpted, stuck together and coloured by

144

confectioners. Gilliers, in 1751, showed how to construct and lay out rococo dessert tables with parterres of sugar work stocked with sweetmeats. Paste was an important structural material for these displays. But Jarrin commented in 1820, 'this mode of decoration and embellishment was once in great vogue, and the most magnificent and costly ornaments have been made of gum paste; but it has fallen comparatively into disuse, and what is worse for the confectioner, the fragments of the art have been transferred to pastry cooks and cooks.' It is obvious that he personally found paste sculpture an interesting skill. Perhaps it was nostalgia that moved him to include a detailed section on making gum and other pastes. It was, he said, an art which required 'great care, dexterity, much patience, some knowledge of mythology, of history, and of the arts of modelling and design—qualifications seldom possessed by the mere pastry cook.'[13]

Jarrin's formulae ranged from the entirely edible fine gum paste and common gum paste (which included starch) through ones including plaster and oil 'fit only for gilding or bronze,' to an 'Alabaster Paste which will resist Damp, and all sorts of Insects' (which makes one wonder about the storage facilities available to confectioners). He used his pastes for modelling flowers, fruit, shells, animals and figures. Jarrin lived to see the art of sculpting with sugar mixtures successfully revived by Carême in the 1830s, renewing a vogue for Chinese temples, hermits' caves, Turkish grottoes and other unlikely ornaments, which did not entirely die out until after the First World War.

Thematic sculptures were doubtless hot topics of conversation to enliven the *ennui* of a banquet. Some carried written mottoes to explain their subjects more fully, but in the early seventeenth century, sugar paste got involved with much more direct communication by conveying script. John Murrell gave these instructions for 'Cinnamon Letters':

> Take paste…colour it with cinnamon, and rowle it in long rowles, as neere as you can all of a bignesse, and therof make faire capitall Romane letters…gild them and make a crosse in the beginning of them.[14]

Figure 45. Wine gums, descendants of chewy nineteenth-century jujubes.

An alphabet mix cut from pastel sugar paste can still be bought in shops supplying sweets for small children and letter shapes (made from chocolate) remain a Christmas novelty in Holland. The paste was originally flavoured with musk and ambergris, which must have made it very attractive, and suggests it was not just intended for children. Stronger perfumes than flowers were, perhaps, a necessity to sweeten the breath after too many sugar banquets. Kissing comfits, as detailed by Robert May in 1685, were sugar paste containing musk, civet, ambergris, and orris powder.[15] These were printed in moulds or rolled into little pellets and then squeezed flat with a seal. Similar little floral cachous lasted well into our own time (even now, scented purple 'Parma Violet' sweets are made as a line for small girls: kissing-comfits for dolls' tea-parties).

The combination of sugar and mottoes continued. Hannah Glasse gave instructions, 'to make little things of sugar, with devices in them. These were made from pieces of sugar paste, tinted whatever colour was preferred, 'in what shapes you like…in the middle of them have little pieces of paper, with some pretty smart sentences wrote on them; they will in company make much mirth.'[16] But the writing migrated from paper to the sweet itself with the Victorian fashion for 'conversation lozenges'. Those who were tongue-tied could always offer their companion a little piece of sugar paste printed with some suitable inscription. 'How do you flirt?' 'Can you polka?' and 'Love me' were amongst those available from Terry's in York; for those wanting to make a really positive response, a large medallion moulded with a heart and the words 'I will' was available. Another novelty was reminiscent of Hannah Glasse's little things with devices in them. As advertised by the firm of Thomas Handisyde in the East End of London, these were 'Handisydes SECRET CHARMS suck carefully and the secret message will appear'. Handisyde produced various shapes and sizes of conversation lozenges, the larger ones cut in hearts, circles, and elegant oblongs with ogee edges.[17] The temperance movement used the idea of motto lozenges to promote their message. 'Drink is the ruin of man', 'Hard work does not need intoxicating liquor', and 'Sobriety is the sure way to riches' were apparently inscribed on paste.[18] The inscriptions were added to the sweets by printing the tops with stamps dipped in dyes.

Accurately measured, carefully mixed and rolled, sugar paste could be divided into lozenges which contained, within reasonable margins of error, a prescribed dose of some drug. By the late nineteenth century, everything from opium (the most potent painkiller), to lettuce (the mildest of soporifics) was conveyed in lozenges, as was ipecacuanha (to make the patient sick), rhubarb (a laxative) and ginger (to comfort the stomach, perhaps necessary after the others had been administered). Both confectioners and apothecaries mixed their own versions, often with combinations of perfumes or drugs which they kept secret. Few of these survive, although the extra-strong mint lozenges still made by Terry's of York had their origins in this tradition, as did 'paregoric'—a patent cough medicine which once contained opium and chloroform. The similar tablets now available are 'paregoric flavour', as the active ingredients can no longer be freely sold.

The handwork involved in making lozenges was skilled but tedious. At the end of the nineteenth century, their manufacture underwent rapid industrialization. The problem with hand-mixing paste was getting exactly the right consistency with the minimum of handling. On this subject, Skuse said (round about 1890) that he felt

> quite unequal to the task of making lozenge makers of his readers; the process is simple enough, but it requires practice…Young beginners, when trying to make lozenges will generally find that what they intended for a nice white peppermint lozenge will turn out, when dry, to have a sort of greyish brown tint; this is caused simply through the sugar being handled and *coddled* about.[19]

He advised beginners to start on cough lozenges, where the addition of dark ingredients meant pallor was not important. But, he added, there was little need for hand-made lozenges, except as high-class goods, because

> recent machinery has rendered lozenge making by hand…a dead letter. Twenty years ago, lozenges were mixed and cut by journeymen confectioners…within the last few years, machinery has been introduced which mixes, rolls, stamps and cuts, all the manual labour that is required is simply a superintendent…turning out many hundredweights a day.

A few years later, in his tenth edition, Skuse gave details of the 'Climax' machine which made two or three tons of lozenges in a day, and needed mixers and kneading brakes to supply it.

******

About this time, the clear gum and jelly category of confectionery began to expand. Two successes were Fruit Gums and Fruit Pastilles, introduced by Rowntree. Both originated when the firm employed a French master confectioner to develop their lines; such sweets are said to have been a French monopoly. Another was Wine Gums, which have never had anything to do with alcohol and were invented in 1909 by a Methodist teetotaller.

Pharmacists created new vehicles for administering the drugs formerly contained in sweetened lozenges, and modern developments in making gum paste show, in common with many sweets, two complementary characteristics. The first is that the sweet itself becomes softer; the second that technology is harnessed to produce ever-larger volumes.

Soft pastes are now made with agents which have different capacities for holding water, and different textures—chewy or short or soft. These include pectin (derived from fruit), gelatine (replacing isinglass, sometimes used in the past), or any one of a modern panoply of modified starches designed to gel, boil, congeal and be chewed in a specified way, and sometimes replacing gum altogether. These have given sweet-making 'cream paste' (whose softer texture is provided by glucose and gelatine). It is the component which provides the colourful 'building-brick' look, built up in layers in Liquorice Allsorts and Dolly Mixtures; it also provides centres for some soft comfits, and has spawned a range of 'chews' of the Opal Fruit (now Star Fruit) type.

Technology has contributed both to marketing and production of sweets which originated from sugar paste confections. It has made all aspects of retailing easier through the development of 'roll wrapping', (introduced in the USA in about 1915).[20] This is the method by which a column of little disc-shaped sweets is wrapped in foil, swaddled with a paper label, and dropped into a carton or encased in a plastic outer. Problems of keeping the sweets clean and dry, preventing them abrading and chipping, and easing distribution and display were solved in a trice.

Technology also contributed a new category of 'tablets' to paste sweets. These still rely on sugar, flavourings, and binder such as gelatine, but the ingredients are mixed into doughs and granulated, or 'slugged' by compressing the mixture first into large tablets, and then breaking them into granules to dry. Slugging is a dry process, allowing the addition of volatile ingredients, such as sherbet powder, to the mixture. The sweets are given their final form by compressing the mix under pressure in tabletting machines which shape small portions of granulated mixture in polished dies. The use of the latter has freed paste from the flat lozenge shape and the slightly rough surface, to give concave dimples and a smooth sleek gloss to Refreshers, and a ring or 'lifesaver' (life-belt) shape to Polos and Navy Mints. Despite this, the art (or science) of confectionery is too conservative to allow all that has gone before to vanish under the onslaught of the machine. Words and little sentences are now compressed with the sugar to make 'Love Hearts', for little girls to giggle and flirt with:

> Be Mine, My Gal, Marry Me, Love, You Alone, Yours, Heart Throb, My Angel, Wake Up, OK Toots, Funny Face, Always, Grow Up....

The language, perhaps, lacks the elegance of English in previous centuries, but the idea is straight from the banquet-table.

Figure 46. Love Hearts, a message in sugar paste.

RECIPES

SUGAR PLATE

500g icing sugar • 15g powdered gum arabic or gum tragacanth
flavours and colours as desired

To achieve the intended flavour and colour, you can experiment with kneading the petals of edible flowers into the mixture, if they are available—make sure they have not been treated with pesticides. Otherwise, use rose water, orange flower water, vanilla extract, or oils from lemon, orange or lime peel.[21]

Mix the icing sugar and gum together roughly, and then sieve into a large bowl so that the two are well amalgamated. Divide the dry mix into portions (keeping a little back for working) depending on how many colours and flavours you want. Make each portion into paste by adding a drop of colour and the desired flavouring. If you are using one of the flower waters, add this in teaspoonfuls, mixing and kneading until you have a pliable paste. If using an essence or an oil, add a drop or two, and then make the paste up with tap water. Knead each portion until it is smooth and coherent, adding a little more icing sugar/gum mixture or water as necessary to achieve a good consistency. Wrap each batch in plastic film until you need it.

Make up into little rolls, putting two or more flavours together in layers as desired, and cut down into little nuggets. Dust a board and rolling pin with icing sugar, roll out the paste, cut into any shape desired, and leave to dry.

JOHN MURRELL'S CINNAMON LETTERS

Use bought petal paste (see appendix), kneaded with a few drops of rosewater and a little ground cinnamon. Otherwise, make up paste as directed in the recipe above. Extra icing sugar will be needed for shaping, and gold leaf to decorate, if you wish to extend to such luxury.

Divide the paste into pieces each about the size of a walnut. Roll them out to the required thickness and shape into letters as desired. Make a small cut about 5mm long into the paste at the start and end of each letter: then open the paste out to give serifs. Dry on a wire rack, and gild if desired.

Figure 47. A table centrepiece made from sugar paste. From Guglielmo Jarrin, *The Italian Confectioner* (1820).

CHAPTER X

At the interface: sherbet

'THIS is *gul sekeri*, it means rose sugar, and you use it for making sherbet,' a Turkish friend said, handing me a thick chunk of dark pink candied sugar cut in a rough lozenge shape. 'It's very old-fashioned.' It was also nothing like the sweet I'd known when growing up in west Yorkshire, where sherbet, or 'kali', is a fizzy powder vaguely flavoured with lemon. Enclosed in a cardboard tube, to be sucked up through a hollow liquorice 'straw', or made into a 'dab' (with a lollipop to dip in the powder and lick), the main point about the sherbet I knew is that it fizzes. In the latter form, it is a sweet known to all children, and all who have been children, in Britain. The taste for it is often lost by about ten years old, but before that it is universally adored. Once eaten, never forgotten. A glance at the packaging shows it contains bi-carbonate of soda and tartaric (or other) acid. Roses and sugar candy are certainly not involved.

British sherbet has, in a strange way, remained quite close to a concept which is much older and has a more exotic origin than these fizzy powders suggest. Sherbet lies at an interface between four areas traditionally included in the confectioner's expertise: solid sugar con-fections, syrups, flavoured alcohols, and ice-creams. The word and the substance it describes have been pushed in different directions by different cultures; but the sherbet which the British first encountered in the seventeenth century used a concentrate, candied sugar, an idea which lay at the basis of the development of the modern sweet.

Sherbet comes from Arabic *sharbat*,[1] a drink made by mixing water with a flavoured syrup. The English term is a straight borrowing from *serbet*, as the Turks called their version. So high was it in the esteem of pashas and sultans that snow or ice was specially stored for cooling the

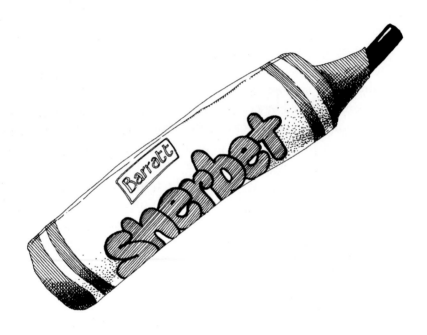

Figure 48. The modern sherbet fountain.

nectar.[2] A complex process of diffusion has given several other words to the European kitchen. Among the bits of related culinary etymology are the Spanish *jarabe*, meaning syrup (both of which can ultimately be traced back to the same Arabic root as *sharbat*); and the French *sorbet*, now meaning a water-ice based on fruit juice or wine. Sherbet in North America also means a species of ice cream. *Shrub*, an English term for an alcohol-based concoction including sugar and lemons, shares a similar derivation.

A parallel development took place with the word julep, which came into English from the Persian *golab*, rosewater. Perhaps because juleps were ephemeral (they were always made for immediate consumption), this has not developed as wide a range of meanings as sherbet; but it has diversified into the modern North American mint julep, a concoction of sugar syrup, bourbon whiskey and mint. Juleps appear to have been principally medicinal in English usage, whilst sherbets were mostly for refreshment.

Travellers to the east were fascinated by sherbet. A seventeenth-century observer, de Thévenot, noted in Turkey that the locals drank *sorbet*, which he described as a very good drink; later he witnessed it being made at Rosetto (modern Rashid, on the western edge of the Nile delta). After the sugar had been clarified with egg white

> they divided that Liquor [the clarified syrup] into three parts, of which they put a third into a great Kettle or Caldron over the fire; and seeing Sugar from time to time was like to boil over, they made it settle, by throwing in two or three Egg-shells full of Milk. When they knew it to be boiled enough...they took it off; it looked then very yellow, and two men set a stirring of it with wooden peels; so that the more they stirred it, as it grew cold it became thicker and whiter. When it was a little thickened; they put into it about two glass-fulls of the juice of Limon boiled...Then they stirred it again to mingle all well together, and a little after they put into it about two spoonfulls of Rose-water in which some Musk had been dissolved, several adding therto Ambergreass. Then they stirred it till it became like a Paste, and afterwards put it into Pots; the same they did with the other two parts. ...When they have a mind to make it of a violet-Colour, after the juice of Limon they put of the Syrrup of Violets into it.[3]

This process would make something approximating to the modern *gul sekeri*, and is perhaps what was meant by another observer in 1626 when he recorded:

> They have in Turkey and the East certaine *Confections*, which they call *Servets*, which are like to *Candied Conserves* and…these they dissolve in *Water*, and therof make their *Drinke*, because they are forbidden *Wine* by their Law.[4]

Authors mention sherbets made from violets, verjuice (sour grape juice), mint and vinegar, and sour fruits, especially lemons or citrons. Some of these confections were imported to England: 'Sherbets (made in Turkie) of Lemons, Roses and Violets perfumed', were advertised in 1662 as being sold, together with tea, coffee and 'chocolatta' at the coffee house in Exchange Alley.[5] Rose sherbet can no longer be bought in Britain, so anyone wanting to try it will have to make their own, following, perhaps, the recipe given at the end of this chapter.

Sherbet was apparently first known in Britain in a form which modern palates would find rather strange. This recipe was translated in 1682:

> *To make Sorbec of Alexandria.*
> Take a good large piece of Veal, that is to say, half a Fillet, or a slice cut round the Leg,…take away the fat, put this in a clean Earthen pot, with about 3 quarts of water, and let it stew till it is reduced to about a pint and a half of a pint, then take 2 pound of Sugar and put it into a Skillet, and make it boil with the juice that came from the Veal, after it is well scummed, and all the fat taken from it, and is strained through a clean cloath, boil all this together and scum it, then boil it to a perle gros, and put it into Bottles, and when it is cold stop it up very close for your use.[6]

This formula reappears a few years later under the name sherbet,[7] elaborated a little with spices, lemon peel, and based on calves foot jelly, but otherwise the same. The product must have been a semi-jellied syrup. It sounds unappetizing, but it was probably not unlike a modern gelatine-set table jelly. The sugar would help to preserve the mixture, which was probably thought restorative.

Recipes for shrub, an alcoholic version of sherbet, were also developed. The following comes from Eliza Smith's *Compleat*

Housewife. Although first published in 1727, it probably reflects culinary practices some decades earlier:

> To make Shrub
>
> Take two quarts of brandy, and put it in a large bottle, adding to it the juice of five lemons, the peels of two, and half a nutmeg; stop it up and let it stand three days, and add to it three pints of white wine, a pound and a half of sugar; mix it, strain it twice through flannel, and bottle it up; it is a pretty wine, and a cordial.[8]

A version of shrub is still produced commercially in Bristol, but it is easy to make one's own.

Sherbet seems to have carried the meaning of an alcoholic drink for many years. In 1775, the anonymous author of *Valuable Secrets Concerning Arts and Trades* gave a recipe for 'How to make Sharbat, a Persian Species of Punch', which in this context was an alcoholic drink based on rum, brandy, shrub or arrack. The author commented, 'There are some who put acids, others do not; and among the acids, some chuse tartar only, others lemons, and others seville oranges.'[9] Tartar—as tartaric acid, or cream of tartar—became one of the vital ingredients of sherbet drinks and sweets in the nineteenth century, and alcohol disappeared from the formula, at least in Britain.

Stronger acids than tartar, lemon or orange juice were also used in drinks. Perhaps this came from the practices of apothecaries. From the fifteenth century onwards, they had described some of their medicinal syrups as *juleps*, hinting at exotic origins similar to that of sherbet. The physician Nicholas Culpeper stated that juleps were mixed from distilled waters (liquids distilled from mixtures of herbs or flowers thought suitable for the patient's condition) and syrups, likewise containing medical ingredients, to be drunk at pleasure. He also remarks, 'If you love tart things, add ten drops of oil of vitriol to your pint, and shake it together, and it will have a fine grateful taste.'[10] The acid was apparently considered cooling (in the Galenic sense of hot and cold, not physically), because then he wrote:

> The syrup of violets is of most use, and of better effect, being taken in some convenient liquor: and if a little of the juice or syrup of lemons be put to it,

or a few drops of oil of vitriol, it made thereby the more powerful to cool the heat, and quench the thirst, and gives to the drink a claret wine colour, and a fine tart relish, pleasing to the taste.[11]

This mixture was considered good for many ailments including jaundice. Lemon juice is perfectly safe, but one should not be tempted to make experiments with vitriol or other strong acids just because Culpeper did.

It is safer (and easier) to consider a late version of mint sherbet such as one given by Theodore Garret in the 1890s:

Put 2lb of moist sugar in a pan with 1 qt of cold water and the beaten white of two eggs, and boil them till reduced to a somewhat thick syrup. Next mix with it 1 pint of the best vinegar and a small bunch of freshly gathered mint tied in a small piece of muslin. Boil the whole for fifteen minutes longer, then strain the Sherbet and leave it until cool. Pour into bottles and cork them well. This Sherbet should be taken mixed with cold water, and is a very refreshing beverage in the summer time.[12]

Garret's recipe incorporates clarification (the froth formed by the egg white would be strained out at the end), an operation which can be avoided by using white granulated sugar, and the proportion of vinegar is high. I have reduced it in the version in the recipe section at the end of this chapter. Vinegar and mint is said to be one of the oldest recorded combinations amongst sherbet recipes.[13]

Sweet-sour drinks cooled with snow; solid rose sugar imported from Turkey; syrups containing meat jelly, or violets and vitriol: what is one to make of these? They add up to the elements which are vital to sherbet: implications of a drink or refreshment, an image of exotic novelty, and flavours and textures which surprise the consumer. These are constants over hundreds of years, during which different versions were passed around the Arab world, to Turkey, to Europe, and to North America, subtly altering along the way, one country emphasizing the temperature, another the texture, and others the flavours.

It was in the 1800s that sherbet began the transformation from a drink into an entirely British confection of the type now loved by children. The process began with the discovery that 'fixed air' (carbon dioxide) could be pumped into water to make soda-water. Fizzy drinks became the rage. Soda water, from bottles or siphons, and 'pop' or ginger beer, (which relied on a mild secondary fermentation) had become a feature of English life by the 1830s.

This was a time when the English, following a not entirely honourable pattern of applying technology to foods, seized on some products of the rapidly developing chemical industry and began incorporating them into drinks on a routine basis. A basic mixture of acid (usually from cream of tartar or tartaric acid), and alkali (bicarbonate of soda) was evolved; it is now better known as baking powder. Inert as long as it is kept dry, if water is added, a chemical reaction starts in which the acid and alkali neutralize each other, releasing carbon dioxide to produce the fizz or effervescence. Such effects seem to have exerted a fascination. In 1851, the *Illustrated London News* reported from the Great Exhibition:

> A drinking glass is exhibited, with a partition for soda and acid, to be mixed separately, the junction of two streams effecting combustion only at the moment of entering the mouth. Few people could 'stand this' we should think.[14]

An acid and alkali mixture in powder, which could easily be dispensed to order (no need for special bottles or fancy machinery) developed quite early in the century. Mayhew commented on this whilst examining the development of the street-trade in ginger beer:

> [It was] not known to any extent until about thirty years ago. About that time (1822) a man, during a most sultry drought, sold extraordinary quantities of 'cool ginger-beer' and of 'soda-powders' near the Royal Exchange…Soda-water he sold 'in powders', the acid and the alkali being mixed in the water of the glass held by the customer, and drunk whilst effervescing.[15]

Perhaps because of the activities of soft-drink vendors, sherbet became confused with lemonade in the mind of the consumer. Mayhew also noted, when listing summer drinks sold from stalls on the streets:

Figure 49. A continuous-action soda-water machine, illustrated in E. Skuse, *Confectioners Handbook* (4th edition, *c.* 1892). For £30, the machine would supply enough water to fill 40 dozen bottles every day. There is a pump and agitator on the left, to supply pressure and the alkali, while the vessel on the right (with an agitating handle on its top) was the point of entry for acid.

the principal is Lemonade…Indeed, the high-sounding names given to some of these beverages—such as 'Nectar' and 'Persian Sherbet'—are but other names for lemonade, in a slightly different colour or fashion.[16]

'Persian sherbet', according to William Finemore's notebook, was flavoured with oil of orange and attar of roses, whereas raspberry could be made with raspberry juice and cochineal. Mayhew found, when he began investigating recipes, that lemonade as made 'by those vendors who deal in the best articles,' was composed of carbonate of soda, tartaric acid, loaf sugar, and essence of lemon. It was kept in powder in a jar and mixed with water in the glass, upon which it effervesced. The alternative was to use lemonade powders bought from

160

chemists. He continued, '"Sherbet" is the same admixture with cream of tartar instead of tartaric acid.' One of his informants commented on 'shocking roguishness in the trade', citing the substitution of vitriol for tartaric acid. Perhaps the influence of apothecaries had not entirely disappeared.

Lemonade or sherbet powder was sometimes called lemon alkali, reflecting the important ingredients. In some northern dialects, this became 'lemon kali'; eventually, northern terseness abbreviated this even further to kali (pronounced kale-eye), a name by which sherbet powder is still known to many children. Abbreviation seems to be a characteristic of sherbet in British tradition, both in name and substance. Curiously, in North America, it was the cold, liquid elements of the definition which were extended, transforming the confection into a smooth, light ice of fruit juice with beaten egg white, milk, or gelatine, and sometimes sparkling wine.[17]

The formula for sherbet as known in Britain now is simply sugar plus fizz from bicarbonate of soda, and an acid, usually tartaric acid, plus colours and flavours. It is still sold by weight from jars under the trade name 'Rainbow Crystals'. The flavoured sugar is coloured and arranged in layers in the jar, which look pretty when the jar is new, but eventually mix to a uniform orange-beige as the level falls. Unlike Victorian sherbets mixed with water for drinks, it is consumed dry. Only when the powder encounters saliva do the crystals react and give off carbon dioxide. Combustion, as the *Illustrated London News* would have said, takes place in the mouth.

Today, interest has moved to the means by which sherbet powder can be conveyed to the mouths of small children with the minimum possibility of mess or getting wet *en route*. The most basic and moist, which can still be observed in playgrounds, especially in the north, is a sherbet dab: a bagful of sherbet with a lollipop to dip in it (those without lollies simply lick their forefingers and dip instead—it is not a hygienic sweet). The 'Sherbet Fountain', a paper tube with a hollow liquorice stick sealed into the top as a straw, recalls the origin of sherbet as a drink. Sherbet lemons—bright yellow, hard-boiled sweets with sherbet in the middle—trade on the connections between sherbet and lemonade.

The development of sweets of the type known to the trade as compressed tablets[18] provided another vehicle. Since the final stages of their manufacture involves virtually no moisture, sherbet powder can be added, preserving the full potential for effervescing until the sweets are eaten. The popular brand Refreshers maintains the implications of a drink in a sweet; another, Love Hearts, has emerged from the conversation-lozenge tradition.[19] Lemonade in powder is just a memory and *gul sekeri* a curiosity, but sherbet has followed the convoluted path of novelty and technology to arrive at every corner sweet shop.

RECIPES

NEVIN HALICI'S GUL SERBETI

110g scented rose petals • 50ml lemon juice • 150g caster sugar
1 litre water.

Cut off and discard the white base of the rose petals and put the petals in a bowl. Add the lemon juice and rub well with the hands for 5–10 minutes. Leave to stand for 30 minutes.

Bring the sugar and the water to the boil, boil for 1 minute, then remove from the heat. Let the syrup cool a little then pour it over the roses. Leave in the refrigerator for 10–12 hours. Strain through muslin and pour into decanters. Pour a little sherbet on to a plate. Dip the rim of a glass into it and then into icing sugar. Allow to dry then fill the glass with cold sherbet and serve.[20]

ELIZA SMITH'S SHRUB

450ml brandy • juice of 1 lemon • zest of half a lemon
a small chunk of nutmeg • 400ml medium-dry white wine
180g sugar

Put the brandy in a jug or bowl, add the lemon zest and juice, and the nutmeg. Cover. Leave for 3 days; stir in the wine and sugar, making sure the sugar dissolves properly. Strain into a clean bottle.

Mix a little with sparkling mineral water or soda and ice for a long summer drink, or use the infusion for flavouring whipped cream to make a syllabub. Add more sugar to taste.

THEODORE GARRET'S MINT SHERBET

450g granulated sugar • 500ml water • 100ml white wine vinegar
a small bunch fresh mint.

Dissolve the sugar in the water and bring to the boil. Add the vinegar and the mint. Simmer for 15 minutes, strain and cool. Bottle, and store in the fridge. Serve diluted to taste with cold water, plus ice and a sprig of fresh mint.

Figure 50. The Liquorice Allsort, using a variety of presentation techniques for liquorice: sandwiched with soft sugar paste, covered in hundreds and thousands, the cut string, the tube and the chequerboard.

CHAPTER XI

Against the cough: liquorice and marshmallow

LIQUORICE and marshmallow have medicinal applications dating back millennia. Only recently have they become sweets, and marshmallow, as now known, has a very short history in Britain. Let's begin with liquorice.

> In the licorice fields at Pontefract
> My love and I did meet
> And many a burdened licorice bush
> Was blooming round our feet[1]

When John Betjeman wrote this verse, he may have used some poetic licence, but the liquorice fields at Pontefract in west Yorkshire did exist. Since liquorice, as sold over the sweet-shop counter to children, is a black, shiny, tough sweet with a strong flavour and no obvious connection to bushes (or any other form of plant life), this surreal detail begs the question of what it really is.

Liquorice is based on the juice extracted from the roots of *Glycyrrhiza glabra.* This forms an untidy bush, perennial and about two feet high, with undistinguished, pointed, oval leaves. It was grown as a field crop around Pontefract until about the time of the Second World War. That a plant which is native to the Middle East and southern Russia should flourish at all in the damp, chilly climate of industrial Yorkshire seems as unlikely a scenario as a poet arranging a tryst there. However, it is not so much climate as soil that is important for liquorice cultivation. It should be deep, fine and fertile to allow the long roots to grow properly. Liquorice roots contain a substance called glycyrrhizin, which has the property of tasting very

Figure 51. A liquorice bush. Illustration taken from Pomet's *Complete History of Drugs* (1747).

sweet: according to food scientists, fifty times sweeter than sugar. Although this occurs in other plants, liquorice contains unusually high levels. The old Scottish word for liquorice, 'sugarallie', celebrates the sweetness: it is a shortened version of the sixteenth-century 'sugar alicreesh'.

The roots of liquorice can be used in confections, boiled with the other ingredients and strained out after a while, or dried and added in powder form. Or the juice can be extracted from fresh roots by cooking in water, reduced until it becomes a thick paste, and dried. The latter is known as 'block liquorice juice', and is the form it was and is usually imported. Block juice is hard, black and shiny when broken. It looks exactly like tar.

Formulae for simple liquorice confections usually require about one to four per cent block juice mixed with sugar, gums, wheat starch, colouring and flavourings.[2] Liquorice confectionery does not have to be black: without added colour, it turns out a slightly translucent, mid-chestnut; some North American liquorice is red. It does not have to be sweet: much of that sold in Holland, Germany and Scandinavia is salty, and tastes most peculiar to the British palate. Nor does it have to be pungent: the use of strongly-flavoured syrups such as molasses, and additions of aniseed oil (the usual flavouring for liquorice in Britain) are at the discretion of the manufacturer.

Confections containing liquorice, although now classed with sweets, were primarily used as cures for throat and lung diseases. The Chinese used it 3,000 years ago, and it was known to the Roman world. It is still valued for treating coughs and chest complaints; this perhaps explains the affection in which it is held by the inhabitants of the chilly, foggy, damp coasts around the North Sea, where every country has developed favourite liquorice sweets.

What was it like in the past? Early recipes show that it could be combined with other ingredients to make sticky, syrup-like medicines or electuaries, which were sucked or swallowed for throat complaints. In the sixteenth century, Alexis of Piedmont's 'excellent conserve against the cogh' was a recipe of this type. The formula included marshmallow roots, 'lickeraus', hyssop, sage and other herbs, boiled up with barley starch, mixed with honey and perfumed with musk, to which one could also add sugar in powder or penides. It seems to be an example of putting everything possible into a prophylactic mixture—rather like the twentieth-century belief in multi-vitamins. Alexis claimed:

> This secret is of suche excellencie, that if a man use it in the winter, as afore is saied, it is not possible for him to bee vexed or turmented wyth the cogh, rumes, murres, catarres, or any other like disease.[3]

With an endorsement like that, it is not surprising that children have always been encouraged to eat liquorice.

Most seventeenth-century confectionery books included one recipe for liquorice, suggesting that it was considered useful to know about but that one didn't do creative things with it: a utilitarian medicine, not a sweetmeat for the banquet. It was, it seems, troublesome to handle. The roots were tough, needing much cleaning, soaking and boiling to make a good extract. These instructions are from *A Queens Delight*:

To make juyce of Liquorish
Take English Liquorish…bruise it with a hammer, and cut it in pieces; to a pound of Liquorish thus bruised, put a quart of Hysop water, let them soak together in an earthen pot a day and a night, then pull the Liquorish into small pieces, and lay it in soak again for two dayes more; then strain out the Liquorish and boil the liquor a good while. Stir it often; then put in half a pound of Loaf-sugar finely beaten, four grains of Musk, as much Ambergreece…boil them together till it be good & thick, still have care you burn it not; then put it out in glass plates, and make it into round rolls, and set it in a drying place till it be stiff, that you may work it into rolls to be cut as big as Barley corns.[4]

Long rolls of liquorice have survived to the present day, as in the ubiquitous bootlaces, cables, twists and whips; so have the pieces 'cut as big as Barley corns', which are made by several companies in England, Holland, France and Italy.

Other recipes required spices, gums, and rosewater, as in this suggestion from 1608:

To make pectorall rowles for the Cough
Take liquorish pouder finely searsed one ounce, of the spices of Diatra-gacanthum frigidium ij drams, of Gum-arabecke and Tragarant in fine powder of each a dram, white starch half a dram, Anniseeds in fine pouder one ounce mingle with the rest, then take of suger six ounces, of Pennits an ounce and a halfe, Suger-candy one ounce powdered and mingled with the former powder, then take Gum-tragacant steeped in Rose water and beat it into a past, and so make it into long rowles and so dry them, and keepe them.[5]

Simplified and freed from hyperbole, this is a liquorice-flavoured sugar paste. Even then, aniseed was important in English liquorice recipes. The recipe also shows how sugar was considered good for you, offering it in three forms—ordinary sugar, pulled-sugar pennits, and sugar candy. It also includes three forms of tragacanth: as 'the spices of Diatragacanthum frigidium', as powder, and as binding agent.

Liquorice often travelled in the form of concentrated juice. Pomet described its preparation and some of the places it came from:

They make of *Liquorice* and warm Water, a strong yellow Tincture, which afterwards is evaporated over the Fire, to a solid Consistence, till it becomes black, and is what we call black *Liquorish* Juice, which comes to us ready made from *Holland*, *Spain* and *Marseilles*, in cakes of different Sizes, which sometimes weigh four Ounces, or half a Pound. The Liquorish Juice which has the most Virtue, is black without, and of a shining Blackness within…*Liquorish* is brought to us out of *Spain*, and many other countries of *Europe*, but the best is that which grows in *England*.[6]

The translators added a note that in England the plant was chiefly cultivated around Pontefract although some was grown near London, and that two sorts of juice were in the shops.

The author of *A Queens Delight* stipulated English liquorice, which at the time might well have come from Pontefract. The Yorkshire antiquarian and physician Nathaniel Johnston (1627–1705), who was living in the town by 1653, wrote in his journal that 'the soile nearest the town is mostly planted with licorice or rootes.'[7] Legends say that liquorice was grown at Pontefract by monks in the Middle Ages; this is possible, but no evidence has been produced to show that it was actually so.

Of the concentrated juices, Spanish liquorice was apparently better quality than home-grown by the time Pomet's work became available in English. His translators commented that 'the one call'd *Spanish*' was of a finer colour and consistency than the home-produced, which was made from the stringy parts of the root and mixed with the pulp of prunes. In the modern industry it is recognized that the flavour of the juice depends to some extent on country of origin. Spanish liquorice has 'a smoother, less harsh background flavour'.[8]

'Spanish' is still a dialect word for liquorice of any kind in west Yorkshire; used originally, perhaps, to distinguish imported juice from local. Liquorice in general has a curious property of acquiring names from external sources: a Dutch variety, shaped like tiny lozenges, is known as 'laurier', perhaps because the dried juice was imported packed in boxes of bay leaves, and 'salmiak' is liquorice containing sal ammoniac (ammonium chloride).

******

The observant reader will have noticed that Alexis of Piedmont included marshmallow roots in his excellent conserve against the cough. Marshmallow, *Althea officinalis*, is another plant which has a long history as a cold cure. It grows near salt marshes and was valued for its mucilaginous roots; the related common mallows had similar uses. In English, they are mentioned in documents predating the Norman Conquest. Roots were infused in sweetened wine or in milk for the treatment of chest complaints, or they could be preserved as suckets in sugar syrup.

Although advertisements and trade cards of late eighteenth-century confectioners sometimes list 'true paste of marshmallow' amongst their products, recipes do not appear in texts until a few years later. By then, it seems, mallow itself was not an acceptable ingredient, possibly because it makes a heavy and mildly bitter confection. Jarrin said that, 'Marsh mallow is not used on account of its unpleasant taste; apple jelly is equally good, and possesses the same healing qualities.'

His recipe for 'Marsh Mallow Paste' was based on gum Senegal and apple juice, flavoured with neroli (orange flower). After the gum had been dissolved and strained and mixed with the juice and sugar:

> dry it to a thick consistence, taking care to have a little fire, covered with ashes, under it; then whisk to a snow six whites of eggs, and add them to your paste. Continue to stir the mixture to prevent it sticking…You will know when it is done, if on applying some of the paste to the back of your hand it does not stick; this mode of making it is rather tedious, but it is the best.[9]

The recipe works well, and I have devised a version, given at the end of the chapter. The quantity of gum required makes it expensive to make. The low proportion of sugar means it has a slightly medicinal flavour, strange to modern palates accustomed to sweet, airy marshmallow. The texture is closer and chewier, the flavour of the gum comes through, and the original, throat-comforting nature of the confection is more apparent.

Marshmallow made this way is similar to the knots of *pâte de guimauve* still sold in France. Trying the recipe makes one appreciate why such confections became very specialized aspects of the industry: good results demand both skill and patience.

Jarrin's recipe for liquorice paste was based on the same principles and ingredients as his marshmallow. The liquorice was made into a decoction with apples and barley, which was used in place of the apple juice, and once the egg whites had been added and the mixture beaten and dried, it must have produced a lighter-coloured, less tough mouthful than the liquorice now made in Britain.

Pale liquorice was not unknown elsewhere. Pomet mentions it:

> We sell besides, other kinds of Liquorish Juices, as those of *Blois*, both white and yellow, and those of *Rheims* or of *Paris*, which are cut into flat Pastiles, or made round like a small Wax-Candle. The white Juice of Liquorish, as 'tis call'd, made at *Paris*, is a Composition of Liquorish Powder, Sugar, Almonds, and *Orrice* Powder…[10]

This sounds rather good (one imagines it a kind of liquorice marzipan), but unfortunately, he did not give a recipe. Another liquorice confection which was probably pale in colour, with an aerated texture, is implied in a recipe given by Hannah Glasse:

Liquorice cakes
Take hysop and red rose water, of each half a pint, half a pound of green liquorice, the outside scraped off, then beat with a pestle; put to it half a pound of anniseeds, and steep it all night in the water; boil it with a gentle fire till the taste is well out of the liquorice; strain it, put to it, three pounds of liquorice powder, and set it on a gentle fire till it is come to the thickness of cream; take it off and put to it half a pound of white sugar candy seered [sieved] very fine; beat this together as you do biscuit, for at least three hours and never suffer it to stand still; as you beat it, you must strew in double-refined sugar, finely seered, at least three pounds; half an hour before it is finished, put in half a spoonful of gum dragon steeped in orange flower water; when it is very white then it is beat enough; roll it up with white sugar, and if you will have it perfumed put in a pastil or two [11]

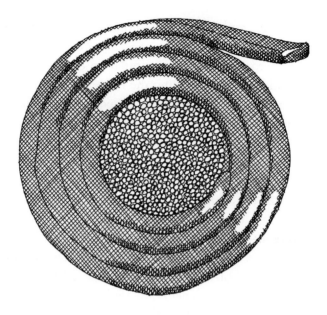

Figure 52. A Catherine wheel. The liquorice string is spiralled around a brightly coloured sweet.

The use of gum and orange flower water, with all the beating, suggests this recipe may have been influenced by the same tradition as early marshmallow, and implies the result was relatively light and easy to chew. Liquorice which relied on gum alone would have been hard. The close, chewy texture now characteristic of liquorice is probably a fairly recent development, due in part to the addition of wheat flour during boiling.

British liquorice has become the most abstract of sweets. Manufacturers have concentrated on the graphic combination of very black liquorice with soft sugar paste in white or brilliant colours. This is best seen in Liquorice Allsorts, which are mostly sheets of liquorice and brightly coloured paste layered together and cut into striped cubes, together in a box with chunks of liquorice cable, aniseed gums covered in pink or blue nonpareils, and round paste-and-liquorice sweets. The origin of this mix is obscure: it is said to have come about when a salesman for the Bassett company got a case of samples hopelessly muddled, some time around the turn of the century.[12] This sounds disingenuous for an industry in which companies have been forced to be highly competitive. Still, accidents do happen. Other shapes much used in Britain are bootlaces and cables, often tied in knots, or spiralled round big bright sweets to make 'Catherine wheels'. Short pieces of liquorice are panned to make the long comfits known as 'torpedoes', coloured in vibrant contrast to the dark centre.

The appearance in the sweet-shop tray of liquorice sticks made visually interesting by dipping the ends into da-glo-bright sugar icing, might be thought simply part of this tradition of contrasting colour. Instead, it returns the discussion to the original medicinal uses of liquorice. Culpeper recorded preparing *lohocks*, compounds based on sugar and herbs for treating chest complaints. These were 'thicker than syrup, and not so thick as an electuary'.[13] The name, he said, signified nothing more than something to be licked up; the patient took it by dipping the bruised end of a liquorice stick into the mixture and sucking it off gradually.

This idea has been persistent in both Britain and North America, illustrated by Charles Apell's instructions for making 'Liquorice Root Suckers', published early in this century in the USA. These were based on boiled sweets, variously coloured and flavoured and lightly striped with white pulled sugar (an echo of pennets). Apell instructed that these should be allowed to cool a little:

> When your batch is cold enough to keep its shape put on your spinning board and spin out round and cut on kiss machine and have girls stick your licorice root in your drops while they are warm. Have your licorice root cut in sticks 3 inches long.[14]

Folk memories of apposite uses for liquorice have proved remarkably resistant to change over both time and space. They recur in 'Pontefract cakes' (also known as 'Pomfret cakes' or 'Yorkshire pennies'), still made in the town. These are shiny, chewy liquorice drops stamped with a seal whose impression is usually indistinct, but which consists of a gate and an owl (elements taken from the coat of arms of a local family, the Saviles). The drops are believed to date from the mid-eighteenth century when an apothecary in the town, George Dunhill, improved the local product by adding sugar to it. Stamping sweets with a seal was then common practice; it flattened them, added decoration and, in the case of medicinal confections such as liquorice and lozenges, the apothecary could use some exclusive mark to signify the product was genuine.

Starch-moulding, developed in the nineteenth century, opened up new possibilities for shapes. The technique is little used in British liquorice and it has been left to continental European manufacturers to exploit. The Dutch, in particular, produce a charming range of *katte* (cats) and 'farm liquorice' in the shape of animals, houses and people. In 1890, Theodore Garrett did give a very simple formula for starch moulding:

> *Liquorice drops:*
> Dissolve 1/2 oz gum Arabic in 1/4 pint of water, mix in 1 oz of powdered Liquorice and 1/2 lb of lump sugar, put them into a sugar-boiler, and boil to a thick syrup. Have a shallow and wide box full of powdered starch, make it quite level, and then with a marble make indentations all over. Fill the hollows in the starch with the hot syrup, and dry the drops in a drying-oven.[15]

By the time this was written, liquorice had become the speciality of those few companies prepared to make the necessary investment in machinery and training to handle it. The trouble with liquorice is that it is difficult to work, especially on a large scale. In 1830, William Gunter dismissed it, remarking:

> Paste of liquorice is rarely called for and is hardly a confection. The juice of the liquorice, with some delicate acid, is added to dissolved gum Senegal. Little sugar is used.[16]

The comments made by Skuse on liquorice goods go a long way to explain the problems:

> Makers of repute are comparatively few and confine themselves almost solely to producing variety from the root in question, their mixings and

manipulations are their own and in most cases, the result of years of experiment. No useful purpose would be served by giving details of processes which mean a large outlay, as those interested to this extent would be better guided by a practical man having the latest experience in this particular branch.[17]

The story of liquorice has since been one of increasing concentration in manufacture. At the start of this century, Pontefract had eleven producers, all making Pontefract cakes; the number is now reduced to two. The town remains the British centre for production of the sweet but its cultivation of the plant declined and was given up (except as a curiosity) by the 1950s. British firms have looked to Spain, China and especially the Middle East for this ingredient.[18] Yet the connection between Pontefract and liquorice persists. The fields have gone, but inertia is a potent force in the location of industries.

Marshmallow has also moved away from its medicinal origins. From the original version given by Jarrin, it has transformed into a frothy, pastel, cloud-like substance. It is softer and lighter, a consequence of the gelatine and modified starches which have replaced the gums as gelling agents, and has become so insubstantial that Lees and Jackson, in a technical discussion, stated that 'the two most important ingredients...are air and moisture'.[19] The gelling agents give structure, holding flavoured, coloured sugar syrup in a foam around innumerable air bubbles. Around 1900, Skuse referred to confections of this type as 'American marshmallows' and they probably were. Charles Apell, publishing in North America, gave a dozen formulae for marshmallow sweets, including types such as 'marshmallow bananas' which were starch-moulded. There is no hint that anyone considered them suitable treatment for colds; nor, I think, would such an idea be taken seriously now.

RECIPES

LIQUORICE LOZENGES (1608)

15g powdered liquorice root • 8g powdered gum tragacanth
125g icing sugar • a pinch of powdered aniseed (optional)
30ml rosewater.

Mix the dry ingredients roughly, and then sieve together. Add the rose-water and knead lightly until you have a coherent paste. A little extra rosewater may be needed. Make into little rolls or lozenges straight away (the paste dries if left for more than an hour or so) and put on a wire rack to dry. Store in an airtight box.

The suggestion in the original recipe of a whole ounce of aniseed seems rather excessive, especially as liquorice itself has a flavour reminiscent of aniseed. It can be left out for those who don't like it.

Liquorice root can be bought from some herbalists; see appendix.

Figure 53. Trademarks and stamps of former Pontefract liquorice producers. The two in the centre incorporate the common motifs of the castle or gatehouse, and the second from the right includes the Savile owl.

JARRIN'S MARSHMALLOW PASTE

100g gum arabic, soaked overnight in 200ml water
100g granulated sugar
100ml apple juice, made by cooking about 250g apples, cut into
pieces, with 150ml water, and then straining off the liquid
2 egg whites • about 15ml orange flower water • cornflour for dusting
Equipment: a slab or tray dusted with cornflour; a hand-held electric
beater; a large pan with a heavy base; a flat-ended wooden spatula.

Take the soaked gum and stir to check it has dissolved properly. If lumps remain, put the bowl containing the gum mixture in a pan of hot water and heat gently to encourage them to dissolve.

In a medium pan, mix the apple liquid and the sugar. Heat gently, stirring. Once all sugar has dissolved, stir in the gum water. Simmer, stirring frequently, for about 15 minutes until the mixture has reduced and thickened.

In a large bowl, beat the egg whites to soft peaks. With the beaters running, pour the gum-apple-sugar mixture onto the whites in a thin slow stream. Continue to whisk for a few minutes, until thick and glossy. Add the orange flower water. Scrape the mixture back into a pan with a heavy, heat-retaining base. Place over the lowest possible heat and continue to cook gently. Stir frequently with the spatula. If the mixture begins to stick to the base of the pan, take it off the heat and stir thoroughly with the spatula until it shows clear once again. Keep heating and stirring until eventually the mixture becomes very thick and begins to hold its shape. Test by dropping a little on the back of your hand: it should no longer be sticky.

When dry enough, turn the marshmallow onto the cornflour-dusted slab or tray, and spread it as neatly as possible into an even layer. Allow to cool, then dust the top with cornflour and cut into strips.

See the notes in the appendix for details of handling gums.

Figure 54. The toffee hammer, for breaking slabs of Bonfire toffee. In the background, a familiar tin of Farrah's Harrogate toffee. This firm in fact went out of business for a brief moment in 1997, but it is now revived and production is expanding.

CHAPTER XII

A late developer: toffee

AGED about six, peering over the top of the counter in the local paper shop one October day, my eyes levelled with a new sight: a large, shallow tray of deep golden toffee, smelling of syrup and butter. It hadn't been there earlier in the year, and before very long it had vanished, the contents smashed into irregular chips with a special hammer, weighed out and sold. And the container? I don't know what happened to the container. Did the proprietors wash it and reinstate it for kitchen duty, or did they return the empties to some toffee-boiling company elsewhere?

Probably it came from elsewhere because selling tray-toffee has been a tradition for most of this century, many companies supplying the demand. I haven't seen a toffee-hammer wielded for a long time, though it was once a feature of every shop selling sweets, at least in the north country. Hygiene regulations do not encourage the display of toffee in places where it runs the danger of sticking to the local paper. Even companies who specialize in tray-toffee no longer expose it quite so directly to the atmosphere. Unless the supplier is local and turnover fast, toffee in an open tray is a liability. Apart from the fact that it might be sneezed on, it goes sticky in a few days.

Made round the corner and sold in hours, tray-toffee had wonderful freshness. Toffee really is best in the first few days after making: shards of crisp sugar between the teeth and a browned-butter smell.

The flavour of toffee (and butterscotch and caramels) is created by a reaction which takes place during boiling. Proteins (such as those contained in dairy products) combine with sugar in something known to chemists as the 'Maillard reaction'. This particular piece of culinary magic produces a brown colour and attractive smells and flavours. The inviting deep bronze and the heady aromas of newly baked bread crust and toast are due to this same reaction. It is sometimes known colloquially as caramelization.

Toffee is one of the easiest sweets to make. It is probably more significant for the role it has played in British childhood over the last two centuries than for any great insights it provides into the alchemy practised by confectioners, although it does show that using molasses, butter or acids such as vinegar to prevent sugar graining was widely grasped at a basic level of the craft, perhaps as early as the start of the nineteenth century.

The really interesting thing about that toffee in the tray (apart from eating it) was the way it appeared unexpectedly and then vanished. All year round, one could buy 'toffees' and I found the relationship between chewy little lumps wrapped in pretty Cellophane and the inelegant, ephemeral slabs in large open trays difficult to comprehend. Then the shopkeeper explained that it was Bonfire toffee, and that made everything clear. It was special for November 5th, Guy Fawkes Night, to go with the parkin (sticky oatmeal ginger-bread) and parkin pigs (ginger biscuits cut in pig shapes) which our mothers were baking, following a good Yorkshire tradition.

To an adult enquiring into the origins of sweets, the concept of Bonfire toffee makes very little clear. Why should it be associated so definitely with a late autumn festival? Toffee is easily made from non-seasonal ingredients such as brown sugar, treacle and butter, which by the last century were sometimes affordable even for poor households. And why was it in a big flat tray, not cut in neat pieces? Maybe toffee became popular simply because it was relatively cheap and easy to make, both for small confectioners and at home.

Speculation is possible on its origin as a festive food, perhaps formerly associated with Halloween or All Souls (31st October and 1st November, dates important in both the pagan and the Catholic year). Special foods for these days undoubtedly existed, such as 'soul cakes',[1] the small fruit cakes made for the feast of All Souls, so why not toffee? Jamieson, in his *Etymological Dictionary of the Scottish Language* (1825)[2] defined *taffie* as a mixture of treacle and flour boiled together, eaten at Halloween.

The ingredients could have been more seasonal than they appear to us. Before the eighteenth century, butter would have been most plentiful in the early autumn, as would honey (molasses or treacle were often substituted once they became common). It's easy to imagine that the poorer members of the community boiled up a simple sweetmeat for All Saints Day, maybe something resembling a cross between one of the solid medieval gingerbreads and a robust treacle toffee.

What is certain is that in the Victorian period an ancestor of Bonfire toffee or 'Plot' toffee (Plot Night was a local name for November 5th) was popular in west Yorkshire. Joseph Wright gave a definition of something which was called 'sucker' in Leeds dialect in 1861. This was:

> A compound of treacle, sugar, vinegar and butter, boiled and spread out in 'pudding tins,'[3] till cool, when it is broken up and is ready for use. On the anniversary of the Gunpowder Plot, the boiling of 'succour' is very general, even amongst the better class of tradespeople.[4]

They may have called it succour, but the details make it instantly recognizable as toffee. The following recipe was recorded some time between 1808 and 1833 by Mrs Ann Hailstone who lived in Bradford. It is not clear if the custom of toffee boiling for November 5th had evolved by the time she was writing.

Toffy
One lb of brown sugar 2 tablespoonsful of treacle dissolved in a gill of water on the fire, and then add 8 ounces of fresh butter boil the whole till it will drop crisp. You may add a few drops of essence of lemon.[5]

It is an advantage to have someone to share the work when sugar boiling. Professional confectioners, making sweets on a day-to-day basis, had their families, journeymen and apprentices as helpmeets. Poor people used sweet-making as an excuse for a social. Marian

McNeill quoted this description of candy-making as an evening's entertainment:

> In rural districts in Scotland…candy-making is a regular adjunct to courting. It draws together all the lads and lasses round for miles, and the fun and daffing that go on during the boiling, pulling, clipping, cooling, are, both the lads and lasses declare, worth the money…A few of the lasses club their sixpences together, a night is set, a house is named, and, of course, the young men who are specially wanted are invited to lend a hand and a foot too, for dancing is not an uncommon adjunct to such gatherings.[6]

The north Wales tradition was to have a toffee-pull around Christmas or New Year, with friends and family joining in. Toffee-boiling nights as an excuse for a gathering were also recorded in Yorkshire. Taffy-pulls or candy-pulls became a custom in North America too, and it was the hard work which Irma Rombauer and Marion Becker seem to have recalled:

> If you have a hankering to re-create an old-time 'candy-pull,' be sure you have a reasonably stout pair of arms, or an adolescent in the family who wants to convert from a puny weakling to a strong man. This way, taffy pulling is fun and seems easy.[7]

By the time music-hall and then cinema provided alternative entertainment and Ogden Nash had cynically quipped that 'Candy is dandy but liquor is quicker', taffy-pulls had become a quaint custom on both sides of the Atlantic.

Taffy, first recorded in 1817, is considered to be the earliest version of the word toffee. Some writers at the time speculated that the word described the toughness of a pulled sweet, and should really be 'tough' or 'toughy,' although this is now discounted. Taffy in North America (where the word toffee never became established) definitely means a pulled sweet. It tends, at least in modern versions, to be pale, made from white sugar, and often has a softer texture which is chewy or 'creamy,' as in salt-water taffy, which bears no relation to toffee as known in Britain.

A few pulled-toffee recipes survive in Britain. A Welsh example (which does have a very hard texture when it is fresh) is given by

Bobby Freeman in her book on Welsh cookery.[8] It is made with equal quantities of black treacle and brown sugar. The basic principle of boiling coarse sugar and then pulling it is not far removed from that involved in early versions of pennetts. A modernized version, omitting the instructions for pulling, is given at the end of this chapter.

Early uses of the words taffy or toffee cited in the *Oxford English Dictionary* refer to boiling treacle or molasses to a consistency at which it would set as a solid cake. This points to a possible alternative origin of the name, indicating a link with molasses through the word *tafia*. In the late eighteenth century this meant a molasses-based drink similar to rum and was recorded in some dialects especially in north-western England. Early writers were very definite about the essential role of molasses or treacle in toffee. The word toffee could also have carried some more generalized notion of a syrup: it is still used by some sugar-boilers[9] as a general term for a high-boiled syrup. Is this the usage which has stuck in the names of one or two Scottish sweets, such as 'taffy rock bools' (also known as Hawick Balls, made of sugar, butter and mint), and horehound toffee? Or did these rely on molasses in earlier versions?

In the 1890s, Skuse wrote in his *Confectioners Handbook*:

> I do not think I could select a better, older or more popular sweet than Everton Toffee to commence my recipes, because it is a toffee which is known all over the world; is a great favourite with young and old, easily made and requires no machinery.[10]

The story of this sweet is recounted in several versions along these general lines: the original Everton Toffee was made and sold by one Molly or Mary, née Johnson, who married a Mr Bushell in the mid-eighteenth century. She had a shop in Everton, then a village just outside Liverpool. So too did her competitor John Cooper. Molly Bushell is said to have been given the recipe by a kind physician when she was ill. Precise details and the number and names of the people involved vary according to the teller. Whatever the truth, there was a strong tradition of making toffee in Everton, and it was sold by several

THE OLD ORIGINAL TOFFEE SHOP AT EVERTON, A.D. 1753.
THE HOUSE IN WHICH TOFFEE WAS FIRST MADE.

PATRONISED BY HER MAJESTY THE QUEEN, AND THE ROYAL FAMILY.

THE WORLD-FAMED ORIGINAL

EVERTON TOFFEE,

ESTABLISHED 1753,
AS SUPPLIED TO

HER MAJESTY THE QUEEN,

HIS ROYAL HIGHNESS THE DUKE OF CAMBRIDGE,

LORD JOHN RUSSELL,

&c. &c.

AND MANUFACTURED ONLY BY

R. H. WIGNALL,

(LATE OF THE ORIGINAL TOFFEE SHOP.)
WHO IS GRANDSON TO

MOLLY BUSHELL,

THE ORIGINAL INVENTOR,

And the only person in the World in possession of the Genuine Original Family Recipe, of which not even a single copy has been taken, consequently all others are only imitations.

DEPOTS FOR THE ONLY GENUINE ARTICLE,

98, LONDON ROAD,

(NEAR THE MONUMENT,)

AND 88, RENSHAW STREET,

NEAR TOP OF BOLD STREET.

MANUFACTORY, EVERTON.

TIN CASES ALWAYS ON HAND READY PACKED,

AND SENT TO ANY PART OF THE WORLD ON RECEIPT OF POST-OFFICE ORDER.

WHOLESALE AND FOR EXPORTATION,

Figure 55. Advertisement for Everton toffee, from a Liverpool trade directory, 1864.

families in the village during the nineteenth century. The account displays strong elements of myth (more than one local speciality has a 'physician' story attached to it), although the idea of toffee as a home-made medical confection once again echoes the history of pennetts.

Before 1850, Everton toffee had become famous well beyond Lancashire. Eliza Acton gave two recipes. Her Everton Toffie No 1 was as follows:

> Put into a brass skillet or small preserving pan three ounces of very fresh butter, and as soon as it is just melted add a pound of brown sugar of moderate quality; keep these stirred gently over a very clear fire for about fifteen minutes, or until a little of the mixture, dropped in a basin of cold water, breaks clean between the teeth without sticking to them: when it is boiled to this point, it must be poured out immediately, or it will burn. The grated rind of a lemon, added when the toffie is half done, improves it much; or a small teaspoonful of powdered ginger…will vary it pleasantly to many tastes. The Real Everton toffie is made with a much larger proportion of butter, but it is the less wholesome on that very account.[11]

Everton toffee was extremely popular. The essence of the recipe remained the same through the century, although Skuse shows a confectioner's expediency in adding water to dissolve the sugar and cream of tartar to help prevent graining. He also recommended the lid be put on the pan once the syrup boiled and the mixture cooked for ten minutes. This was a trick which allowed the steam trapped in the pan to dissolve any residual crystals, before the toffee was finally uncovered and boiled to hard crack.

Whatever its origins, Everton Toffee is similar to butterscotch, another mystery word in the toffee lexicon, one which seems to have nothing to do with Scotland. Marian McNeill's 'Edinburgh recipe' for butterscotch is identical, give or take an ounce of butter, to Acton's Everton Toffie No 1. Skuse recorded that Doncaster butterscotch:

> is made just the same as Everton toffee, the difference is simply in the packing; while one is run into frames or cut up in large bars, the other is cut in small pieces about 1/2oz each, and wrapped in tinfoil, six or twelve of which made up into an attractive packet is sold at 3d. or 6d. each.[12]

Figure 56. A roller toffee cutter. The blades were adjustable by means of spacers. From Skuse, *Confectioners Handbook* (10th edition, *c.* 1900).

A special roller was used for cutting butterscotch into small blocks. Doncaster butterscotch was made by the firm of Parkinson & Son. The company—but not necessarily the butterscotch—was begun in 1817 by a confectioner called Samuel Parkinson. By 1851 Doncaster butterscotch was famous, sold to crowds who attended the races, and (according to Parkinson's) tasted and approved by Queen Victoria.

The first mention of butterscotch cited by the *OED* is 1855, in a glossary of dialect from Whitby. The derivation of the word itself is not from an affiliation with Scotland but rather the English 'scotch', meaning cut, slit or notch. Perhaps Skuse's observation on the habit of cutting the sweetmeat into small pieces is relevant here. Robert May's *The Accomplisht Cook* (1660) explains how to carbonado a shoulder of mutton: 'half boil it, scotch it and salt it, save the gravy, and broil it on a soft fire'. The meat is scored, scotched or cross-hatched with parallel cuts to give a pattern of diamonds so the broiling develops a burned and characterful crust. In *Coriolanus*, Shakespeare wrote: 'He scotcht him and notcht him like a Carbinado'. Another speculation on the name is that it is really 'scorched', because the butter burns during cooking, but dictionary derivations of 'scotch' and 'scorch' do not support this.

If the high-class confectioners specializing in expensive sweetmeats for desserts took much interest in making toffee, they did not record it in their books. The nearest they got is an occasional recipe for a rich and elegant cream-based sweet. An example appeared in the late eighteenth century in the book *Court and Country Confectioner*.

Coffee Cream Bomboons
Take about a pint of coffee made with water, put in it a pound of loaf sugar, set it on the fire and boil it to the 9th degree, then you add a full pint of double cream and let it boil again, keeping it continually stirring till it comes

to caramel height; to know when it is come to that point, you must have a bason of water by you, dip your finger in it, and put it quickly in your sugar, then in the water again to remove the sugar, which will have stuck to it; take a bit of it in your teeth, if it is hard in its crackling take it off, it is to the height required.[13]

Since 1794, a coffee-flavoured, chewy, toffee-type sweet has been known in Holland under the trade name of Hopjes. The idea is said to have originated with the Austrian Ambassador to the Netherlands, a Baron Hop.[14] Either coffee-flavoured sweets were quite widespread at this time, or the confectioners attached to the households of various ambassadors were passing ideas around amongst each other. This occasionally reappeared in books in the first half of the next century. Jarrin, having added a few recipes to a later edition of *The Italian Confectioner*, recorded that his 'coffee à la crème tablets…are excellent and have been much approved.'[15] He does not appear to use the words 'toffee' or 'butterscotch'.

******

For confectioners of Jarrin's epoch, 'caramel' indicated the highest degree of sugar boiling, and it is still used today to mean browned sugar. 'Caramels', however, means something quite different, a confection much closer to toffee.

Early toffee recipes had an in-built disadvantage: they were very hard on the teeth or, rather, on the lack of them. Mayhew noted the point when boiled, pulled-sugar sticks, toffee, and almond hardbake (caramelized sugar containing roasted almonds) were some of the most popular confections. A street-seller of sweet-stuff told him that for the sake of his elderly customers (aged about 50 or over):

> I'm sometimes a thinking I'll introduce a softer sort of toffy—boiled treacle, such as they call Tom Trot in some parts, but it's out of fashion now, just for old people that's 'boy's still.' It was rolled in a ha'penny stick sir, and sold stunnin'[16]

Across the Atlantic, confectioners seem to have had the same idea. Sometime during the mid-nineteenth century, a chewier toffee evolved in the eastern USA. The result is now known collectively as caramels. In 1887, the North American author Catherine Owen said that, 'Caramel is really sugar boiled till it changes colour, but the candy understood as "caramels" is something different.'[17]

Caramel, as a sweet of the toffee type, often includes sugar boiled to caramel, but the name actually refers to caramelization, in the sense of the brown colours and pleasant flavours produced by the Maillard reaction. Early caramel recipes were based on butter and cream (the North American dairy industry was pumping out suitable produce). Like fudge, they often involved chocolate. Some also reflected early toffees and required treacle or molasses. The texture was still quite hard. This one is Catherine Owen's:

Chocolate Caramels
Cream well together a quarter of a pound of grated chocolate, unsweetened, half a teacupful of butter, one teacupful of sugar, one teacupful of molasses, and one teacupful of milk or cream. Boil all together until the candy cracks in ice water, then pour half an inch thick into tin pans well oiled. When nearly cold mark into squares with a greased knife. In summer these require to be set on ice to cool and harden.[18]

Such confections became known as 'Philadelphia Caramels'. Recipes for these were sought-after. Skuse announced in about 1890:

I have great pleasure in giving my customers the benefit of these recipes for caramels. They were until very recently strictly an American sweet, but since their introduction into England, they have gained great popularity, being sold very freely in the lowest and poorest quarters of London, at two-pence per ounce…These few American recipes cost the writer the price of nearly forty handbooks, besides a great deal of trouble and correspondence to get them all.[19]

The Confectioners Handbook cost 7s 6d, so Skuse paid out about £15, the equivalent of several weeks' wages for a labourer. Here is one of his expensively obtained recipes:

Vanilla Caramels, No 1
Put in your boiling pan 6lbs of best sugar and two quarts of sweet cream, mix it well by stirring with the spatula, then add 4lbs of glucose, put it on

the fire and stir constantly…let it boil quarter-of-an-hour, add 1 1/2lbs fresh butter, then commence to try the sugar…(the thermometer cannot be used in making these goods, on account of the stirring); as soon as the sugar will crack…take the pan off the fire, add two tablespoonsful of the extract of Vanilla, stirring very briskly; then pour…

Not everyone was so fussy about their ingredients. The trade author Robert Wells said the ingredients for Philadelphia caramels were sugar, cream, glucose, butter, cream of tartar, cocoa paste, and a small amount of white wax of paraffin.[20] Nor did it take long for production of caramels to industrialize, at least in the USA. This is clear from Charles Apell's book, in which he instructed the would-be industrial confectioner on the equipment required:

In the making of caramels on a wholesale scale you must have stirring kettles and cook by steam, and when making caramels of skimmed milk or whole milk you have got to have a mixing tank to mix your sugar, glucose and milk…Then you must have a rotary pump to pump your mixture up to your tank in your cooking room; then have a pipe system from your tank above each cooking kettle and also a suction pipe and fan to take away the steam from all your cooking kettles; and as a slab for cooling is too slow you must have iron frame trucks that hold 8 or 10 pans with end bars to hold the candy in the pans. Then have two cold fan air blowers to cool them.[21]

Confectionery had moved into an era in which machines and purpose-manufactured ingredients played an increasing part. As far as fats were concerned, Apell recorded that he had 'tried everything from cottonseed oil to cremole and parasub,' but recommended C.B. butter and Nucoa butter, 'as you will find by experience that they don't leave a taste in the mouth when you have eaten a caramel.'[22] It is not clear if the two 'butters' recommended had any association with cows. What Apell's recipes do show is caramels produced on a massive scale in various flavours, wrapped or unwrapped, covered with icing, pulled or unpulled, in many grades.

'Oh do you know the Toffee King that lives in Halifax?' ran a rhyme at the start of this century. It was, apparently, the Americans who dubbed John Mackintosh Toffee King when his company began exporting sweets in about 1904. He had established one of the best-

THE LATEST TOFFEE TESTING MACHINE TESTING THE SMILE VALUE OF TOFFEE DE LUXE

Figure 57. An advertisement for Mackintosh toffees, drawn by W. Heath Robinson. In the 1920s and 1930s, the firm would take the front pages of newspapers such as the *Daily Mail* to proclaim their wares.

known British toffee companies at the end of Queen Victoria's reign. His aim was to make good confectionery to be sold in conditions of great cleanliness, begging the question of what the average confectioner's shop was like at the time. He combined elements from recipes for soft American caramels with ones for harder English toffee.

The toffee-boilers of Everton had always recognized the potential of a good recipe: many companies had established niches as household names. They remain today, though often absorbed into larger firms as brands: Callard and Bowser's Butterscotch, Keiller's 'Kinema' toffee, Tucker's Devonshire Cream Toffees, Sharp's 'Kreemy' toffee, Bluebird, Batgers, Anglo-French...the list is long. Toffee-boilers varied from those who made a tray or two for their own shop up to the toffee kings: Mackintosh of Halifax, or Sharp's of Maidstone, who were recognized as the largest sellers of toffee in the world in 1921. Toffees and caramels had great advantages at this early stage of sweet industrialization. It was still possible to begin a business on a small scale with toffee, whereas chocolate manufacture was firmly in the hands of large companies.

Most companies concentrated on individually wrapped toffees as opposed to bulk tray-toffee sold by weight. They were popular, kept well, and sold at a lower price than chocolate while maintaining a luxurious image. This was done partly by advertising and packaging. Robert Opie examined the role of packaging, especially tins, in marketing confectionery, and commented of toffees:

> splendid and glamorous tins abounded with bright colours and decorative patterns. The use of a tin also enhanced the status of the toffees, making them a more acceptable gift in comparison with the prestigious box of chocolates.[23]

Manufacturers also kept toffee firmly associated with the luxury ingredients of cream or butter in the public mind by promoting an image of toffee as a 'creamy' product, even when little cream was actually involved in its making.

Toffee-eating and schoolboys seemed indivisible. The novelist Compton Mackenzie recalled the sweet-eating habits of his youth:

> When I consider the risk of discovery involved in chewing gently upon a caramel during the exposition of a knotty passage of Thucydides I marvel at our audacity. To start with, the laborious process of divesting the caramel of its waxed paper covering was a challenge to fortune. Then if that was accomplished and the caramel was safely inside one's mouth, the next ten minutes were fraught with peril, because if suddenly called on to answer a question it might easily happen that the jaws at that moment were locked by caramel.[24]

Both methods of education and tastes have changed. Few now translate from the Classics and sneaking a sweet in class is low on the scale of schoolboy misdemeanours.

As the generation who had grown up with toffees as a novelty aged, the sweet had to evolve once more. Several 'chocolate' bars involving layers of chewy toffee or caramel were introduced in both North America and Britain. The archetype is probably the Mars bar, introduced in 1932. Several other bars, and Rolos (bits of chocolate-coated toffee, sold from 1937), followed. Most branded chocolate selections include at least one with a toffee or caramel filling.

RECIPES

MARY HAILSTONE'S TREACLE TOFFEE

500g soft dark brown sugar • 2 tablespoons of black treacle
100ml water • 250g salted butter cut into cubes
lemon essence (optional).
*Equipment: a tin approximately 22cm square lined with silicone-coated,
or buttered greaseproof paper; a fairly large pan to boil the sugar.*

Mix the sugar, treacle and water together in the pan, and stir over a low or medium flame to dissolve. When all crystals have disappeared, add the butter and increase the heat. Boil, stirring constantly but gently, until a sample, dropped in cold water, is crisp and does not stick to the teeth. The mixture will foam at the beginning of boiling, which is the reason for recommending you use a large pan. Begin the testing after about 15 minutes. As soon as it reaches hard crack remove the pan from the flame and pour the toffee into the tin. When cold, break up with a hammer and store in an airtight box.

Toffee varies according to types of sugar and treacle used. Soft dark brown sugar and black treacle—probably what were used in the early nineteenth century—give a dark colour and strong flavour.

BOBBY FREEMAN'S *CYFLAITH*, OR WELSH TOFFEE

500g black treacle • 500g brown sugar • 125g butter
one teaspoonful vinegar
*Equipment: a marble slab or metal tray, metal scraper and kitchen
scissors, all buttered, plus a little extra butter for your hands.*

Put all the ingredients in a large saucepan (enamel or copper). Start the mixture over a very low flame, stirring to make sure all the sugar melts. Increase the heat and boil fairly briskly. Begin testing after 10 minutes, by dropping a teaspoonful of the boiling mixture into cold water. When it hardens at once, leaving the water perfectly clear, it has boiled to the required degree. Pour the boiling toffee onto the slab or tray.

Butter both hands and pull the toffee into long golden strands while hot. Be cautious, as the mixture seems to hold its heat for longer than ordinary sugar syrup. Cut into smaller pieces before the toffee hardens. Store in an airtight box; *cyflaith* rapidly becomes sticky.

Always handle hot sugar with caution. If it becomes too stiff to work easily, heat it at the open door of a warm oven about (160°C, Gas 3).

ELIZA ACTON'S EVERTON TOFFEE NUMBER 1

90g butter • 500g light brown sugar
grated lemon zest or powdered ginger (optional)
Equipment: a tin 20cm square, buttered.

Melt the butter and add the sugar. Stir over a low flame until the sugar has melted. Cook, stirring gently all the time, over a low to medium heat for 10–15 minutes. Test by dropping a little of the mixture into a basin of cold water. When it sets hard and snaps, pour it immediately into the tin and allow to cool before breaking into pieces with a hammer and storing in an airtight box.

If a flavoured toffee is desired: add about 1/2 teaspoon of powdered ginger, slaked in a little cold water, when the sugar and butter have melted. For a lemon version, finely grate the zest of a lemon and add it after the mixture has boiled for about 5 minutes.

BORELLA'S COFFEE BONBONS

500g granulated sugar • 500ml freshly brewed coffee
500ml double cream.
Equipment: a tray 20cm square lined with silicone-coated paper.

In a large pan, stir the sugar and coffee together over a low flame, until all the sugar is dissolved. Increase the flame and boil to feather (116–117°C). Add the cream and continue to boil, stirring constantly but gently in one direction, until the sugar reaches hard crack (149°C). Pour into the tray (don't scrape the pan, as this spoils the appearance of the sweets). Mark into small squares when almost set; then break into pieces when cold. Store in an airtight tin.

Beware of the mixture graining once it reaches soft crack. The results, if it does, resemble aerated fudge: pleasant but untidy, and probably not what was intended. The coffee aroma suffers during the prolonged boiling. If you are not concerned with historical accuracy, and want to cut down on time, use 2 teaspoonfuls of instant coffee dissolved in 300ml water instead of fresh coffee.

CATHERINE OWEN'S CHOCOLATE CARAMELS

125g dark chocolate • 60g butter • 250g sugar
250g golden syrup (use molasses if you like the distinctive flavour, or a mixture of the two) • 300ml full cream milk.
Equipment: a 20cm square tin lined with silicone-coated paper.

Mix everything together in a large pan and melt over gentle heat. Bring to the boil, and cook, stirring constantly and gently in one direction. The mixture will foam at first, but subsides as it thickens. After 10–15 minutes begin testing by dropping small amounts in iced water. When it becomes brittle on cooling, remove from the heat and pour into the prepared tin. When almost cool, butter the blade of a heavy knife and mark into squares. Allow to cool completely, then break along the marks. Store in an airtight container.

E. SKUSE'S VANILLA CARAMELS

500g granulated sugar • 200ml double cream • 330g glucose syrup
125g butter • about 1/2 teaspoonful vanilla essence
Equipment: a 20cm square tin lined with silicone-coated paper.

Over a gentle heat, mix the sugar and cream together in a large pan. Add the glucose, increase the heat and allow to boil, stirring gently in one direction. After about 10 minutes, add the butter. Keep stirring, and begin testing the mixture by dropping bits in cold water. As soon as it reaches hard crack, remove from the heat and add the vanilla. Stir briefly and pour into the tray. When almost cold, mark into squares using a heavy knife (oil the blade lightly to prevent it sticking).

For a softer, chewier caramel, boil to hard ball, 121°C.

CHAPTER XIII

For the look of the thing

THE ALLURE of the sweet shop depends on more than taste and anticipation. Sugar confectionery, well made, is beautiful: it sparkles, gleams, glows and shines. Enjoyment is made visible. Colour and light deliver variety. Shapes and names display ingenuity. Quality and 'good taste' derive from cute association with places and people. Motifs, mottoes and advertising slogans add novelty. Large windows and glass jars show off tints from the subtlest pastel to deep, florid hues. As there were technical developments in colouring agents, printing and glass making, so the forms of display altered and responded.

As a vehicle for added colour, no edible substance compares with sugar. Refined sucrose is transparent in syrup, and pure white as a solid. For over 400 years confectioners have made sweets as varied and attractive as possible by colouring them. The edible palette was at first muted. Colours which were safe came from plants—roses, violets, saffron, spinach, sandalwood and turnsole. It was recognized that some colours could be harmful; in 1617 John Murrell said that sap-green, rosa-paris, 'blew bise' and yellow smalt were 'fit to garnish but perillous to eate.'[1] The frequent appearance of formulae for colours in manuals shows craftsmen expecting to make at least some of their own and engaging in an ever-widening search to produce sweets which were brighter and more vivid than the next man's.

The colour red must have been vital. The combination of red or pink and white, often in stripes, remains one of the most eye-catching features of traditional boiled sweets. Apart from simple eye-appeal, red colouring agents were easily available. Turnsole, sandalwood and brasil wood made various shades for early confectioners; another option was roset[2] (sugar with beaten rose petals), providing both colour and

Figure 58. The brasilwood tree, from Pomet's *Complete History of Drugs* (1747).

perfume. Cochineal,[3] brought to Europe from Central America in the late sixteenth century was a significant introduction. Mixed with other substances, usually alum and tartaric acid, it formed the basis of a brilliant red-pink known as carmine, still a favourite in confectionery today. Carmine coloured anything from pink sugar paste to counterfeit cherries made from apple pulp and the syrup drained from preserved cherries.

Yellow was a decoction of saffron, which gives a beautifully bright tint but was expensive. Other flowers could be used instead; Giles Rose translated instructions for using the stamens of lilies; and marigold, primrose or cowslip petals were sometimes incorporated to give both colour and perfume. The favourite yellow of Georgian confectioners was gamboge. This is made from a gum derived from trees of the *Garcinia* species, native to south-east Asia (*gamboge* is a corruption of Cambodia). Apart from being a vivid colour, it is also a violent emetic.

For green, extracts of beet or spinach leaves were generally recommended. Green, acid fruits that were being cooked for preserving had their colour enhanced by the use of untinned copper vessels. The acid combined with copper from the pan, making them a pretty viridian, whilst adding a potentially toxic copper content. Verdigris (made deliberately, or scraped from copper which had become green in the air) was added to confections as a colouring; and green could also be made by mixing yellow and blue.

Apart from the natural blue-purple implied by the use of violets, this tint is little mentioned before 1700. There was a dubious practice of cooking quinces in pewter plates which was alleged to make them purple, but it probably made them poisonous as well, because pewter is a lead alloy. Once blue does enter the confectioner's colour-box, it is often in the form of smalt's blue. Smalt (sometimes called blue starch because of the tinge it gave to starch for linen, enhancing whiteness), was produced by colouring glass with cobalt, then pulverizing it. Indigo, plant-based, was also used, as was Prussian blue (called stone blue). Discovered in Berlin in the early eighteenth century, this is a compound which includes cyanide.

Gold and silver leaf were also used with sweetmeats, for decoration and because they were thought medicinal. However, this was by no means the case with many colouring agents. By the early nineteenth century, confectioners and food manufacturers were using ingredients of dubious benefit to health with such abandon that queries were raised about their safety. The pioneer food scientist and campaigner against food adulteration, Frederick Accum, commented in 1820:

> In the preparation of sugar plums, comfits and other kinds of confectionery, especially those sweetmeats of inferior quality frequently exposed to sale in the open streets for the allurement of children, the grossest abuses are committed.[4]

White comfits, he said, were made whiter by the addition of pipe-clay; red sugar drops were coloured with pigment which included red lead, and other sweets (including preserved fruits imported from abroad) owed their colour to copper compounds.

Confectioners themselves were complacent, sometimes warning against the use of harmful colours but still discussing and using them. James Wallace prefaced his remarks with a disclaimer:

> In giving the various sorts of colouring used in Confectionary, we do not recommend anything pernicious, although it may be in some of the recipes, we merely give them to show that such things are used, at the same time beg

197

THE GREAT LOZENGE-MAKER.
A Hint to Paterfamilias.

Figure 59. Cartoon from *Punch*, 1858, ridiculing the constituents of Victorian confectionery.

to say, that the quantity of any deleterious article used in colouring being so diminutive, that not the slightest injury can follow.

He listed some pigments:

Rose pink, vermilion, woad, Spanish red, madder &c., are used in colouring...also Indian lake, arnatto, saffron, archel, auripigmentum, and yellow masticot.[5]

A series of scandals during the 1850s, including a case of lozenges that proved fatal to several people, led to a review of colours and ingredients generally. The long-term effect was modern food-safety legislation; in the shorter term, it provoked a trend towards advertising confectionery as 'pure' or 'wholesome'.

After about 1860, apparent variety was produced to simple boiled sugar syrup by adding new synthetic flavours and colours. The latter were chemically synthesized pigments of an intensity and reliability which earlier confectioners would have thought impossible. These were coal-tar dyes. Now considered suspect themselves, they were none the less a substantial improvement on colours that had hitherto been accepted.

In fact, brilliant colour in boiled sugar never quite recovered from the adulteration and poisoning scandals of the last century. Those astonishing shades were too intense to be true and they persisted in retaining a slightly down-market image. Perversely, fashion decreed that when bright dyes became cheap, the wealthy revised their opinion in favour of quieter shades at the very moment when confectioners could stop worrying about poisoning customers. Taste has changed. A display of fine chocolates, varied in shape but all brown except for decorative morsels of nuts or candied fruit, is today more desirable than the gemstones of glimmering sweeties.

******

Names are important in retailing. Brands and trademarks convey meaning: a guarantee of consistency, subliminal messages about style and status, continuity and identity. Exclusive properties now shelter behind ramparts of protective legislation, separating the products of one company from those of their competitors.

Brands did not exist before the last century, but concepts of excellence were already attached to places or individuals. Originally, some sweets (as with other foods and consumer goods) were distinguished by the idea that certain places were the source of better versions, because they grew the appropriate raw materials, the inhabitants had particular skills in processing, or had access to trade secrets. The use of a geographical name was in some measure a guarantee of the product being original and genuine, as in 'paste of Genoa' (quince paste) or 'Venice treacle'. Different countries were seen as producing superior quality or having more style at certain periods: so things would be done in the Spanish, or Naples, or French manner. Only secrecy ensured a monopoly over a product. Tangled stories of acrimony, such as those associated with the toffee-makers of Everton, shows what happened when an item became successful.

The craftsman anxious to enlarge his trade could also take advantage of the aspirations of his customers. Perhaps, at first, the mere possession of sweetmeats based on expensive imported spices or fruit was glamorous enough. No hints of chic were needed beyond an exotic foreign name such as marmalade—as much a status symbol to sixteenth-century cognoscenti as, say, balsamic vinegar from Modena in a modern delicatessen. Alternatively, the product could be boosted by claiming aristocratic origin. Written recipes, especially in the seventeenth century, were attributed to noble households whose wealthy, well-travelled inhabitants, exposed to many luxuries, were arbiters of taste. Confectioners themselves asserted such links: Mary Eales with Queen Anne, Borella with the Spanish Ambassador. Jarrin mentioned how, in Paris, he had made a figure of Napoleon 'led by Victory' for a dinner for the Emperor returning triumphant from Germany. Claims of association with reputable businesses were also useful. Several London tradesmen at the start of the nineteenth century publicized their associations with Gunter & Negri, the leading confectioners.

There was a discernible trend at about the same time towards employing national heroes and significant places or events as props for marketing. Gibraltar Rock, Wellington's Pillars, Nelson's Buttons and Buonaparts Ribs were popular sweet types made for twenty or thirty years after the wars which inspired them. 'North Pole' sweets (two entirely distinct versions of these existed) also enjoyed a vogue, provoked perhaps by polar exploration. William Finemore included 'Chrystallised Chrystall Palace Gems' in his notebook, most likely in 1851. Curious, whimsical names with no particular meaning seem characteristic of the trade. Both bull's eyes and humbugs were first noted at approximately this juncture.

The same tendencies are on show in modern British confectionery. Pontefract Cakes, Kendal Mint Cake, Hawick Balls (though recently [1997] deceased), Moffat Toffee[6] and Edinburgh Rock are current instances of naming by place. Jeddart Snails[7] and Berwick Cockles combine geography and whimsicality, but the Black Bullet, a spherical, high-boiled mint sweet made in north-east England, almost certainly has a prosaic derivation as a diminutive of the French *boule*. Foreign associations leant towards North America early this century, for example to glamorize caramels and chewing gum. Toffees used film stars as role models, or emphasized links with enviable activities such as travelling by ocean liner. But Bournville was so named when Cadbury's bought the site, because the best chocolate was thought to come from France. Associations with royalty and the aristocracy have continued: Farrah's Harrogate Toffee announced that it was 'patronised by H.M. Queen Mary', Duchy Originals launch a range trading off the repute of their royal proprietor, and royal warrants remain on much packaging. Today, however, companies are as likely to take merchandizing opportunities from cartoons, television, music and sport, while the whimsical end of the market, from nineteenth-century Fairy Kisses to Dolly Mixtures in the 1950s and the wobbly jelly tarantulas now available, seems boundless.

******

Confectioners, having laboriously clarified sugar, boiled and coloured it, and worked it into different textures and shapes, found themselves up against problems of storage and distribution. The first could be partly avoided by fast turnover. Smart confectioners commanded a good passing-trade, and made sweets to order for balls or parties. Likewise, journeymen confectioners and sweet-stuff makers probably relied on selling their output within a few days. Some sweets store well, for instance comfits and sugar paste—and candied sugar also has a long shelf life in a dry place—but high-boiled sugar and toffee soften and must be sold quickly. Fruit preserves were notoriously difficult to keep, as Giles Rose made clear in 1682:

> I would advice you to put your dried Preserves in Boxes of Wood, but always between two Papers; when you have taken them out of your Stove, and be sure to keep them in a dry place, and keep their papers changing from time to time, till the syrup hath done running, and the paper continues to dry.[8]

Liquid preserves were even trickier. Edward Lambert instructed in about 1744:

> Look over these Fruits so kept in Syrup; and if you perceive any Froth on them you must give them a Boil; and if by Chance they should became very frothy and sower, you must first boil the Syrup and then altogether.[9]

Instructions to watch against preserves fermenting or mouldering are given in many confectionery books, suggesting they were frequent and accepted hazards.

Containers are essential; they help maintain low humidity, hold sweets together, and protect them during transport. Before the nineteenth century, options were limited. Fruit in syrup was mostly stored in earthenware gallipots, and small sugar confections and pastes in oblong or round boxes made of thin sheets of matchwood (similar to those sometimes still used for imported candied fruits). Early examples appear utilitarian, although their use as subjects in still-life paintings suggests they symbolized hidden luxury and pleasure.

'Jar glasses' (small, cylindrical glass containers) were in use by the seventeenth century but are rarely mentioned.[10] They were expensive, limited to wealthy households or enterprises. Glass jars probably did

202

not become common until the late eighteenth century when, though used as storage containers, their emphasis had switched to a means of display. Examples are seen in contemporary prints. They include straight jars presumably for conserves or jams, small, stemmed glasses for jellies and larger ones with lids for sweets and comfits. Tall straight-sided jars and little bottles are also shown. Glass was used more and more to show off the bright colours and clarity of newly fashionable, transparent acid and fruit drops to brilliant advantage in the 1830s and '40s. As the century wore on, increasing window space with the use of plate glass allowed ever more visible display.

Despite difficulties of storage and packing, finished goods were sent long distances to clients on account, or agents or other confectioners who resold them.[11] This trade must have been mostly used for small, light items, especially those with supposed medicinal properties such as lozenges, whose makers advertised in early newspapers. John Piercy made 'Lozanges or Pectoralls' in London in 1662 with agents in many provincial towns including Exeter, Norwich and Bristol.[12] In the late eighteenth century, when transport was still not easy, sweets were sent from London to Leeds for sale. For really grand occasions, the best means of ensuring quality was to transport the confectioner to the party, as the Marquess of Buckingham did James Gunter to Stowe in 1805.[13] Eventually, railways made matters easier.

Another important innovation, from the 1850s onwards, was the airtight tin—especially for toffee. Functional yet decorative, these became coveted in their own right. Commemorative versions were produced for national events, or the patterns designed so that a set of tins with themed pictures was available.

Transparent wrapping is a product of our own age. Cellophane was introduced in the 1920s and plastics followed later. These allow sweets of all kinds to look after themselves on the supermarket shelf in the ubiquitous, utilitarian multi-pack.

Confectioners in the nineteenth century wrote of another method of keeping some sweets in good condition: submerging them in syrup

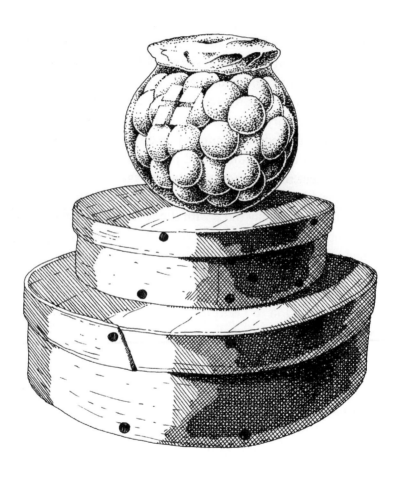

Figure 60. A drawing of sweetmeat boxes and a gallipot, taken from the painting 'Still Life with Sweets and Pottery' by Juan van der Hamen y Léon (1596–1631), in the National Gallery of Art, Washington DC. The boxes most likely contained quince paste or other fruit 'cheese'; the jar, a preserve of fruit such as cherries in syrup.

and allowing a layer of sugar crystals to grow on their surface. The technique was fully exploited by the 1820s, when sugar was still clarified by craftsmen in their own workshops. It needed a high-quality syrup, not one from scrap sugar that had been boiled and re-boiled. The extra labour and expense had to be justified but, as Skuse said of crystallized creams and gums, it is a simple process, 'whose sparkling appearance adds to their beauty, and has the advantage of rendering them almost impervious to the action of the atmosphere.'[14] After the Second World War, when confectioners benefited from airtight tins and Cellophane wrappings, crystallizing had lost its practical importance and was regarded as just another way to sell more sugar.

******

Wrappers, although treated as so much waste paper, account for much of the colour perceived in confectionery by the modern observer. This is a phenomenon of the last hundred years. Before, a scrap of paper wrapped round a sugar stick or twisted into a cone (the origin of the triangular paper bag) was the most one could expect when buying sweets in the street. These wrappers were themselves waste paper. Henry Mayhew recorded how one street-seller of sweet stuff bought paper from stationers or secondhand book shops, including Acts of Parliament, 'a pile of these a foot or more deep, lay on a shelf. They are used to wrap the rock &c. sold.'[15]

Smarter confectioners used paper wrappers with cut or fringed ends twisted around sweets. A French custom of making these up as packets of bonbons for presents at New Year is mentioned by Jarrin. The London confectioner Tom Smith is said to have commercialized the idea in Britain. His bonbons consisted of several sweets wrapped together in tissue paper, with mottoes enclosed. They were first introduced as a Christmas novelty in the late 1840s.[16] Shortly afterwards, Smith added a 'bang', evolving the modern Christmas cracker. The theory is that the idea was provoked by a spark leaping out of the fire one night. However, exploding 'cracker bonbons' were apparently known some years earlier.[17]

Figure 61. A selection of glass jars offered to confectioners in the catalogue issued in 1930 by Thomas Mills & Brother, Inc. of Philadelphia.

Before the onset of national brands, advertising and the expansion of sales were for the benefit of the individual confectioner. He might use word-of-mouth recommendation, newspaper advertisements and distribution of trade cards to entice new customers to his shop. Although national marketing of medical confections was of long standing, it was really the large-scale manufacture of chocolate that stimulated assertion of the desirability of one sweet product across the nation as a whole.

Although chocolate sweets had coexisted with chocolate for drinking in the eighteenth century, production was small, mostly of little drops or nuggets, and confined to sophisticated confectioners in large towns. When several entrepreneurs—Fry, Cadbury, Terry—applied their business zeal (and, in many cases, stern religious principles) to processing cocoa, it became the recognizable ancestor of modern eating chocolate, a perfect substance for mechanical production. Manufacture is slow and repetitive, the result stable at ambient temperatures without airtight packaging. By the mid-nineteenth century, chocolate bars could be distributed by the new railway network and stocked by any shop, in the knowledge that it would keep for several months.

The problem was that there was little precedent for eating chocolate. Flora Thompson remembered as a child in the 1880s surveying the contents of a gingerbread stall at a village feast:

On it were gingerbread babies with currants for eyes, brown-and-white
striped peppermint humbugs, sticks of pink-and-white rock, and a few boxes
and bottles of other sweets…One year, side by side with the gingerbread
babies, stood a box filled with thin, dark-brown slabs packed in pink paper.
'What is that brown sweet?' asked Laura, spelling out the word 'Chocolate'.
A visiting cousin …already knew it by name. 'Oh, that's chocolate,' he said
off-handedly. 'But don't buy any; it's for drinking. They have it for breakfast
in France.' A year or two later, chocolate was a favourite sweet even in a
place as remote as the hamlet.[18]

Chocolate was essentially a new product which industrialists wanted
to sell in ever-increasing quantities. It was also uniformly brown at a
time when fashion had a love affair with vivid colour. Makers of
boiled-sugar sweets could take advantage of the latest food colourings,
but the subtleties of hue and shine in chocolate told the story of processing and quality only to the knowledgeable few. The answer to
chocolate's disadvantages lay in the packet, enhanced by new processes
of cheap colour printing.

Initially, chocolate was packed as unwrapped bars in wooden boxes
with paper labels, displayed on the shop counter. Individual paper

Figure 62. A drawing based on a
label produced by the York confectioner, Terry, which shows the girl
eating her sweets out of a paper
cone or triangular bag, c. 1890.

207

wrappers developed soon afterwards. Gold printing and metal foils repeated the luxury message which gold leaf had given to sweets in earlier centuries. Designs used the latest images, and graphics publicized the desirability of chocolate. Even more status was attached to special boxes, decorated with pictures, lined with tissue and paper lace.[19] As the package, not the contents, occupied more and more of the foreground, so advertising has shifted almost entirely from the taste of confectionery towards style by association.

Figure 63. *Liliputiens*, French barley sugar sticks in handsome metal foil twisted wrappers.

CHAPTER XIV

The sugar archives

I CANNOT imagine nostalgia for the confectionery aisle of a super-market, where the best selling lines are piled as high as Sunday papers and are as nauseating *en masse*. But there is a fond affection for a traditional sweet shop. Memory has filled it with satisfyingly exuberant colour, bold stripes, and masses of little shapes. The collective nose of our memory presses against a little square window pane, watching a kindly confectioner weigh a penn'orth of sugar-plums. This bow-fronted anachronism is kept alive in the picture on the 'Quality Street' tin, where Miss Sweetly in her pink crinoline and Major Quality in his red army tunic have been flirting since 1936.[1]

These figures were a direct appeal to the past at a time when the small independent confectioner was on the point of vanishing. Perhaps Mackintosh (who began as a craft confectioner) was nostalgic for the 'good old days' when all towns had a sweet shop with a boiling-room at the back. But what were those shops like? Dazzled ourselves by colour and display, we tend to assume that sweet shops have always been a riot of colour.

Originally, a confectioner's shop was more likely a place of hidden treasures. In the reign of Queen Anne, the prosperous gentlewoman Rebecca Price owned 'a Sweetmeat Cupboard large and high with Six Shellow boxes therein.'[2] In an effort to keep the contents wholesome, many sweets were in wooden boxes, filed between layers of paper, sealed in gallipots under bladder and wax, or ranged in cupboards. Only when newly made, or the boxes opened, were colours and shapes revealed. It was up to the consumers to show them off on special stemmed glass dishes or in china bonbonnières.

Figure 64. 'Dandies sans sis-sous', by Charles Williams (worked *c.* 1797–1830). The ladies are saying, from the left, 'Much obliged to you gentlemen, adieu!' 'Bye Bye! Dandies! nice Cakes!' The dandy on the left asks his friend, 'Tim you'll pay my Lad D…n me if I have any Brass!!' 'And D…n me Bob if I have any copper! We must brus my Lad!' is the rejoinder. ['Brus' is a cant word for brush or brush off, to run away.] Meanwhile the shopgirl is offering a paper twist full of, 'Your Sugar-plums Sir that makes Nine and sixpence.' The shop sold cold meats, pies and pastry as well as sweetmeats.

The beginnings of shops as we know them were documented by Daniel Defoe. He deprecated 'modern Extravagancy in this respect, wholly unknown to our Ancestors in Trade'.[3] In a pastrycook's shop, for which £20 would effectually furnish all 'needful things for sale', fittings could cost over £300. Defoe gave the details: sash windows, painted tiles, large mirrors and carved and gilded embellishment. Lighting was important: two large branched candlesticks, 'three great glass lanthorns and eight small ones', twenty-five wall sconces and 'a large pair of silver standing candlesticks in the back room'.[4] For serving sweetmeats, six fine large silver salvers were supplied, together with 'twelve large high stands of rings…to place small dishes for tarts, jellies &c. at a feast'. Small plate and china completed the display. The things which were actually essential—two ovens and the stock of foods—cost about £45 altogether.

Such flash and glitter is still expected of a sweet shop. The use of salvers reflected eighteenth-century desserts where biscuits, marzipan and preserved fruit were piled in high pyramids on shallow china or silver dishes. As more glass jars were used, filled with transparent jellies, fruit preserves, little candies and comfits, so they were placed in the window to glint in the light streaming through those expensive glass panes. Inside, candlelight reflected in the mirrors sparkled among glass and gilding. The sweet shop was a grotto.

Windows were dressed to their utmost on Twelfth Night, January 6th, more important than Christmas Day until Prince Albert's time. Defoe mentioned that 'twelfth-day' was an 'extraordinary shew' for pastry cooks. In 1825, William Hone described confectioners' shops on Twelfth Night, with displays of decorated cakes as well as sweets:

> their upright cylinder shaped show-glasses, containing peppermint-drops, elecampane,[5] sugar-sticks, hard-bake, brandy-balls, and bulls'-eyes are carefully polished; their lolly-pops are fresh encased, and look as white as the stems of tobacco-pipes; and their candle-sticks are ornamented with fillets and bosses of writing paper.[6]

No doubt only the opulent could afford real ostentation although the stock of small shops and street-sellers was perhaps no less eye-

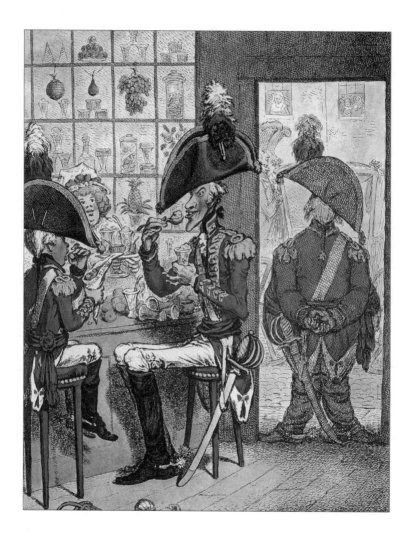

Figure 65. 'Hero's recruiting at Kelsey's; – or – Guard-Day at St James's', by James Gillray, 1797. The soldiers are eating, on the right, sherbet or ice-cream, and on the left, sugar-plums plucked out of triangular bag. The jars and ornaments in the window are very similar in style to those depicted in the Williams cartoon above, and the drawing of Twelfth Night, below.

catching, exploiting bright colour and the techniques of pulling and striping sweets. The equipment of their stalls and barrows consisted of simple, robust trays and canisters. Henry Mayhew estimated the total fixed capital (barrows, stalls, pans, weighing-scales, etc.) of the 200 or so people employed in this trade in London at £70 4s 6d, less than a third of the amount Defoe quoted for fitting out a single extravagant eighteenth-century shop.

When writing of the history of sweets, Ron Lees identified 1851 as a significant year:

> The Great Exhibition of 1851 marked a turning point in the way that sweets and chocolate were made. The trade changed from an industry based on retailers who manufactured goods on their premises to factory production with the development of networks of wholesale and national distribution and company owned chains of shops.[7]

In the late twentieth century, most retail confectioners simply sell sweets produced by other companies. The message of confectionery has become one of brash commercialism: myriad colours and shapes, visible through clear plastic, the flash of tinfoil, rustle of paper, lurid graphics on children's lines, 'classic' designs for chocolate bar wrappers, kitsch illustrations on boxes and tins. Unlike the slow organic development of older sweetmeats, it speaks of deliberate positioning in the market. Chocolate dominates: think of brand names for confectionery, Cadbury's Dairy Milk, Nestlé's Milky Bar, Lindt Excellence, Rowntree's Black Magic, Terry's All Gold, Suchard, Fry's—and countlines,[8] such as Mars bars or Kit-Kat. Toffees might be remembered, or a few individual brands of sugar confectionery, with their slogans: Murray Mint, the too-good-to-hurry-mint; Polo, the mint with the hole.

The bow-fronted shop of the Mackintosh tin bears no resemblance to the aisles of supermarkets, or even the pic'n'mix counter in Woolworths. It conveys a memory of a time when sweets were magical enough to be universally desired, yet had reached the point of being inexpensive enough to be attainable by almost everyone. The

213

Figure 66. 'Twelfth Night', by George Cruikshank, from *The Everyday Book* by William Hone, 1827. So rapt were the onlookers by the glittering display of gilded cakes and confectionery in the shop window that ragamuffins were able to pin unnoticed the clothes of two of them together.

contents of the package are a different matter. They are the products of a factory-based confectioner, shaped as much by food technology as by some amiable alchemist of the boiling-pans.

Sweets were once disposed in elaborate arrangements for desserts and special occasions, to be witnessed and eaten by the fortunate few. Now the display is at point-of-sale, proffered to the multitude. Over-exposure leads to trivialization, and the story of sugar confectionery in Britain is no exception. Yet there remains nostalgic regard for sweetness. The contents of sweetie-jars remain available symbols of affection, status and well-being. In the present-day sweet shop, confections pile on shelves like books full of once-treasured stories: bowdlerized and rewritten until the meanings have almost vanished. Half-remembering the value bestowed, we love sweets for what they once symbolized. But now it is children who listen, moving rapidly from one colourful sticky item to the next, until all the contents of the sugar archives have been tasted and enjoyed.

Figure 67. An advertisement for Quality Street, from Mackintosh. This was the front page of the *Daily Mail* on Saturday, May 2, 1936.

APPENDIX

Practical notes

Ingredients

Sugar: most of the recipes in this book call for white granulated sugar or icing sugar. Both consist of almost 100 per cent pure sucrose, and are processed from either cane or beet. Sugar cubes, colloquially known as 'lump' sugar, are not the same thing as lumps of sugar broken from a loaf. They are made from granulated sugar, coated with just enough water to make the crystals stick together, pressed into a mould. Granulated sugar is quite adequate for all recipes here.

Many brown sugars are produced from fully refined white sugar mixed with a small proportion of cane molasses. Those processed from beet are always made this way. Those from cane may be produced by this method, or can be made by halting the refining process at an earlier stage. The latter are often labelled as 'unrefined'. They have undergone an initial process of clarification, but not all the molasses has been extracted. They are imported directly from their country of origin, which will be stated on the label.

Molasses and treacle: molasses and black treacle are substances which are similar in composition and flavour. Only those produced from cane sugar are sold.

Glucose syrup is available from pharmacists and specialist kitchenware shops.

Cream of tartar and tartaric acid: ream of tartar is widely sold as an ingredient for baking; tartaric acid, from pharmacists, is essential for acid drops.

Gum arabic and gum tragacanth: these are imported from North Africa to Britain as irregular lumps which vary slightly in colour. Large pieces dissolve faster if crushed: use a mortar and pestle for this. Gums have generally been picked over before retailing, but sometimes have scraps of bark or grass attached. These bits of savannah are undesirable in confectionery. If in doubt, strain the gum solution through cloth before using. Pharmacies and specialist kitchen shops sometimes stock powdered gums, which need no cleaning and dissolve easily. They are also twice the price.

Sugar paste: this can be bought ready-prepared from specialist kitchen shops. Ask for 'petal paste' or 'flower paste' for modelling; it is formulated to dry quickly with a brittle, porcelain-like finish. Paste intended for cake covering is too soft.

Almond oil: this can be bought from pharmacies.

Rose water and other flavourings: rosewater and orange-flower water can be bought from specialist delicatessens, shops supplying Middle-Eastern communities, and chemists. Look for those which are distilled in preference to ones made up with essences. Geranium-flavoured water can also be bought from shops supplying North African communities. Grocers and super-markets stock ranges of flavouring essences including peppermint and vanilla. Look for true vanilla extract.

Liquorice root powder can be bought from G. Baldwin and Co., 173 Walworth Road, London SE17 1RW. They also supply almond oil, rose and orange-flower water.

Colours: the liquid colours sold by grocers and supermarkets are generally adequate for boiled sugar. If a deep tint is required in sugar paste, use specially prepared colours in powder or concentrated liquid form. They can be bought at specialist kitchen and cake-icing shops.

Gold and silver leaf: gold leaf can be bought in books of 20–30 sheets from companies supplying bookbinders and sign-writers. It is expensive but a little goes a long way. One stockist is Cornelissen & Son Ltd, Fine Artists' Materials, 105 Great Russell Street, London WC1B 3LA. Specialist kitchen shops sometimes stock single leaves. This is an expensive way of buying leaf, but a reasonable alternative if you just want to experiment with a little. Other compounds with gold or silver finishes are available from shops specialising in cake decorating materials; enquire about their edibility before using them. Silver leaf is available from Pakistani and Indian specialist shops under the name *vark*.

Equipment

Pans: most households have a saucepan suitable for boiling small amounts of sugar. Copper was preferred by professional confectioners in the past, but almost any metal will do. Pans with non-stick linings are not suitable. It is important that you can lift the pan easily and quickly for pouring boiled sugar. Cleaning pans after working with sugar is simple: fill them with hot water and leave to soak for a couple of hours, by which time most of the mixture will have dissolved into the water.

Marble slab: this is not essential. A sturdy baking tray (not one with a non-stick coating) is adequate for small amounts of boiled sugar. If you feel that interest will extend beyond the odd batch of toffee (or you make a lot of pastry as well), it may be worth investing in a slab from a specialist kitchen shop.

Moulds, cutters, scrapers, palette knives: specialist kitchenware shops, and chef's suppliers carry the best ranges, but simple cutters and moulds are widely available from supermarkets and household shops.

Sugar boiling thermometers: always use a specially designed thermometer for sugar. This has a scale running up to 200°C/ 400°F, plus some indication of the stages of boiling. A basic one costs a few pounds. They are not scientific instruments, and the readings may not be precise to more than a degree or two. Some impression of the accuracy of the thermometer can be gained by putting it in a pan of boiling water and observing how much the reading varies above or below 100°C. Modern thermometers are reasonably robust, but always handle them carefully.

Spoons: a flat-ended wooden spatula is best for stirring toffee and fudge. A metal skimmer with holes is necessary if you want to experiment with testing for candy height or soufle in the old-fashioned manner.

Paper: silicone-coated baking paper is useful for lining tins when pouring out toffee, fudge or fruit paste; I also use it for candy mixtures. It is available from supermarkets and household supply shops. Oiled greaseproof paper is a reasonable substitute.

Sugar boiling

Preparation: have all ingredients and equipment ready before boiling. Be cautious with cream of tartar (too much makes the confection sticky) and glucose (too much leaves a slight aftertaste).

A bowl of cold water is essential for testing the sugar. It is useful to have a jug filled with water hot from a freshly boiled kettle close to hand: keep the sugar thermometer, a couple of spoons and a pastry brush in this, before and after use.

Ensure that all sugar crystals are fully dissolved *before* you start boiling a mixture. If undissolved sugar crystals remain in the syrup, they can induce graining. Stir until they vanish, then take a wet pastry brush and wash down the sides of the pan. Only then should the sugar thermometer be put into the syrup.

Use the scale on the thermometer to estimate when to make a cold-water test. If is not quite right, boil a minute or two longer and try again. It is the texture of the syrup, not the temperature as read by thermometer which is really important. If the temperature has gone a little past the desired stage, remove the pan from the heat, dilute the syrup with a little warm water, and re-boil to the correct stage from a lower temperature.

When boiling toffee and other mixtures for which a thermometer can't be used, watch them carefully and test frequently.

The tests are:

Thread: dip a spoon into the mixture. Take a little off it between your finger and thumb and move them apart slightly to see if you can make a short thread between them.

Soft ball: drop a little syrup into a bowl of cold water. It will form a soft ball under water, but deform when taken out.

Hard ball: drop a little syrup into cold water. It will form a hard lump which keeps its shape in the air.

Crack: drop a little syrup into cold water. It will form a clear, pliable sheet.

Hard crack: drop a little syrup into cold water. It will form a hard, glass-like solid which can be snapped cleanly in two.

Pulling sugar

Always be cautious. Pour the batch onto an oiled slab or tray, and allow it to form a skin. Turn it sides to middle a couple of times with an oiled scraper or palette knife, to help it cool evenly, until you can just touch it. Remove *all* rings from your fingers and oil or butter your hands; leave about a teaspoon of oil or butter to one side so that

221

you can pick up a little more if necessary. Begin to work the sugar cautiously, using your finger tips to start with. If it feels too hot, wait a minute or two longer. Try to keep the sugar under control and work it evenly. Beware of the ends forming into hard blobs which won't incorporate into the mass. It is helpful to have an assistant, especially when cutting and shaping sugar, because it goes from being relatively soft and malleable to stiff and intractable quite quickly. Some confectioners wear special gloves for handling hot sugar. These can be bought from Continental Chef Supplies (see below).

Safety

Never leave a pan of boiling sugar unattended. Do not allow children to handle hot sugar unsupervised. Molten sugar is very hot and can inflict unpleasant burns.

Equipment

Continental Chef Supplies, Unit 4C, South Hetton Industrial Estate, Co. Durham DH6 2UZ produces a catalogue with a section on sugar-working equipment, including cutters, moulds, stencils, and gloves for working with hot sugar.

Notes and references

Notes to the Introduction

1. I am indebted to Andrew Millward for access to this, and background information concerning the family.

Notes to Chapter I

1. Cadbury Brothers (1949), p. 11.
2. I have found no real indication of when tobacco, newspapers and sweets began to be sold from the same shops, although in *Sketches By Boz*, from the 1830s, Charles Dickens mentions a tobacconist who also dealt in walking sticks and Sunday newspapers.
3. F. M. McNeill (1971), p. 239.
4. Mayhew (1851), p. 216.
5. Dickens (1969).
6. In the Castle Museum, York; Terry's were founded in 1767.
7. Would Queen Mixtures and Fairy Rock have survived the Gay Liberation movement?
8. Shops which sell tobacco and newspapers in continental European countries often don't sell confectionery, which sometimes leads the British to conclude that other European nations don't have sweets.

Notes to Chapter II

1. According to *OED*, 'sweetie' or 'sweety' is first recorded in the early eighteenth century, and could mean things such as biscuits as well. Although now seen as childish in southern English, it has survived as the everyday word for sweets in Scotland.
2. 'Banquet', in the modern sense of a large ceremonial meal, has been used in English since the fifteenth century. For a detailed discussion of the sweetmeats and customs associated with banquets, see C. Anne Wilson (1991).
3. These seem to have appeared in Europe quite early in the history of sugar confectionery. The few detailed descriptions which survive show them to have been very elaborate.
4. '*How to get on in Society*', John Betjeman (1978).
5. Mayhew (1864), p. 217.
6. Links also remain in the subconscious of English-speakers who refer to various drugs, legal or otherwise, in similar terms, such as 'sweets' as slang for amphetamines; presumably, a combination of appearance, use, and effect is implied by such usage.
7. John Ayto (1993). Joseph Wright in *The English Dialect Dictionary* records several examples of the use of 'spice' from Yorkshire and the surrounding counties, with a distinct

concentration on spice meaning sugar sweets in south-west Yorkshire. Iona and Peter Opie (1959) also commented that sweets were always called spice in the West Riding.

8. Iona and Peter Opie (1959).

9. Anne Roenblat and Alexandre Révérend (1991).

10. Allison James (1979).

11. Joseph Wright in *The English Dialect Dictionary*, and the Opies (1959) both noted isolated uses of the word candy for sweets.

Notes to Chapter III

1. Glucose is also sometimes called dextrose or grape sugar; alternative names for fructose are laevulose, or fruit sugar.

2. Dates given by the *OED* range from the late thirteenth century to the mid-fifteenth for these.

3. Cited in the *OED*.

4. According to prices quoted by C. Anne Wilson (1991).

5. Noel Deerr (1949), vol. 1. p. 93.

6. Interpretation after Deerr.

7. It is mentioned in account rolls dating from the early fourteenth century, quoted in the *OED*.

8. Modern sugars available from importers of oriental foods include lumps of coarse, clear, yellowish sugar, sometimes colloquially called 'rock sugar' and used in Chinese cookery, and *masri*, (from *Masr*, the Arabic name for Egypt), a sugar in large, roughly oblong or octagonal crystals.

9. William Gunter (1830), pp. 227–8. The East India Company experimented with importing sugar in the early nineteenth century, only to discover that it paid a higher rate of duty than that from West Indian sources. Rates of duty were equalized in 1825.

10. William Finemore is thought to have been a master confectioner in Devonport, before moving to London to work as a journeyman. He kept a manuscript notebook on confectionery between the years 1839–56.

11. Finemore MS.

12. Both white and brown sugars are produced from either cane or beet: see appendix for details. The non-sucrose content of brown sugars—mostly water and uncrystallizable non-sucrose, plus tiny quantities of minerals—is about 8 per cent of the total.

13. Figures from Deerr (1949), p. 532.

14. Figures from The Biscuit, Cocoa, Chocolate and Confectionery Alliance.

15. Tobias Venner (1620), p. 104.

16. Venner, ibid. The nearest available equivalents to 'red' sugar now are probably jaggery or gur, both names for partially refined sugar from India, made into small dark red-brown loaves which are sandy when pulverized.

17. Sir Kenelm Digby (1669), p. 217 in the Prospect Books edition (1997).

18. Loose sugar and cheaper pot sugar were recorded in the accounts of the household of Robert Waterton, Lord of the Manor of Methley (near Leeds), *c.*. 1416, discussed in *Sciant*

Presents, the newsletter of the Yorkshire Archaeological Society, autumn 1983. Pot sugar was also cited in the York manuscript. In the mid-eighteenth century, potting described the transfer of crude sugar to containers for the molasses to drain off.

19. Knut Boeser (1994). Nostradamus originally published in France in 1557.

20. Randle Cotgrave (1611); Deerr (1949), p. 95, says that material from disintegrated loaves, scrapings off loaves, and general waste 'was used to fill up the space between the loaves, which were packed in chests. From this process comes the term *cassonade,* or "chest sugar," for an inferior white, which became standardized with special reference to a product of the French West Indies', but Mintz (1985), p. 83, stated that, 'Less refined brown sugar, partially cleaned and crystallized, was imported in chests—the "casson sugar", later called "Cassonade", one finds in the inventory lists of grocers in the mid-fifteenth century.'

21. Pierre Pomet, 'chief druggist to the late French King Lewis XIV' (1747), p. 57. Louis XIV died in 1715; Pomet was published in French in the seventeenth century.

22. Deerr (1949), p. 464.

23. Geoffrey Fairrie (1925), p. 165.

24. Pomet (1747), p. 58.

25. Edward Lambert, (*c.* 1744), p. 2.

26. Guglielmo Jarrin (1820), p. 1.

27. Finemore MS.

28. Gunter (1830), p. 227.

29. In grape-growing areas, must—grape juice condensed to a dark, sticky syrup by prolonged boiling—was an alternative to honey as a sweetener. Known as *defrutum,* the idea survives in Turkey as *pekmez,* a dark sweet grape-based syrup.

30. The word molasses, at this time, could also mean molasses fermented and distilled to make a spirit, now known as rum.

31. Discussed more fully by C. Anne Wilson (1985).

32. William Warde (1562).

Notes to Chapter IV

1. In the confectionery section of *Delightes for Ladies* by Sir Hugh Plat.

2. This may have been due to the residual molasses content of unrefined sugar, which would alter the composition towards a slightly higher content of monosaccharides. Small but significant amounts of the latter must have been retained after clarification.

3. York XVI.O.10, *c.* 1500 AD; Harleian MS 2378 is apparently very similar in content, but I have not been able to examine it.

4. By the seventeenth century sugar plate had become a mixture of powder sugar and gum, similar to modern sugar paste.

5. Published 1573. The background is discussed by Lynette Hunter in Wilson (1991).

6. Elizabeth David (1979).

7. Boeser (1994). Nostradamus provided a very early example of testing sugar by dropping a sample into cold water.

8. Anon. (1602).

9. Plat (1609); there were earlier editions of this book between 1600–1609.

10. 'W. M.' (1655), p. 46.

11. Anon. (1653).

12. 'Thread' now indicates a short distance of less than 1cm; a much longer one was recognized in the past, and confectioners were sometimes instructed to look for a thread which held between fully-opened finger and thumb.

13. No one has satisfactorily explained the name, but for more discussion see Chapter V.

14. It is not recommended that the reader attempt this test; burnt fingers are the most likely result. This recipe also gives instructions for 'pulling', stretching and folding concentrated syrup to make it opaque.

15. Nicholas Culpeper (1817), p. 316. Practical trials of this test are not recommended.

16. John Partridge (1585).

17. Such as Hannah Woolley (1684).

18. Syrup candies from about 110°C upwards, and grains easily when the temperature rises above 121°C (hard ball).

19. Madeleine Masson (1974), p. 278.

20. Discussed by Peter Brears, in Wilson (1991), p 104.

21. Karen Hess (1981). This undated manuscript is thought to have been written in England during the mid- to late seventeenth century and to have been taken to North America shortly after composition. Candy height is when the sugar 'will draw between your fingers in great flakes like bird lime'; and casting height, when the syrup was tested with a stick '& sometimes swing your stick from you, and when your sugar is at casting height, it will flie from your stick in great flakes like flakes of snow, or like fethers flying in the Ayre'. The use of exactly the same words by both Margaret Savile and the writer of Martha Washington's manuscript must indicate some common [printed] source.

22. Information in *Le Maître d'Hôtel* (1659, Pierre David) was used for *Le Confiturier Royal*, reprinted in 1667 as *Le Parfait Confiturier*, and attributed to La Varenne.

23. Rose (1682), p. 130.

24. Rose (1682), p. 183.

25. Anon. (1681), p. 10.

26. Francois Massialot (1702).

27. Massialot (1702), p. 3.

28. John Nott (1726), art. 'Sugar'. Much information in this was plagiarized from Massialot.

29. Massialot (1702), p. 4.

30. Borella (1770).

31. Frederick Bishop (*c.* 1850), p. 332.

32. E Skuse (*c.* 1890), p. 11.

33. Specific gravity of syrup was measured in degrees Baumé until an international system of units of density replaced this in the mid-twentieth century.

34. Jarrin (1837).

35. William Jeanes (1861), p. 222.

36. May Whyte (1910), p. 1.

37. Skuse (*c.* 1890), p. 11.

Notes to Chapter V

1. Charles Dickens, *A Christmas Carol*.
2. York XVI.O.10.
3. Reddish-purple colouring probably derived from the plant *Crozophora tinctoria*.
4. One suggestion is that it derives from the gesture used for testing syrup at manus Christi height, which echoes that of a blessing; see Hess (1981).
5. Sir Hugh Plat (1653). This was originally published in the last decade of the sixteenth century, but I have not been able to examine an earlier edition.
6. Anon. (1608), p. 16.
7. 'W.M.' (1655), p. 27. Experiments with wormwood, *Artemisia Absinthium*, are not advisable. It was used as an ingredient of absinthe in nineteenth-century France. This drink was linked with mental deterioration; the cause was eventually traced to thujone, a toxic substance present in wormwood.
8. S.W. Stavely (1830).
9. Quoted by F.M. MacNeill (1971).
10. Mrs McLintock (1736), p. 35. Modern equivalents for measurements are not certain: lib. indicated approximately 1lb 1 oz, 500g; and a mutchkin was about 7 fluid ounces, 0.212 litres.
11. MacNeill (1971), p. 244.
12. According to Time-Life (1981) and quotations given in the *OED*.
13. The Picayune (1901).
14. Louisa Thorpe (1922), p. 72.
15. Jarrin (1836), p. 245.
16. Catherine Owen (1887), pp. 9–10.
17. 1936 The Macmillan Company, New York; quoted in Time-Life (1981).
18. E Skuse (*c.* 1900), p. 120.

Notes to Chapter VI

1. Charles Perry (1993). The word may go further back in time and space to India, where it appears in texts from about AD 300, but these cannot be analysed with any certainty because, according to Deerr (1949), translators have not been systematic in the interpretation of words relating to sugar types.
2. *OED*.
3. Culpeper (1817), p. 316.
4. A very similar confection exists in France, where it is known as a *berlingot*.
5. Pomet (1747), p. 58.
6. William Salmon (1692), p. 629. Salmon also mentioned the use of 'penids' for treating coughs.
7. Wallace (1831), p. 41.
8. Comparing these two authors (only available to me in late editions) suggests that some recipes from Wallace were plagiarized by Stavely (whose book is smaller and less detailed);

but they may both have had access to a third, unidentified source. Plagiarism and/or an undercurrent of rivalry amongst confectioners is a phenomenon which can be observed in many books.

9. McNeill (1971) p. 243

10. Stavely (1830), p. 28.

11. Jarrin (1820), p. 17.

12. Stavely (1830). Stavely worked in Nottingham and his book was printed in Derby.

13. James Wallace, (1831), Wallace styles himself 'late of Philadelphia'; his book was published in London and various English provincial towns. The author states that he had 'repeatedly, both in England and America, been importuned to publish his methods in Pastry, Confectionary, Sugar-Boiling, Icing, Candying, Colouring, &c &c.'

14. A history of over 200 years was claimed for this by F. Marian McNeill.

15. Jeanes (1861), p. 180.

16. Quoted by Wright (1903); the definition of humbug varied slightly over the country, but generally indicated a hard-boiled sweet made from a basic brown sugar and water mixture, sometimes with treacle or molasses added. This definition is from west Yorkshire. 'Humbug' in the context of sweets has not been explained: the usage appears to be mid-nineteenth century, but there is no obvious connection with the word's other meaning of sham and pretence.

17. Mayhew (1864), p. 215. Mint as a flavouring for confectionery remains popular throughout Britain in the late twentieth century, but the habit of using spices—ginger, cloves and cinnamon—in boiled sugar has continued to the present day in Scotland.

18. See chapter IX.

19. Mayhew (1864), p. 216. Sir Robert Peel, a former Prime Minister, died in a riding accident in 1850.

20. Skuse (c, 1890), p. 32.

21. A sugar thermometer is of little help. It will give a reasonably accurate reading up to about 135°C, but after this the starch affects the syrup which becomes elastic and rosy, and a thermometer no longer reads true.

Notes to Chapter VII

1. Fred. K. Steel & Co. Ltd., (1932), p. 62.

2. Skuse (c. 1890), p. 13.

3. Compare glass, the name commonly given to quartz crystals (silicon dioxide) heated with soda or potash and rapidly cooled so that the mixture remains transparent. It shares some of the characteristics of clear boiled sugar. Physicists categorize all such substances as 'glass', edible or not.

4. Rose (1682), p. 191. A second confection, perfumed with syrup of capillaire (maidenhair fern) given under the same name is less convincing, requiring sugar boiled 'a little higher than for a Preserve',—about 121°C—to be put into cold water when boiling had finished.

5. Gilliers (1751), p. 71.

6. *Caramella* and *caramelos* are, respectively, the Italian and Spanish collective names for hard-boiled sugar sweets to the present day.

7. Jarrin (1820), p. 15.

8. Sulphuric acid, which was added to a few confections to sharpen the taste or alter the colour. Don't try this at home!

9. Skuse (*c.* 1890), p. 13.

10. ibid., p. 36.

11. I have not been able to identify 'penbric': presumably some type of marble.

12. *Illustrated London News*, 19.7.1851.

13. Mrs Mary Eales (1718).

14. C. Anne Wilson (1985); techniques for storing quinces in honey are thought to have a history which reaches back more than two thousand years.

15. An earthenware storage jar.

16. They are still used for making preserves in most Mediterranean and Middle-Eastern countries.

17. Plat (1609), p. 32.

18. Eliza Smith (1758), p. 206.

19. Plat (1609), p. 41.

Notes to Chapter VIII

1. Lewis Carroll (1865).

2. Ayto (1993), p. 116.

3. Roald Dahl (1984), p. 32.

4. This could mean an alloy, or thin sheet metal or tin-plate.

5. Plat (1609), p. 42. Plat made practical observations on many crafts. This particular case is especially interesting; the section is written very differently to the rest of the text and contains much detail, as if the author went out with a notebook, interviewing and observing comfit-makers at work.

6. Recorded in York XVI.O.10.

7. A 16 fl oz pint.

8. Plat (1609), pp. 43-4.

9. York XVI.O.10.

10. This type of comfit, made from almonds, white sugar and rosewater is still produced in some countries, such as Iran and Afghanistan. As late as 1818, the French confectioner Madame Utrecht-Friedel gave a recipe for *grains de coriandre sucrés en frisure* [p. 94].

11. York XVI.O.10.

12. Massialot (1702), p. 113.

13. McLintock (1736).

14. Pomet (1747), p. 59. Oricce, *Iris florentina.*

15. Plat (1609), pp. 44–5. There are various reasons for spots forming on the surface of comfits: insufficient drying between charges of sugar is one. Oil leaking from nuts used as centres can also cause this.

16. York XVI.O.10.

17. Brasil wood, a red dye derived from the wood of a tree of the same name.

18. Plat (1609), p. 47. Gold was thought to be an elixir of life until well into the seventeenth century.

19. Jarrin (1820), p. 115.

20. Eliza Acton (1847), p. 538.

21. York XVI.O.10.

22. Rose (1682), p. 276.

23. Pomet (1747), p. 58.

24. An especially good selection of comfits, including long ones, can be seen in 'Still Life with Cakes and Parrot' by Flegel (1563–1638) in the Altepinakothek, Munich, illustrated in Claire Clifton, *The Art of Food* (1988).

25. G.E. Brereton and J.M. Fenier (1981).

26. Plat (1609), p. 28.

27. In Dutch tradition, pink and white comfits known as *musjies*—little mice—are scattered over buttered rusks and eaten to celebrate the birth of a child.

28. Quoted by Jennifer Stead in Wilson (1991), p. 146.

29. W. Goethe (1970). p. 458.

30. It has recently become more popular in England. Distributing favours (from amongst the sugar decorations on the wedding cake, rather than as bags of comfits) is a custom which seems to have a longer history in Scotland.

31. Gunter (1830), p. 61.

32. Plat (1609), p. 38.

33. Anon. (1608), p. 33.

34. Plat (1609), p. 43.

35. Stavely (1830), p. 39.

36. Frederick Accum (1820), p. 224.

37. *The Magazine of Domestic Economy* 1839, vol. 4, pp. 110-1.

38. Skuse (*c.* 1890), p. 64.

Notes to Chapter IX

1. John Murrell (1617).

2. Described by William Woys Weaver (1989).

3. Theodore Garret (*c.*1890), p. 728.

4. Harold McGee (1984), p. 422.

5. see chapter VII.

6. Acacia gum, originating from the Senegal region of West Africa, the better grades of which were used in pharmacy.

7. Jarrin (1820), p. 67.

8. Warde (1562), f. 63.

9. In the York manuscript, it meant a sheet of candied sugar.

10. Plat (1609), p. 25.

11. W. M. (1655), pp. 64–5.
12. Anon. (1608), p. 26.
13. Jarrin (1820), p. 215.
14. Murrell (1617), p. 89.
15. Robert May (1685), p. 276.
16. Hannah Glasse (1783), p. 58.
17. Examples are in the Museum of London.
18. Ron Lees (1988).
19. Skuse (*c.* 1890), pp. 69–70.
20. Alma H Austin (1938).
21. Small bottles of these oils can be bought from kitchen supply shops.

Notes to Chapter X

1. For details, comments on shrub, julep and punch, and eastern recipes for sherbet, see Alan Davidson in C. Anne Wilson (1993).
2. Elizabeth David (1994).
3. M. de Thévenot (1687), p. 8.
4. Francis Bacon (1626), §705; he meant flavoured candied sugar as discussed in Chapter V.
5. *Mercurius Publicus* 1662-3, Number 11, March 12–19, p. 177.
6. Rose (1682), p. 266.
7. For instance, in John Nott (1726).
8. Smith (1758), p. 240.
9. Anon. (1775), p. 245.
10. Nicholas Culpeper (1684), p. 277.
11. Culpeper (1817), p. 189.
12. Garret (*c.* 1890), vol. VII, p. 446.
13. According to Davidson in Wilson (1993).
14. *Illustrated London News,* 23. 8.1851, p. 254.
15. Mayhew (1864), p. 196.
16. Mayhew (1864), p. 198.
17. It is tempting to speculate that both the egg white and the milk elements of North American sherbet ultimately come from some confusion over the former use of these as clarifying agents for candied sherbets, and the alcohol and gelatine from eighteenth-century recipes.
18. See chapter IX.
19. An old-fashioned French sweet manages to combine the two great childhood favourites of liquorice and fizz in the *Coco Boer*. This little round box with a coloured metal top contains a bright brown-yellow powder which is an extract of liquorice root combined with bicarbonate of soda.
20. Nevin Halici (1989), p. 166.

Notes to Chapter XI

1. 'The Liquorice Fields at Pontefract', Betjeman (1978).
2. R. Lees and E.B. Jackson (1973).
3. Warde (1562), f. 35, Book 1.
4. W.M. (1655), p. 13.
5. Anon. (1608), p. 55. *Diatragacanthum frigidium* appears to refer to a compound including tragacanth, which was considered to be cooling; the prefix 'dia' was an apothecaries' term, latinized from Greek, indicating a compound consisting of the stated substances—in this case, tragacanth.
6. Pomet (1747), Book II, p. 54.
7. *Sciant Presents*, the newsletter of the Yorkshire Archaeological Society, No. 15, 1986.
8. Lees and Jackson (1973), p. 102.
9. Jarrin (1820), pp. 65–6.
10. Pomet (1747), Book II, p. 54.
11. Glasse (1783), p. 146.
12. Robert Opie (1988), p. 116.
13. Culpeper (1684), p. 281. An electuary is a medicine where powder is mixed with a very thick syrup or jam: spoonable rather than drinkable.
14. Charles Apell (1912), p. 291.
15. Garret (*c.* 1890), Vol. IV, p. 863.
16. Gunter (1830), p. 41.
17. Skuse (*c.* 1900), p. 159.
18. Liquorice is cultivated on a large scale in Turkey and Iran to supply the Pontefract liquorice industry.
19. Lees and Jackson (1973), p. 299.

Notes to Chapter XII

1. Peter Brears (1987).
2. *OED.*
3. Presumably tins for making Yorkshire pudding—large and shallow in shape.
4. Wright (1903).
5. York Minster Library, Hailstone Collection QQ5.1.
6. McNeill (1973), p. 239.
7. Irma Rombauer and Marion Becker (1963), p. 733.
8. Bobby Freeman (1996), p. 245.
9. For instance, in Blackpool.
10. Skuse (*c.* 1890), p. 13.
11. Acton (1847), p. 537.
12. Skuse (*c.* 1890), p. 14.
13. Borella (1770), p. 37.

14. Robert Opie (1989), p. 39. Chewy coffee-flavoured sweets of the toffee type are also made in Pamplona, Spain under the trade name 'Dos Cafeteras' and 'Cafe con Leche'.
15. Jarrin (1844), p. 21.
16. Mayhew (1864), p. 216.
17. Owen (1887), p. 65; she mentions that her caramel recipes are adapted from an earlier publication, *The Art of Candy Making*.
18. Owen, ibid.
19. Skuse (*c.* 1890), p. 36.
20. Robert Wells (1896).
21. Apell (1912), p. 5.
22. Apell, ibid.
23. Opie (1988), p. 16.
24. Compton Mackenzie (1954), p. 64.

Notes to Chapter XIII

1. Murrell (1617), p. 111. Sap-green was prepared from buckthorn berries; rosa-paris, blew bise and yellow smalt all appear to have been artists' pigments; the latter was probably a nickel compound.
2. Plat (1609), p. 35 used roset to make 'a faire murrey colour' in sugar plate.
3. Derived from *Coccus cacti*, a species of beetle found in Central America.
4. Accum (1820), p. 224. Accum exposed numerous adulterations and frauds in all types of foods, making himself unpopular with manufacturers. His book, widely read, added to the hostility manufacturers already felt towards him. After accusations of mutilating books from a library, he was forced to leave England. It is possible that this controversy was actively exploited by vested interests to discredit him and drive him out of the country.
5. Wallace (1831), p. 59. Rose pink: possibly one of several yellows known as 'pink', perhaps in this case, Dutch pink, extracted from quercitrion bark; woad: *Isatis tinctoria*, blue dye; Spanish red: a type of ochre; madder: a preparation of the root of *Rubia tinctoria*, which gave 'Turkey red' in textiles; Indian lake, a crimson pigment prepared from lac, the dark red resin used in lacquer, treated with alum and alkali; arnatto, or properly, annatto, a yellowish or red-orange food colouring from central America; archel, orchil, a green-yellow pigment derived from lichen; auripigmentum, a bright yellow mineral, trisulphide of arsenic; yellow masticot was red ochre.
6. A clear sweet with an acid, sherbet-like centre.
7. A clear brown mint-flavoured sweet, curled into a rough snail shape, from Jedburgh in the Scottish Borders. For some unknown reason, geographical names for traditional confectionery specialities have been very tenacious in this area.
8. Rose (1682), p. 284.
9. Lambert (*c.* 1744), p. 13.
10. For instance by Plat (1609).
11. Several examples are cited by Hoh-cheung and Lorna H. Mui (1989), p. 247.
12. *Mercurius Publicus,* June 1662, p. 410.

13. David (1994), p. 317.
14. Skuse (*c.* 1892), 4th edn., p. 45.
15. Mayhew (1864), p. 216.
16. Maurice Baren (1992).
17. From 1841, according to the *OED*. They have been popular ever since, occasionally to celebrate potentially explosive events. Annie Perrier-Robert (1986) shows French advertisements for an exploding cardboard model of the Bastille and a 'Bombe Orsini Explosible en chocolat'. The latter was inspired by the attempted assassination of Napoleon III in 1858, when the Italian activist Orsini organized a plot to throw bombs at him. Both items were filled with *dragées de Verdun*.
18. Flora Thompson (1946), p. 210.
19. For a detailed discussion on the development of packaging, see Opie (1990).

Notes to Chapter XIV

1. The year in which Mackintosh's of Halifax introduced them as a trademark.
2. Masson (1974), p. 348.
3. Daniel Defoe (1732), p. 269.
4. Defoe, ibid., p. 271. Supplying all lanterns and sconces with reasonable quality candles would, alone, have been a heavy expense.
5. Originally a sweetmeat flavoured with *Inula Helenium*, horse-heal, but in the mid-nineteenth century William Finemore's recipe for 'Elecompane' was a grained confection of sugar, flavoured with lemon.
6. William Hone (1825), p. 47.
7. Lees (1988), p. 102.
8. So called because they are retail lines which are counted, i.e. sold by number, not weight.

Bibliography

Accum, Frederick A. (1820), *Treatise on the Adulteration of Food*. Facsimile published 1966 by the Mallinckrodt Collection of Food Classics. Philadelphia.

Acton, Eliza (1847), *Modern Cookery for Private Families* (6th *edn*).

Anon., MS York XVI.O.10, The Minster Archives, York.

Anon. (1602), *A Closet for Ladies and Gentlewomen or, the Art of Preserving, Conserving and Candying*. Printed for Arthur Johnson, London.

Anon. (1653), *A Book of Fruits and Flowers*. Facsimile with an introduction and glossary by C. Anne Wilson published 1984. Prospect Books, London.

Anon. (1775), *Valuable Secrets Concerning Arts and Trades*. London.

Apell, Charles (1912), *Twentieth Century Candy Teacher*.

Austin, Alma H. (1938), *The Romance of Candy*. Harper and Brothers, New York.

Ayto, J. (1993), *The Diner's Dictionary*. Oxford University Press.

Bacon, Francis, Viscount St Albans (1626), *Sylva Sylvarum*.

Baren, M. (1992), *How It All Began*. Smith Settle, Otley.

Betjeman, John (1978), *John Betjeman's Collected Poems*. Compiled and with an introduction by Lord Birkenhead. (4th edition). John Murray, London.

The Biscuit, Cake, Chocolate and Confectionery Alliance (1965), *Annual Report*; (1990), *Annual Review*. 11 Green St, London W1Y 3RF.

Bishop, Frederick (*c.* 1850), *Wife's Own Book of Cookery*. London.

Boeser, Knut (ed.) (1994), *The Elixirs of Michel Nostradamus*. Bloomsbury, London.

Borella (1770), *The Court and Country Confectioner*.

Brereton, G.E. and Fenier, J.M. (1981), *Le Menagier de Paris*. Clarendon Press, Oxford.

Brears, Peter (1987), *Traditional Food in Yorkshire*. John Donald, Edinburgh.

Brunskill, Elizabeth (1953), 'A Medieval Book of Herbs and Medicine, Part II', *The North-Western Naturalist*, NS vol. 1, pp. 177–89.

Cadbury Brothers (1949), *Sweet-shop Success: a handbook for the sweet retailer.* Sir Isaac Pitman and Sons, London.

Coe, Sophie and Michael (1996), *The True History of Chocolate.* Thames and Hudson, London.

Cotgrave, Randle (1611), *A Dictionarie of the French and English Tongues.* London, printed by Adam Islip.

Culpeper, Nicholas (1684), *The English Physician Enlarged.* London.

———— (1817) *Culpeper's Complete Herbal and English Physician Enlarged.* London.

Dahl, Roald (1984), *Boy.* London, Penguin Books.

David, Elizabeth (1979), 'Banketting Stuffe', *Petits Propos Culinaires* 3, pp. 39–44.

————(1994), *Harvest of the Cold Months.* Penguin Books, London.

Deerr, Noel (1949), *The History of Sugar* 2 vols, Chapman and Hall, London.

Defoe, Daniel (1732), *The Complete English Tradesman.*

Dickens, Charles (1969), *Sketches by Boz illustrative of every-day life and every-day people.* From the edition of 1839, with an introduction by Thea Holme. Oxford University Press, London.

————(1843), *A Christmas Carol.*

Diderot, Denis, *A Diderot Pictorial Encyclopedia of Trades and Industry,* ed. Charles C. Gillespie, Dover, New York, 1987.

Digby, Sir K. (1669), *The Closet of the Eminently Learned Sir Kenelm Digby, knight, opened.* 1910 reprint, Warner, London; 1997 reprint, Prospect Books.

Eales, Mrs M. (1718), *Mrs Mary Eales's Receipts.* Facsimile 1985 Prospect Books from the edition of 1733.

Fairrie, Geoffrey (1925), *Sugar.* Fairrie and Company, Liverpool.

Finemore, William (*c.* 1839–1856), MS of notes relating to confectionery.

Freeman, B. (1996), *First Catch Your Peacock.* YLolfa, Ceredigion.

Garret, Theodore F. (*c.* 1890), *The Encyclopaedia of Practical Cookery.* 8 vols., L. Upcott Gill, London.

Gilliers, J. (1751), *Le Cannameliste Français.* Nancy, France.

Glasse, Hannah (1783), *The Compleat Confectioner.* J. Cooke, London.

Goethe, W. (1970), *Italian Journey 1786–1788.* Translated by W.H. Auden and E. Mayer, Penguin, London.

Gunter, William (1830), *The Confectioner's Oracle.* London.

Halici, Nevin (1989), *Nevin Halici's Turkish Cookbook.* Dorling Kindersley, London.

Hess, Karen (ed) (1981), *Martha Washington's Booke of Cookery and Booke of Sweetmeats.* Columbia University Press, New York.

Hone, William (1825), *The Every-day and Table-book.*

Illustrated London News, 19.7.1851; 23. 8.1851.

James, Allison (1979), 'Confections, Concoctions and Conceptions,' *Journal of the Anthropological Society of Oxford,* Vol. X, No. 2.

Jarrin, Guglielmo A. (1820), *The Italian Confectioner.* 1st edition. John Harding: London.

———(1836), *The Italian Confectioner.* New edition.

———(1837), *The Italian Confectioner.* New edition, revised and enlarged.

———(1844), *The Italian Confectioner.*

Jeanes, William (1861), *The Modern Confectioner.* London.

Lambert, Edward (*c.* 1744), *The Art of Confectionary.*

Lees, Ron (1988), *A History of Sweet and Chocolate Manufacture.* Specialised Publications, Surbiton.

Lees, R. and Jackson, E. B. (1973), *Sugar Confectionery and Chocolate Manufacture.* Leonard Hill, Aylesbury.

McGee, Harold (1984), *On Food and Cooking.* Allen and Unwin, London.

Mackenzie, Compton (1954), *Echoes.* Chatto and Windus, London.

McLintock, Mrs (1736), *Receipts for Cookery and Pastry-Work.* Glasgow. Reprinted 1986 with an introduction by Iseabail Macleod. Aberdeen University Press.

McNeill, F. Marian (1971, first published 1929), *The Scots Kitchen.* Blackie and Sons, Glasgow.

The Magazine of Domestic Economy (1839), vol. 4, W.S. Orr and Co., Paternoster Row, London.

Massialot, François (1702), *New Instructions for Confectioners.*

Masson, Madeleine (ed.) (1974), *The Complete Cook,* by Rebecca Price. Routledge and Kegan Paul, London.

May, Robert (1994), *The Accomplisht Cook or the Art and Mystery of Cookery.* Facsimile of the 1685 edition with foreword, introduction and glossary supplied by Alan Davidson, Marcus Bell and Tom Jaine. Prospect Books, Totnes.

Mayhew, Henry (1864), *London Labour and the London Poor*. Charles Griffin and Co., London.

Mintz, Sidney (1985), *Sweetness and Power*. Viking, New York.

Mui, Hoh-cheung and Lorna H (1989), *Shops and Shop-keeping in Eighteenth Century England*. Routledge, London.

Murrell, John (1617), *A Daily Exercise for Ladies and Gentlewomen*.

Nott, John (1980), *Cooks and Confectioners Dictionary*. Facsimile of 1726 edition with introduction and glossary by Elizabeth David. Lawrence Rivington, London.

Opie, I. and P. (1959), *The Lore and Language of Schoolchildren*. Oxford University Press.

Opie, Robert (1988), *Sweet Memories*. Pavilion Books, London.

———(1989), *Packaging Source Book*. Macdonald Orbis, London.

———(1990), *The Art of the Label*. Simon and Schuster, London.

Owen, Catherine (1887), *Catherine Owen's Lessons in Candy Making*. Good Housekeeping Press, Springfield, Mass.

Oxford English Dictionary, 1991.

Partridge, John (1685), *The Widows Treasure*.

The Picayune (1901), *The Picayune's Creole Cookbook*. reprint of the 1901 2nd edn. Dover, New York.

Perrier-Robert, Annie (1986), *Les Friandises et Leurs Secrets*. Larousse, Paris.

Perry, Charles (1993), 'Moorish Sugar', *Spicing up the Palate* (Proceedings of the Oxford Symposium on Cookery and Food History 1992). Prospect Books, Totnes.

Plat, Sir Hugh (1609), *Delightes for Ladies to adorne their Persons, Tables, Closets and Distillatories with Beauties, Banquets, Perfumes and Waters*. 1948 edition with introductions by G.E. and K.R. Fussel. Crosby Lockwood and Son, London.

———(1653), *The Jewel House of Art and Nature*. London.

Pomet, Pierre (1747), *A Complete History of Drugs written in French by M. Pomet Chief Druggist to the late French King Lewis XIV Done into English from the originals*. 4th edition, London J. & J. Bonwicke, S. Birt, W. Parker, C. Hitch and E. Wicksteed.

Raffald, E. (1782), *The Experienced English Housekeeper*. Facsimile edition, 1970, E & W Books, London.

Roenblat, Anne, and Révérend, Alexandre (1991), *Les Bonbecs*. Syros Alternatives, Paris.

Rombauer, Irma, and Becker, Marion (1963), *Joy of Cooking* (4th edition). Dent, London.

Rose, Giles (1682), *A Perfect School for Instructions for Officers of the Mouth*.

Russell, John (1868), *The Boke of Nurture*. Ed. F.J. Furnivall. Early English Text Society.

Salmon, William (1692), *The New London Dispensatory*.

Sciant Presents. Newsletter of the Yorkshire Archaeological Society, autumn 1983; No, 15, 1986.

Skuse, E. (*c.* 1890), *The Confectioners Handbook*. (3rd edn). London.

———(*c.* 1892), *The Confectioners Handbook*. (4th edn). London.

———(*c.* 1900), *The Confectioners Handbook*. (10th edn). London.

Smith, Eliza (1758), *The Compleat Housewife or Accomplished Gentlewoman's Companion*. Facsimile of the 16th edition of 1758, 1983 Arlon House, King's Langley.

Stavely, S.W. (1830), *The Whole New Art of Confectionary*. 11th edition, Nottingham.

Steel, F.K. & Co. (1932), *A Handbook of Chocolate and Confectionery*. Stroud.

de Thévenot (1678), *The Travels of Monsieur de Thévenot into the Levant*. London.

Thompson, Flora (1946), *Lark Rise*. Guild Books, Oxford.

Thorpe, Louisa (1921), *Bonbons and simple sugar sweets*. Sir Isaac Pitman and Sons, London.

Time-Life Books (1981), *The Good Cook. Confectionery*. Amsterdam.

Utrecht-Friedel (1818), *Le Confisieur Royal, ou L'Art du Confisieur*. Paris.

Venner, Tobias (1620), *Via recta ad vitam longam, or a plaine philosophical discourse*. London.

'W.M.' (1655), *The Compleat Cook* and *A Queens Delight*. Facsimile 1984, Prospect Books, London.

Wallace, James (1831), *The Confectioner's Guide and ladies' and housekeeper's instructor* (10th edition). Bungay.

Warde, William, translator (1562), *The Secretes of the Reverende Maister Alexis of Piedmont*.

Wells, Robert (1896), *The Bread and Biscuit Bakers and Sugar Boiler's Assistant*. 3rd edition, revised. Crosby Lockwood and Son, London.

Whyte, May (*c.* 1910), *High Class Sweetmaking.* Birkenhead.

Wilson, C. Anne (1991), *Food and Drink in Britain.* Constable, London.

———(1985), *The Book of Marmalade.* Constable, London.

———(ed.), (1991), *Banquetting Stuffe.* Edinburgh University Press.

———(ed.), (1993), *Liquid Nourishment.* Edinburgh University Press.

Woys Weaver, William (1989), contribution in *The Confectioners Art: catalogue of an exhibition at the American Craft Museum, 1988– 1989, curated by Merle Evans.* The American Craft Museum, New York.

Wright, Joseph (1903), *The English Dialect Dictionary.* Henry Frowde, London.

Index

References in italics refer to illustrations or tables. Names of authors referred to in the text are indexed, but not the titles of their books.